How to Plan PRIMARY LESSONS

How to Plan PRIMARY LESSONS

ESSENTIAL PRACTICE AND THEORY FOR NEW TEACHERS

LORNA SHIRES

Sage

1 Oliver's Yard
55 City Road
London EC1Y 1SP

2455 Teller Road
Thousand Oaks, California 91320

Unit No 323–333, Third Floor, F-Block
International Trade Tower Nehru Place
New Delhi 110 019

8 Marina View Suite 43–053
Asia Square Tower 1
Singapore 018960

Editor: James Clark
Assistant Editor: Esosa Otabor
Production Editor: Gourav Kumar and Tanya Kapoor
Copyeditor: Sarah Bury
Indexer: Cathryn Pritchard
Marketing Manager: Lorna Patkai
Cover Design: Wendy Scott
Typeset by KnowledgeWorks Global Ltd
Printed and bound by CPI Group (UK) Ltd, Croydon, CR0 4YY

Library of Congress Control Number: 2024934419

British Library Cataloguing in Publication data

A catalogue record for this book is available from the British Library

ISBN 978-1-5296-2662-9
ISBN 978-1-5296-2661-2 (pbk)

This book is dedicated to my parents, Hilary and Dave, my children, Niamh and Jack, and my granddaughters, Peggy and Bea.

CONTENTS

ABOUT THE AUTHOR

Dr Lorna Shires has been a schoolteacher and headteacher and led a university programme of initial teacher education. She has many years' experience of teaching trainees and new teachers in school and at university at both undergraduate and postgraduate level, and working with teacher educators in both types of setting.

ACKNOWLEDGEMENTS

This book is the culmination of many years teaching, leading teachers and training teachers. I am most grateful to all the teachers and headteachers I have worked with, whose insights have shaped the approach this book adopts to understanding how teachers think about teaching and develop their professional judgement.

I would like to thank the team at Sage, especially Esosa and James, for their interest and support. I would like to thank Sarah Bury for her clarity and wisdom and Tanya Kapoor for her patience.

Finally, as ever, thanks to Gav.

HOW TO USE THIS BOOK

This book is written for new teachers in training or the early years of their career, and the more experienced teachers who work alongside them and induct them into the profession. The aim of the book is to provide a systematic account of lesson planning as a professional activity where knowledge, techniques and ways of thinking can all be found in one place. Think of it, perhaps, as a kind of professional handbook that will support you, as you join the teaching profession, by sharing with you the essential theory and practice used by expert teachers.

However, this book does not set out to prescribe one method of lesson planning. Instead, its aim is to support you on your journey to 'thinking like a teacher'. Knowledge is power. As you learn more about it, planning will become more interesting and more memorable because you understand the how, what, why and when of planning and have clear ideas about how to get better at this most fundamental professional skill.

When planning to teach a lesson, there are some important principles to keep in mind:

- The use of the words 'lesson plan' brings to mind paper templates and proformas to be completed late into the evening. A better phrase is, perhaps, lesson preparation. What is important is not whether you have filled in all the boxes on the template, but whether you have thought the lesson through in terms of important pedagogical questions.
- This book addresses both essential theory and practice: skills are developed from knowledge. The book describes many techniques proven to have worked by teachers. Your role is to select from these techniques and to practise and perfect them over time so that your teaching repertoire is wide. With time, you will be able to select the most appropriate technique for any particular lesson and any particular class at any particular moment.
- However, no technique brings about learning by itself. Your role is to fully understand the content that you have to teach. Not just a cursory understanding of the topic of that lesson, but in terms of conceptual understanding and how it is sequenced in the curriculum of each Key Stage.
- Teachers do not just teach children, nor do they just teach a curriculum. Getting better at teaching is more complex than many other practical and professional skills because teaching has a dual focus: you are teaching something to someone. Teaching is a complex cognitive skill that requires social understanding and an enjoyment of both the curriculum and the company of children as they learn. It is important to remember that the pupils never 'get back' a lesson which they did not understand, and so it is important

to be sensitive to your pupils as they learn in your classroom so that you can adapt your teaching in response to their individual needs.

- Becoming a good teacher does not happen overnight; it takes time and practice. However, with time you will perceive what is happening in the classroom better and make better decisions about how to implement your plan.

The book is set out into three parts. Part 1 introduces the four big questions (What is learning? What is teaching? What is a curriculum? What is backwards planning?) that guide and shape the 'what', 'how' and 'why' of lesson planning. Each chapter explains the evidence, research and theory that form the basis for practice. Parts 2 and 3 introduce the key components of a successful lesson that should be planned in. Rather than try to work out what teachers mean when they explain ideas about teaching and learning, these chapters set it out clearly and accurately. The history of each idea and its theoretical background is summarised to make clear its importance and relevance to your professional knowledge. Following Part 3 is a Conclusion that addresses how you can keep improving as a teacher. It includes how you should develop your ability in terms of adaptive teaching and SEND, but also how to continue to develop your professional judgement so that you know how to use your knowledge wisely. At the end of the book, you will find a list of the most important professional words every teacher needs to know, understand and use as they plan, teach and assess.

The most important goal you should aim for in the early years of your career is to plan good lessons day by day and to truly master your teaching skills. Several years ago, my young teenage son met one of his sporting heroes, an All Black rugby player, who very kindly signed an autograph for him. Recognising my son as a keen young player, he offered him these words of wisdom then, which I offer you now:

'Work hard on your skills, and make sure you're always having fun.'

PART 1
ESSENTIAL THEORY

Introduction

This book is divided into three sections. Part 1 explains and summarises the theoretical knowledge it is essential a new teacher knows and understands. Parts 2 and 3 then explain how this essential knowledge is used by teachers in actions as they plan, teach and assess, and how such knowledge and skill should be planned into the lesson by the teacher before it begins. A conclusion ends the book by looking at how to continue to get better as a teacher.

Part 1 addresses the four big questions that shape what a teacher does, how they do it and why:

- Chapter 1 addresses the foundational knowledge all teachers need to fully understand – what is learning? It summarises the way learning is understood by the relevant disciplines.
- Chapter 2 summarises what key research has to say about what good teaching is and what good teachers do. It is important to understand the evidence developed from this area of research so that you can reflect it in the way you plan and teach.
- Chapter 3 explains the third area of core knowledge a new teacher needs, which will work alongside the pedagogical knowledge (to do with teaching for learning) that was addressed in Chapters 1 and 2. This is knowledge of the subject-matter of the curriculum. It is important to understand what a curriculum is and how a teacher should work with it because it is the content knowledge that you will work with. In other words, knowledge of the curriculum is a major tool for teachers, and it is important to know how to make sense of the curriculum when you plan your lessons.
- Chapter 4 explains the planning process adopted by expert teachers – backwards planning. This chapter addresses the most frequent misconception in the practice of new teachers – that planning is about devising activities rather than planning for pupil understanding – and demonstrates how backwards planning actually works.

1
WHAT IS LEARNING?

Important Questions

- Why is it important for you as a new teacher to understand learning?
- How do children learn?
- What knowledge about learning will help you 'get better' as a teacher?
- What teaching approaches best support learning?

Introduction

This chapter is the first of four chapters in Part 1. Each chapter in Part 1 explains a different key area of knowledge that it is important to understand as a new teacher. Each chapter explains the most relevant and important theories to the key area of knowledge. Theories are the ideas that shape how we understand and operate in the world. As a teacher, it is important, therefore, to understand key ideas about learning, teaching, the curriculum and planning as the basis for what, how and why you go about teaching.

It can appear self-evident to say that the aim of teaching is to cause learning but learning itself can be hard to define. By the end of this chapter, you will understand how learning is defined and by what processes something is learned. The chapter also considers how to think about teaching approaches to best support learning and what this means for how you might go about teaching a curriculum to a group of children in a primary school classroom.

Why is It Important to Understand Learning?

Learning is complex to understand because we cannot see it directly, but nevertheless it is the prime task of a teacher. However, the *Teachers' Standards* (DfE, 2011) – the professional standards for qualified teacher status and for progression through the profession – do not define learning directly, but state that, 'Teachers make the education of their pupils their first concern' (DfE, 2011), and then lists what a teacher must do: set high expectations; promote good progress and outcomes by pupils; demonstrate good subject and curriculum knowledge; plan and teach well-structured lessons; adapt teaching to respond to the strengths and needs of all pupils; make accurate and productive use of assessment; manage behaviour effectively to ensure a good and safe learning environment and to fulfil wider professional responsibilities. If, as a teacher, you can be very clear and specific in terms of what you understand learning to be, it is likely that you will be more effective as a teacher because you understand what it is you are trying to bring about in your pupils.

It is important to think hard about learning for three main reasons. First, if you uncritically accept metaphors that have been developed to explain how the brain works, for example, like a clock, a filing cabinet, or a computer (Cobb, 2020), your teaching may be shaped by these misconceptions and interpret learning as simply information processing. Second, being a primary school teacher means that you work in a very specific context: in a classroom, with a group of children of a similar age and who have specific knowledge and skills to learn. This means that ways of learning that take place in less formal settings, with one or two children, or where there is no fixed agenda of what is to be learned do not necessarily translate across to the situated context of your work. Finally, you are aiming to bring the children that you teach into a relation separate from you to the subject-matter of the curriculum, and so you have a dual focus as the basis of your teaching because your long-term aim is that your pupils are able to use and apply what you have taught them independently from you in the future.

John Hattie (2009), a professor of education in Melbourne, undertook a very influential meta-meta-analysis of over 800 studies related to how children learn in an attempt to consider how to teach to make learning visible. He identified approaches to teaching that may have a larger impact on pupil achievement. However, he has since updated this work (Hattie, 2023) because he says that the list of teaching strategies, which he described in terms of their impact on achievement, led teachers to focus on their mastery of the techniques, rather than focusing on the impact of the strategies on their pupils in terms of their learning.

What is Learning?

Because learning is so central to understanding human development, it has been studied and researched in a variety of disciplines: history, sociology, psychology and philosophy. Consequently, there are many definitions of, and disagreements about, learning depending on particular situations, purposes and perspectives. It is important, as a primary school teacher, to understand how learning is currently defined so that you can use the component ideas to inform your progress in teaching.

Traditionally, new teachers were taught about behaviourism, a theory founded by John B. Watson (1878–1958) and developed by Edward Lee Thorndike (1874–1949) and Burrhus F. Skinner (1904–1990), which explains learning in terms of conditioning responses (and how positive and negative reinforcements shape behaviours) and its relation to constructivism (which we will look at in this chapter). However, since 2019, a new Education Inspection

Framework (EIF) was introduced that emphasised the role of knowledge and the curriculum, as opposed to the previous inspection framework that focused on the quality of education in terms of pupil outcomes attained. The current EIF has for the first time explicitly stated the definition of learning on which it is based (one drawn from cognitive science) and has also defined how it interprets progress in learning. It is important, therefore, for you to know and understand this definition of learning because it is the approach adopted by the regulator of school standards and widely adopted by schools. However, it also important to understand the theory of constructivism because it provides a broader explanatory context to learning; how learning is linked to the curriculum; explains the processes of learning and important teaching strategies; and shares important ideas with Cognitive Load Theory.

Two Definitions of Learning You Should Know

It is important to know and understand how Ofsted (2019) defines learning and also how learning is explained by constructivism because these are the two definitions of learning most relevant to the work of primary school teachers. Both definitions share the idea that learning represents change.

Constructivist theory views learning as something that happens in the mind of each learner that is shaped by their own experiences and the prior knowledge they bring to a topic. Different constructivist definitions of learning have slightly different wordings, but this expression by Chaiklin (2015: 94) encapsulates it most clearly: 'Learning is used to refer to a psychological event: a relatively permanent change in the way in which an action is achieved, as a result of prior experience.' Change in performance is used as an indicator of learning and many different forms of performance change are interpreted as indicators of learning. In other words, to understand learning you have to be aware of the source of the psychological change in the way the action is achieved. That is, as a teacher, you have to be aware of the processes that underpin learning and observed performance change.

From 2019, the Education Inspection Framework (EIF) for the first time explicitly stated the educational research on which the framework was based. In the initial consultation, training, and final handbook, Ofsted makes clear that its wider approach is taken from cognitive psychology, but its working definition is from one theory in particular, which was first developed by John Sweller – Cognitive Load Theory (Sweller et al., 2011). Ofsted has adopted their definition of learning. It cites the definition in its published research evidence underpinning the EIF and restates it in paragraph 222 of the *School Inspection Handbook* (Ofsted, 2022): 'Learning is defined as an alteration in long-term memory. If nothing has been altered in long-term memory, nothing has been learned' (Ofsted, 2019: 19). It is a small, but significant point to note (and will be mentioned later in the chapter) that Sweller does not use the word 'alter' in relation to long-term memory; he uses it in relation to the teacher's need to break down knowledge into smaller chunks or steps in order to make it teachable. Sweller's actual definition is: 'Learning is defined as a positive change in long-term memory and so if nothing has changed in the long-term memory then learning has not occurred' (Sweller et al., 2011: 53).

What the Core Content Framework Says About Learning

The Core Content Framework (CCF) (DfE, 2019) is a curriculum framework developed by the Department for Education 1. The CCF sets out the minimum declarative knowledge (learn that) and procedural knowledge or skills (learn how to) that new teachers are required to learn. The CCF is developed around five core areas – behaviour management, pedagogy, curriculum, assessment and professional behaviours – but is set out in line with the eight *Teachers' Standards* (DfE, 2011). The second area is named How Pupils Learn (pages 11-12 of the CCF) and is set against Teacher Standard 2: Promote good progress and outcomes by pupils. This section of the CCF sets out what aspects of Cognitive Load Theory new teachers are required to learn. First, it describes learning as 'involving a lasting change in pupils' capabilities or understanding' (DfE, 2019: 11) and then goes onto eight further components to elaborate. The eight components are reorganised in Table 1.1 in terms of the four topics they address: long-term memory, working memory, prior knowledge and teaching strategies.

However, as you might expect, the implications of this model of learning for teaching, the curriculum and planning are also threaded throughout the CCF. It is helpful to think about eight components of the CCF model of learning as learning-focused teaching strategies (i.e. what you can do as a teacher to support the learning of your pupils). The learning-focused teaching strategies from the CCF are mapped in Table 1.2 under five themes: task design, knowledge, misconceptions, vocabulary and motivation.

Table 1.1 The definition of learning as prescribed for new teachers in the CCF (DfE, 2019: 11–12)*

Long-term memory	Working memory	Prior knowledge	Teaching Strategies
An important factor in learning is memory, which can be thought of as comprising two elements: working memory and long-term memory. (3)	An important factor in learning is memory, which can be thought of as comprising two elements: working memory and long-term memory. (3)	Prior knowledge plays an important role in how pupils learn; committing some key facts to their long-term memory is likely to help pupils learn more complex ideas. (2)	Regular purposeful practice of what has been previously taught can help consolidate material and help pupils remember what they have learned. (7)
Long-term memory can be considered as a store of knowledge that changes as pupils learn by integrating new ideas with existing knowledge. (5)	Working memory is where information that is being actively processed is held, but its capacity is limited and can be overloaded. (4)	Where prior knowledge is weak, pupils are more likely to develop misconceptions, particularly if new ideas are introduced too quickly. (6)	Requiring pupils to retrieve information from memory and spacing practise so that pupils revisit ideas after a gap are also likely to strengthen recall. (8)
Prior knowledge plays an important role in how pupils learn; committing some key facts to their long-term memory is likely to help pupils learn more complex ideas. (2)			Worked examples that take pupils through each step of the new process are also likely to support pupils to learn. (9)

*The numbers in the table refer to relevant CCF number in the 'Learn that' column of the 'How Pupils Learn' section of the CCF.

Table 1.2 What the CCF requires new teachers to be able to do so that their teaching brings about pupils' learning

	Elements of teaching that bring about learning				
	Task design	**Knowledge**	**Misconceptions**	**Vocabulary**	**Motivation**
CCF Strand					
High expectations	Set tasks that stretch but are achievable				Create a positive environment in which making mistakes and learning from them and the need for effort and perseverance are part of daily routine Acknowledge and praise pupil effort and emphasise progress being made
How pupils learn	Break complex material into smaller steps Regularly review and practise key ideas and concepts over time Design practice, generation and retrieval tasks that provide just enough support so that pupils achieve a high success rate when attempting challenging work As knowledge becomes more secure, increase challenge of practice and retrieval tasks	Take into account pupils' prior knowledge when thinking about how much new information to introduce Secure pupils' foundational knowledge before encountering more complex content Link what pupils already know to what is being taught	Identify possible misconceptions and plan how to prevent these forming Encourage pupils to share emerging understanding and points of confusion so that misconceptions can be addressed		
Subject and the curriculum	Accumulate and refine a collection of powerful analogies, illustrations, examples, explanations and demonstrations Provide tasks that support pupils to learn key ideas securely Revisit big ideas over time and teach key concepts through a range of examples	Identify essential concepts, knowledge, skills and principles of the subject Focus pupils' thinking on key ideas within the subject Use retrieval and spaced practice to build automatic recall of key knowledge	Be aware of common misconceptions	Teach unfamiliar vocabulary explicitly Repeatedly expose pupils to high-utility and high-frequency vocabulary in what is taught	

(*Continued*)

Table 1.2 What the CCF requires new teachers to be able to do so that their teaching brings about pupils' learning (*Continued*)

	Elements of teaching that bring about learning				
	Task design	**Knowledge**	**Misconceptions**	**Vocabulary**	**Motivation**
	Interleave concrete and abstract examples and slowly withdraw concrete examples and draw attention to underlying structure of problems	Ensure pupils have relevant domain-specific knowledge, especially when asked to think critically within a subject			
Classroom practice	Break tasks down into constituent components when first setting up independent practice and deconstructing this approach Provide sufficient opportunity to consolidate and practise applying new knowledge and skills Make steps in a process memorable to ensure pupils can recall them Plan activities around what you want pupils to think hard about		Teach necessary foundational content knowledge to enable critical thinking and problem solving		
Adaptive teaching	Make use of well-designed resources Build in additional practice Remove unnecessary explanations Ensure all pupils have access to a rich curriculum	Teach necessary foundational content knowledge to enable critical thinking and problem solving Start explanations at the point of current pupil understanding Include a range of types of questions in class discussions to extend and challenge pupils Balance input of new content so that pupils master important concepts			

Table 1.2 What the CCF requires new teachers to be able to do so that their teaching brings about pupils' learning

	Elements of teaching that bring about learning				
	Task design	**Knowledge**	**Misconceptions**	**Vocabulary**	**Motivation**
Assessment	Plan formative assessment tasks linked to lesson objectives and think ahead about what would indicate understanding Structure tasks and questions to enable the identification of knowledge gaps and misconceptions	Use assessments to check for prior knowledge Prompt pupils to elaborate when responding to questions to check that a correct answer stems from secure understanding	Use assessment to check for pre-existing misconceptions Monitor pupils' work during lessons to check for misconceptions Prioritise the highlighting of errors related to misunderstandings, rather than careless mistakes when marking		
Managing behaviour	Check pupils' understanding of instructions before a task begins				Give manageable, specific and sequential instructions Support pupils to master challenging content Provide opportunities for pupils to articulate their long-term goals and help them to see how these are related to their success in school Support pupils to journey from needing extrinsic motivation to being motivated to work intrinsically
Professional behaviours	Strengthen pedagogical and subject knowledge by participating in wider networks Extend subject and pedagogic knowledge when planning lessons Share intended lesson outcomes with teaching assistants ahead of the lesson				

What the Core Content Framework Says About How to Teach to Cause Learning

Because helping children to learn in a classroom is a very specific context, certain aspects of learning are prioritised for the attention of teachers. This is because teaching and learning take place in a formal, group and age-related setting where the purpose is the coverage of a set curriculum. The context in which you will teach impacts the aspects of learning that you need to understand. The key aspect of learning that you, as a new teacher, will focus on is schema formation. A schema is how the brain structures knowledge. It is based on past experience and is accessed to guide current understanding or action. Jean Piaget (1896–1980) is credited as the first researcher to create a theory of learning that included schemas. Three important elements of his theory are that:

1 New information is added to or *assimilated into* current schemas.
2 Cognitive dissonance is caused by *new information* that cannot be easily integrated and schemas are forced to change or *accommodate* this new information.
3 Three factors cause learning and development – biological development that progresses in *stages, interaction* with the worlds and objects, and *interaction* with others.

Understanding how we learn by processing and connecting new and old information inside our brains has been further developed by both cognitive science and cognitive psychology. As a new teacher, it is helpful to begin by focusing on the work of cognitive scientist, John Sweller, and his Cognitive Load Theory, and Vygotsky, whose ideas were termed, after his early and untimely death, as social constructivism.

Cognitive Science and Cognitive Load Theory

John Sweller is an Australian psychologist. His work into Cognitive Load Theory (CLT) began in 1988 when he looked at how we process information as we solve problems. His work on CLT is developed from biological theories of evolution because his view is that how we think and learn have evolved as a natural information processing system. Central to his theory is how knowledge is classified. He draws upon the work of David Geary (2007, 2008), an evolutionary psychologist who developed the concept of biologically primary and biologically secondary knowledge. Biologically primary knowledge is the type of skill that we have evolved to acquire and do not need to be explicitly taught, i.e. how to speak, listen, recognise faces and experience basic social relations. We may be helped to learn them by others, but we are self-motivated and acquire these skills easily, effortlessly and unconsciously without specific teaching. By contrast, biologically secondary knowledge is important to our culture and needs to be learned for us to function in society, i.e. learning to read and write. Sweller argues that, although both types of knowledge are processed in the same way, what is important for teaching is how you deal with secondary knowledge because that is the knowledge to be taught in schools by teachers (Sweller et al., 2011).

CLT – A Theory of Teaching Based on How Learning Happens

Although Cognitive Load Theory contains a definition of learning (see above), it is in fact a theory of teaching. Sweller developed CLT as a theory of teaching based on the mental actions and processes of acquiring knowledge and understanding, which he terms 'human cognitive architecture' (Sweller et al., 2011: 37). Sweller developed five principles for how we process information, and from these generated 13 teaching approaches, which he calls Cognitive Load Theory Effects. Sweller emphasises that teaching approaches have to be tested, so he states where such data have not yet been fully developed (although many of the approaches are now being investigated since his book was published in 2011).

Ten years later, in 2021, the Education Endowment Foundation (EEF) undertook a major review of the evidence of seven different cognitive science approaches to learning that are used in classrooms: spaced learning, interleaving, retrieval practice, managing cognitive load, working with schemas, multimedia learning and embodied learning. The EEF concluded that teachers need to understand the principles of cognitive science, but also found that the application and testing of these ideas in the classroom was still underdeveloped. Importantly, the EEF concluded that elements of cognitive science should not be considered or implemented in isolation as a teaching technique, but instead should be considered in terms of how they work together as ideas in practice so that teachers develop professional judgement about how best to use them (knowing the right thing to do at the right time in the right way for the right reason).

Working Memory and Long-Term Memory

Sweller's view is that the role of education is to increase knowledge of all the different curriculum subjects held in long-term memory and that human working memory limits how we learn (Sweller et al., 2011). The working memory acts as a conduit between what is to be learned and the long-term memory. At any time, the working memory can only store seven items of new information for about 20 seconds. It can only process (combine, contrast or deal with) three or four items of information at any time. Sweller therefore argues that teachers must consider the capacity and duration of working memory: 'Information that cannot be fully processed in working memory cannot be fully transferred to long-term memory inhibiting learning' (Sweller et al., 2011: 54). He argues that many teachers approach teaching as if human working memory does not exist or is irrelevant to learning. He also suggests that the purpose of teaching is to increase secondary knowledge held in the long-term memory. This is because long-term memory changes us, and the limits of working memory are what enable us to do things we were not able to do before.

Intrinsic and Extraneous Cognitive Load

Cognitive load comes from two sources: the intrinsic nature of some information imposes a heavy cognitive load, and sometimes it is not the information itself that imposes a heavy cognitive load, but the way it is presented by the teacher. The latter is known as extraneous cognitive load. Both types of heavy cognitive load are caused by the same thing, which Sweller calls element interactivity. It is when the working memory is being required to process too much information at the same time. It is important to understand these terms associated with CLT so that you can think about how to teach so your pupils learn. These key concepts of CLT are set out in the Table 1.3.

Table 1.3 Key concepts in CLT and what they mean

Key idea in CLT	What it means
Intrinsic cognitive load	The complexity of the information being processed
Extraneous cognitive load	When the information is presented in too complex or complicated a way to be processed by the working memory
Element interactivity	The number of elements to be processed (due either to the nature of the information or the complexity of the teaching)

Learning With Understanding

Ofsted (2022) warn, in the *School Inspection Handbook*, that rote learning of disconnected facts or glossaries represents poor practice when using CLT in teaching because it lacks the proper focus on three important aspects of learning processes: connecting new and existing knowledge, developing fluency and applying what one has learned. Sweller takes the view that element interactivity and intrinsic cognitive load explain the difference between learning by rote and learning with understanding. His view is that understanding is linked to the nature of the information contained within the knowledge of the curriculum. By this, he means that low element interactivity (when the concept or skill can be processes one element at a time) and high element interactivity (when the concept or skill is complex and must be processed simultaneously) will impact on your design of tasks. Being aware of high element interactivity and which elements your pupils have already mastered will help you decide how to approach developing a task that goes beyond single recall of single elements as in rote learning but provide your pupils with opportunities to gain fluency in the concept or skill or to apply what they have learned (Sweller et al., 2011).

Borrowing and Reorganising

Sweller et al. (2011: 44) developed five principles of information processing in CLT:

1 Information storage.
2 Borrowing and reorganising.

3 Randomness as genesis (generating new information).
4 Narrow limits of change.
5 Environmental organising and linking.

The first of these principles relates to the intake of information (working and long-term memory) and the fifth to the storage of information (schema development). Typically, they are emphasised as important knowledge for teachers.

However, Sweller et al.'s second principle – the principle of borrowing and reorganising – helps teachers to understand their role in causing learning in their pupils. They argue that 'we do acquire or borrow the vast bulk of information held in long-term memory from other people, but we alter that information depending on what we have already stored in long-term memory' (Sweller et al., 2011: 48). In many ways, the role of the teacher is to be the person from whom their pupils borrow information and the activities that take place in the lesson facilitate its reorganisation in pupils' schema. The ways in which we 'borrow' information include: imitating other people, listening to what others tell us, reading what others write, and looking at diagrams and pictures that others produce. These processes of borrowing information from others are particularly important in the acquisition of biological secondary information. The vast bulk of such information that is stored in long-term memory is acquired by one of the processes or a combination of the processes. The teaching strategies generated from CLT rely heavily on the borrowing and reorganising principle. Such teaching strategies are largely attempting to present information to pupils that will be most likely to result in facilitating schemas.

It is important to remember when teaching that the information your pupils store as knowledge will never be a precise copy of what you have told them. This is because your pupils' schema is likely to be different from the schema held in your long-term memory – as the person from whom it is borrowed – because it is a combination of borrowed information (new knowledge) combined with information already held in long-term memory (prior knowledge).

Key Takeaways

- Learning is a change in the long-term memory.
- Working memory is where conscious processing takes place. It is limited in capacity and duration.
- Long-term memory contains limitless amounts of information organised into schema.
- Long-term memory is the basis for everything we do and understand.
- Getting better at something is determined by what is stored in the long-term memory. It is also specific to the subject. Therefore, teachers need to teach with the specifics of each subject in mind.
- Teaching should be designed on the basis of what we know about how we learn so that it can be effective.
- Use of any CLT technique in isolation does not guarantee more effective teaching. As a teacher, you need to think about what approach to use with whom and to have thought

through your reasons as to why it will help your pupils learn. For example, if cognitive load is reduced too much, it may result in a long and fragmented process, and similarly, it is important to relate ideas back to the 'big picture' so that pupils can understand the purpose and direction of what they are learning.

Constructivism

Constructivism is a theory of learning developed from the 1920s. It is typically described as cognitive constructivism, representing the work of Jean Piaget, and social constructivism, representing the work of LS Vygotsky. Constructivism does not regard children as empty vessels into which knowledge should be poured, but recognises that children already have organised knowledge. Pupils will integrate new information into their existing ways of understanding the world. Thus, for effective learning to take place, new knowledge must be integrated into their existing schema or conceptual structures.

Piaget's work was based on studying the individual and how the individual's cognitive development progressed. He is best known for suggesting that children progress through stages of development. His work was adapted from the idea of biological adaption (so the mind adapts its structures to cope with new experiences). However, it is the work of Vygotsky that has had the most significant influence on learning and teaching today. His ideas about learning and development have shaped how we teach today. For example, his concept of the Zone of Proximal Development has been developed by others into the teaching activities of scaffolding and modelling (see Chapter 11).

Vygotsky – How Can Teachers Help Pupils Learn the Curriculum?

Vygotsky had worked as a teacher and then as a psychologist in Russia during the 1920s and early 1930s. He died in Moscow in 1934 at the age of 37. His untimely death meant that other researchers and thinkers were left to take up and develop his ideas. Vygotsky's work was first translated from Russian into English in the 1970s and has been recently translated again by Stanley Mitchell and summarised for teachers by Myra Barrs (2021).

Vygotsky's research focused on conceptualising consciousness – how minds are shaped and how the world is conceptualised. His breakthrough was the concept of mediation – that ideas are taken on and worked with. Further, Vygotsky's psychology was also concerned with how people use ideas as 'tools' to act upon the world to shape it. Vygotsky attempted to transcend the *nature versus nurture* dichotomy prevalent at the time of his research. In his view, a child is neither shaped into a social being only by their environment, nor does the child only develop their innate potential by adapting to the environment. From Vygotsky's perspective, the relationship between the child and the environment has a dynamic nature. He saw the learning process in terms of the child playing an active role in learning by interacting with the environment and modifying it with the help of internalised mental tools.

For Vygotsky, learning is a process of internalising ideas and then externalising those ideas by using them in action. As learners, we take in and make sense of what we see as having value and work with those understandings as we act in and on the world. Vygotsky recognised that all the things we do are shaped by what we know and that how we act in the world is in line with how we make sense of it. As such, what we are able to do (the action we can now take) is shaped by what we have internalised and can now externalise, and how we use what we know as tools reveals how a learner may be thinking (Edwards, 2011).

Higher and Lower Mental Functions

Vygotsky (1997 [1931]) was concerned with the development of higher mental functions and his primary concern was with how a teacher helps pupils to develop the higher order concepts (what is taught in school) that they do not have access to in everyday life. He described mental ability as comprising two distinct functions: lower mental functions are those that are inherited and are controlled by external events; and higher mental functions are developed through social interaction and are controlled internally (e.g. thinking and language, which, he argues, are central to the process of learning in school). Lower mental functions are culture-free and have not changed significantly over the course of human history. By contrast, higher mental functions are culture-specific and can vary from society to society. Lower mental functions, such as sensations, reactive attention and associate memory, are part of our biological heritage and are already present at the moment of birth. The development of lower mental functions occurs through maturation and through the accumulation of the individual experience. When learning is based on lower mental functions, the learner is relatively passive and the outcomes of learning are determined by the nature of any stimuli. Learning based on lower mental functions is time-consuming and not very efficient.

Higher mental functions continue to be formed throughout our lifetime as a result of mastering mental tools by working with other humans. The higher mental functions include focused attention, deliberate memory and logical thinking. All higher mental functions are deliberate and involve the use of language. For Vygotsky, the acquisition of higher mental functions is what enables humans to be in control of what they think, say and do.

Each higher mental function appears twice in the course of child development – first as inter-subjective and later as intra-subjective. In this way, each higher mental function goes through a stage when it does not yet belong to a single individual (intra) but is 'shared' among several people (inter). For example, before a child learns to remember on purpose, there will be quite some time when they will only be able to remember with substantial support from their parents or guardians, being prompted with various memory strategies. Without the adult's help, the child cannot yet control their memory. After some time of sharing a mental function with others, the child will eventually internalise this new process and it will become part of their own mental repertoire. There are many ways in which a developing skill or concept can be shared between two or more people. A child may use a strategy or concept with the support of a teacher. Two children may work together to solve a problem. One child may teach another child. A group of children may support each other in learning a new activity. All of these interactions may result in the child mastering a new concept or skill. In this way, the social environment, language and thought are the sources of learning and development so that the mental processes themselves can be the product of co-construction.

The Concept of a Mental Tool

To develop higher mental functions, children must acquire mental tools. Usually these are passed on to the children by other more knowledgeable members of society, such as teachers or their parents or guardians. Whenever teaching takes place, either formally or informally, there is an opportunity for an expert to introduce a tool, to model how to use it, and to monitor its use by a novice. For Vygotsky, the teaching and learning of existing mental tools and the generation of new ones replaces the process of biological adaption as the major mechanism for human development.

Mental tools allow humans to function beyond the limits of their mental capacities. All devices used to improve mental functioning fall into the category of mental tools. They vary in their format and in their complexity. The most primitive tools can be applied to isolated tasks and facilitate only just one mental function. For example, leaving your house keys by the front door will help you to remember just one thing and will only work for a short period of time. On the other hand, the most complex tool, language, can be applied for a variety of tasks and to more than one mental function. Mental tools expand our ability to learn but also help us in terms of our emotional and social behaviours.

Vygotsky's students, following his death, developed his idea of mental tools. They were able to identify many categories of tools that help children learn. For children in school, written speech becomes one of the most powerful tools. Learning to read and write, for Vygotsky, means more than just acquiring one more skill because it actually restructures the child's mind, enabling the child to think in abstract terms, which is essential for learning the school curriculum. Having acquired a mental tool, a pupil becomes responsible for their own learning and requires less and less of the teacher's assistance.

The concept of mental tools makes it clear why Vygotsky sees learning as leading a child's development rather than following it (i.e. it is not a biological adaption). This is because mental tools are not developed by children spontaneously as an outcome of their development. Instead, they are passed on to children and acquired by them through the processes of teaching and learning. When the teaching of and acquisition of mental tools occurs, pitched at the right level for the child, development itself may take a big leap forward, bringing a child to a new level of understanding.

Spontaneous (Everyday) and Scientific (Academic) Concepts

As a more knowledgeable other, a primary school teacher is required to have considerable understanding of the subject they teach in the form of subject knowledge, curriculum progression and conceptual understanding (Karpov, 2014). Vygotsky (1987 [1934]) differentiated between two kinds of concepts – the scientific (academic) concepts and the spontaneous (everyday). This idea lies at the heart of his interpretation of both teaching and the curriculum. According to Vygotsky (1987 [1934]), the role of the teacher is to provide pupils with access to theoretical concepts in all their different forms as they appear in the school curriculum. Vygotsky (1978) recognised that learning happens as an outcome of the tasks designed by the teacher to enable the pupil to integrate subject concepts with their everyday knowledge.

Mercer (2007: 19) developed a powerful metaphor of crossing a bridge for how teachers work in relation to their pupils:

> Teachers have to organise, energise, and maintain a local mini-community of enquiry. Teachers are expected to help their pupils develop ways of thinking that will enable them to travel on intellectual journeys, so they understand and are understood in wider communities of discourse. However, teachers have to start from where the pupils are, to use what the pupils already know and help them to go back and forth across the bridge between everyday and educated ways of thinking.

This metaphor offers a way of thinking about the dual focus of the teacher on both the children in the class (as the mini-community of enquiry) and the subject-matter of the curriculum, and the process of teaching as moving back and forth across the bridge in relational as opposed to transactional terms.

Vygotsky believed that teaching is relational (it has the aim to bring the pupil into relation with the curriculum). The activities of teaching in school operate in the following ways: the teacher works with pupils to assist pupils to develop self-regulation and autonomy, and verbal and written tasks are designed by the teacher to assist pupils to develop understanding. That is, as a teacher, you talk *in* the subject (using the language of the subject in order that pupils learn the subject). At the same time, as the teacher, you are also working with the curriculum in terms of how the knowledge embedded in the school curriculum is represented to pupils in activities and tasks (Young, 2014). In doing so, you assist pupils to develop and use higher-level thinking and cognitive strategies (Shulman, 2000). As such, the teacher talks *about* the learning of the subject to their pupils. Winch (2017: 81) addressed this in terms of the concept of epistemic ascent: 'an understanding of the structure of systematic knowledge from the point of view of the learner rather than the expert'.

In other words, teaching is not as simple as transmission, where the teacher talks to pupils and they memorise what they have been told (Daniels, 2005). On the contrary, Shulman describes the process of teaching in terms of pupils' relation with the content of the curriculum as 'making the internal external; working on it together while it is out and then putting the outside back in' (Shulman, 2000: 133). A Vygotskyian approach to teaching emphasises that the activities of teaching take the form of a social practice because, as Bruner (1975) suggests, it is the activity between the teacher and their pupils that enables learning by pupils in the lesson to proceed.

The Double Move

Marianne Hedegaard is a post-Vygotskyian who has researched his ideas to test how they work in classrooms. In 2002, she set out a way of understanding how classroom teaching and learning are integrated and operate in relation with one another. She terms this approach the 'double move'. The double move is a teaching process where the teacher is working to advance the subject-matter of the curriculum towards the child's everyday knowledge and to extend the child's everyday knowledge towards the concepts in the subject-matter so that they are integrated. Hedegaard's (2002) approach to the double move in teaching and developmental learning is built on two basic assumptions about children's functioning:

- That the child appropriates cultural knowledge, skills, and motives through social interactions with other participants of a cultural practice, usually more skilled adults, and older children
- That the child's own intentional activity is one of the conditions for his or her development of concepts, skills and motives. (Hedegaard, 2002: 17)

The double move approach has its theoretical roots in the work of Vygotsky (Hardman, 2019; van Oers, 2019). The double move assumes that teaching is a complex process by which the pupils' everyday knowledge is extended and transformed by the concepts as they exist in the school curriculum. Therefore, in the terms that Vygotsky (1978) used, teachers distinguish the everyday, spontaneous concepts that a child learns through engaging with the world from the scientific, abstract concepts that need to be taught to the child. Use of language is a major element of teaching actions because teacher talk leads to the development of scientific concepts by the pupil:

> Scientific and everyday concepts are dialectically entailed: a scientific concept in the absence of an everyday concept is merely a verbal definition and has no meaning; similarly an everyday concept in the absence of the scientific concept remains hidden from the consciousness. (Hardman, 2019)

'Scientific' refers to academic concepts introduced by a teacher in school, whereas an 'everyday' concept is regarded by Vygotsky (1978) as not requiring an explicit teaching process in order to develop it (Barrs, 2021). The social interactions between the teacher and pupils and the task designed by the teacher have the function of moving the pupil to the next level of development in terms of their conceptual understanding of the subject-matter. The process of teaching enables the pupil to move to a relationship with the new theoretical knowledge such that they are able to use and employ it in their own local practice as both a learner in a classroom and in their everyday existence. In this way, the process of teaching requires that teachers have knowledge and expertise in the subject-matter of what is taught. In addition, teachers also need to develop a good knowledge of the children they teach and have expertise in creating social interactions and practical activities that draw the knowledge of pupils and of the subject together, while creating a culture in the classroom and a relationship with pupils that enables all to enact the subject and everyday knowledge.

Applying the double move to your teaching needs you to take three actions: first, analyse the subject-matter so that your teaching is based on the academic concepts within each subject; second, make sure you know your pupils' interests and backgrounds; and third, create tasks and activities to illuminate the academic concepts (Hedegaard, 2002). In other words, the double move provides a way to interpret the process of teaching: the integration of scientific concepts in subject-matter with the pupils' personal concepts so that they might take this understanding forward in their lives, and as learners. As such, the social practice of teaching has the long-term aim of offering pupils an understanding of the links between scientific concepts within the subject in order that pupils might gain an understanding of the subject as a coherent, conceptual, model system to be used by them at some future time and independently (Hedegaard, 2002).

The Concept of the Zone of Proximal Development

The Zone of Proximal Development (ZPD) is probably the most widely known and least understood of Vygotsky's ideas. The purpose of the ZPD is to help us understand when the teaching of and acquisition of mental tools should best occur to have the maximum impact on the learning and development of the child. It was defined by Vygotsky in Chapter 6 of his book *Mind in Society* (1978: 86) as 'the distance between the actual developmental level as determined by independent problem solving and the level of potential development as determined through problem solving under adult guidance or in collaboration with more capable peers' or 'what the child is able to do in collaboration today he will be able to do independently tomorrow' (Vygotsky, 1987 [1934]: 211). Typically, the Zone of Proximal Development has been conceived as an interaction between a more competent person and a less competent person on a task, such that the less competent person becomes individually independently proficient at what was initially a jointly accomplished task. This view of ZPD suggests teaching perfection, where an amazing teacher is able to help every child master easily whatever it is that needs to be taught that day. It is not what Vygotsky was attempting to suggest. The use of the term 'developmental' rather than 'learning' is not coincidental. This is because the ZPD is not concerned with developing a specific skill in any task, but is related to overall cognitive development.

Because having a good teacher is important for learning, the idea of ZPD has been used to focus on the importance of the assistance the teacher provides. However, Vygotsky was particularly interested in the role of collaboration and the nature of the help that enables pupils to do more difficult things than they can do independently. In other words, the competence of the teacher is not the purpose of ZPD as such, but thinking in terms of ZPD helps us to understand the meaning of the teacher's assistance in relation to a pupil's learning and development.

The ZPD has two different purposes. First, to identify the different types of psychological functions and the social interactions associated with them for a child to develop. Second, to identify a child's current state in relation to these functions so that they can develop further. In this way, the ZPD is a tool by which a teacher can think about teaching for learning because the teacher is looking to assess the child's current state of development in a way that provides insight into what that child needs to develop. From this, the teacher is able to decide how to model so that the pupil can imitate what it is they are learning how to do. Vygotsky was clear that the pupil is not copying the teacher because the teacher has necessarily analysed 'everything that the child cannot do independently but which he can be taught or which he can do with direction or cooperation or with the help of leading questions' (Vygotsky, 1998 [1934]: 202). Such imitation (from the modelling of the teacher) is possible because the child has not yet sufficiently developed the higher mental functions to work independently but has developed enough so that they can understand how to use the collaborative actions (the modelling by leading questions or worked examples) of the teacher.

The idea of the Zone of Proximal Development is meant to ensure that teaching is focused on pupils' next steps rather than what they can already do. The ZPD is a way of describing the relationship between what the child can do now and what they need to do next. It does not just describe how help can lead to learning, but is concerned with thinking about how the pupil can get better and work at a higher level in terms of academic concepts. The ZPD is not located in the pupil, but is always an evaluation by the teacher of the pupil's capabilities in relation to the next step of learning academic concepts as higher mental functions. It is important to be aware that the Zone of Proximal Development is not created in interaction between pupil and teacher. This is because the pupil getting better at what it is they have to learn is not *created* in the interaction. Rather, the interaction between pupil and teacher *provides the conditions* for identifying how far the child has developed in relation to developing the academic concepts.

Key Takeaways

- Learning in school includes learning from other people.
- The process of learning involves internalising, externalising and then integrating new knowledge (the scientific, abstract or academic concepts in each subject) with the (everyday concepts) pre-existing (prior) knowledge the child has already.
- Teaching is a form of assistance.
- Teachers should think carefully about how language can develop the ability of their pupils to think.
- The ZPD is intended to help teachers think about the relation between teaching and learning.
- Active learning is not about what pupils do but is about activating hard thinking by pupils.

Suggested Activities to Develop Learner-Focused Teaching Strategies

Discuss With a More Experienced Teacher

1 What do you want the pupils to be thinking about in the lesson? How will the lesson move from you talking through something with them to internalised self-talk and internalised thinking with your pupils asking themselves questions?
2 How can you consider what pupils might already know about what you are teaching?
3 Which pupils might experience specific difficulties with acquiring, recalling and using knowledge, and what actions you might take in relation to this?

For You to Think About After a Lesson

1 Did you break complex tasks down into small enough steps?
2 Did you explain the purpose of what the pupils were learning so that they could integrate new knowledge with prior knowledge?

For You to Do

1 Identify the academic concepts that shape the particular subject you are teaching.
2 Research the different types of knowledge that make up the different subjects that you will teach. For example, generative knowledge (what you need to know in order to learn more in the future, i.e. to grasp new information more readily later); substantive knowledge (the abstract concepts that are used to think like an historian or artist, etc.) and disciplinary knowledge (knowing about the origins and social production of knowledge, not just its processes, structures, rules and conventions, i.e. how historians learn about the past and use this knowledge to construct meaning).

Deepening Your Knowledge

Sfard, A (1998) On two metaphors for learning and the dangers of choosing just one. *American Educational Research Association* 27(2), 4–13

Anna Sfard discusses learning theory using two metaphors: acquisition and participation. She suggests that regarding learning as acquisition sees learning as the accumulation of concepts which are the basic units of knowledge. In this, we can see the influence of cognitive models of transmission and the constructivist idea of the construction of meaning through internalisation. The participation metaphor emphasises learning as constant activity in the context of a community of which the learner is an integral part. Her argument is that rather than try to explain learning through one or the other of these metaphors, they both complement each other and should be used together.

Reflection on Important Questions

It is important to have developed your understanding of learning because one of the key purposes of your role as a teacher is to enable the children in your class to learn. Without a set of ideas to explain the processes of learning, it is likely that you will copy the external behaviours of your teachers when you were at school yourself or those you now observe as you learn to teach. If you just copy what other teachers do, rather than thinking about what you do using ideas about how children learn, it will be harder to develop the syntactic knowledge of a teacher. In other words, without understanding learning, 'thinking like a teacher' is much more difficult.

Remember too that, as a teacher, you also 'wear another hat' in that you are also a learner – you learn more every day about teaching, the curriculum, planning and learning itself. It is the integration of this new learning that will help you to keep getting better as a teacher because your capacity to teach well will be expanded.

There are many teaching strategies, but it is important to develop strategies that connect with how children learn. Furthermore, you will not want to think about each strategy as an isolated technique whose performance you must perfect. Instead, you will want to think about how to connect your teaching strategies to your teaching aims. In this way, you will develop your professional judgement, pedagogical reasoning and the ability to make good decisions about learning before, during and after you actually teach a lesson.

Conclusion

Part 1 of this book addresses the four big concepts that teachers need to understand: What is learning? (Chapter 1), What is teaching? (Chapter 2), What is the curriculum? (Chapter 3) and What is backwards planning? (Chapter 4). In these four chapters, we look at the key theoretical and practical concepts that answer each of the questions. It is important for you to understand these concepts because they will form the basis of your actions as a teacher. Furthermore, by looking at the connections across the four questions that make up Part 1, you begin to make sense of your new role as a primary schoolteacher.

Note

1 In 2024 the CCF was subsumed into the new Initial Teacher Training and Early Career Framework (ITTECF) which combines and updates the previous ITT Core Content Framework and the Early Career Framework into a single policy document. This newer DfE document contains some minor text amendments to the 2019 CCF but the majority of the text is the same.

References

Barrs, M (2017) Rediscovering Vygotsky's Concept of the ZPD: Stanley Mitchell's New Translation of 'The problem of Teaching (*Obuchenie*) and Mental development at School Age' *Changing English Studies in Culture and Education* 24 (4), 345–358

Barrs, M (2021) *Vygotsky, the Teacher: A Companion to His Psychology for Teachers and Other Practitioners*. London: Routledge

Bruner, J (1975) *Toward a Theory of Instruction*. Cambridge, MA: Harvard University Press

Chaiklin, S (2015) The concept of learning in a cultural-historical perspective. In Scott, D and Hargreaves, E (Eds.), *The SAGE Handbook of Learning*. London: Sage

Cobb, M (2020) *The Idea of the Brain: A History*. London: Profile Books

Daniels, H (2005) Vygotsky and educational psychology: Some preliminary remarks. *Educational and Child Psychology 22*

DfE (Department for Education) (2011) *Teachers' Standards*. London: HMSO

DfE (2019) *ITT Core Content Framework*. London: HMSO

Edwards, A (2011) *Cultural-Historical Activity Theory*. BERA (British Educational Research Association) https://www.bera.ac.uk/publication/cultural-historical-activity-theory-chat

Geary, D (2007) Educating the evolved mind: conceptual foundations for an evolutionary educational psychology. In Carlson, J S and Levin, J R (Eds.), *Psychological Perspectives on Contemporary Educational Issues*. Greenwich, CT: Information Age

Geary, D (2008) An evolutionarily informed education science. *Educational Psychologist* 43, 179–195

Hardman, J (2019) Vygotsky's developmental pedagogy recontextualised as Hedegaard's double move: Science teaching in Grades 1 and 2 in a disadvantaged school in South Africa. In Edwards, A, Fleer, M, and Bottcher, L (Eds.), *Cultural-Historical Approaches to Learning and Development* (Vol. 6). Singapore: Springer

Hattie, J (2009) *Visible Learning: A Synthesis of over 800 Meta-analyses relating to Achievement*. Abingdon: Routledge

Hattie, J (2023) *Visible Learning: The Sequel. A Synthesis of over 2,100 Meta-analyses relating to Achievement*. Abingdon: Routledge

Hedegaard, M (2002) *Learning and Child Development*. Oxford: Aarhus University Press

Karpov, Y (2014) *Vygotsky for Educators*. New York: Cambridge University Press

Mercer, N (2007) *Dialogue and the Development of Children's Thinking: A Sociocultural approach*. Abingdon: Routledge

Ofsted (2019) *Education Inspection Framework: Overview of Research*. London: Ofsted

Ofsted (2022) *School Inspection Handbook*. London: Ofsted

Sfard, A (1998) On two metaphors for learning and the dangers of choosing just one. *American Educational Research Association* 27(2), 4–13

Shulman, L (2000) Teacher development: Roles of domain expertise and pedagogical knowledge. *Journal of Applied Developmental Psychology* 21(1), 129–135

Sweller, J (1988) Cognitive load during problem solving: Effects on learning. *Cognitive Science* 12(2), 257–285

Sweller, J, Ayres, P, and Kalyuga S (2011) *Cognitive Load Theory* (Vol. 1). New York: Springer Science and Business Media

van Oers, B (2019) The double move in meaningful teaching revisited. In Edwards, A, Fleer, M, and Bottcher, L (Eds.), *Cultural-Historical Approaches to Learning and Development* (Vol. 6). Singapore: Springer

Vygotsky, LS (1978) *Mind in Society: The Development Psychological Processes*. Cambridge, MA: Harvard University Press

Vygotsky, LS (1987 [1934]) Thinking and speech. In Reiber, RW (Ed.), *The Collected Works of LS Vygotsky. Vol. 1: Problems of General Psychology*. New York: Plenum Press

Vygotsky, LS (1997 [1931]) The history of the development of higher mental functions. In Reiber RW (Ed.), *The Collected Works of LS Vygotsky. Vol. 4: The History of the Development of Higher Mental Functions*. New York: Plenum Press

Vygotsky, LS (1998 [1934]) The problem of age. In Reiber RW (Ed.), *The Collected Works of LS Vygotsky. Vol. 5: Child Psychology*. New York: Plenum Press

Winch, C (2017) *Teachers' Know-How: A Philosophical Investigation*. Oxford: Wiley

Young, M (2014) *The Curriculum and Entitlement to Knowledge*. Cambridge: Magdalene College, Cambridge Assessment Network

2
WHAT IS TEACHING?

Important Questions

- What is teaching?
- What is good teaching?
- How do we know?
- What is an evidence-informed teacher?

Introduction

In Chapter 1, we considered what research, theory and evidence tell us about how children learn in school. As well as describing the processes and elements of learning, we identified the importance of the relationship between teaching and learning, and the significance of the *invisibility* of learning (as a cognitive process or hard thinking) to you as a teacher. Unlike learning, teaching is observable. However, 'whether the teaching is effective, and pupils are actually learning is a judgement, rather than a fact' (Mortimore, 2014: 55). In many ways, the act of teaching is your *work* as a teacher – that is, it is what *you actually do*. While your teaching will be shaped by educational policy, key ideas from theory and evidence from research, you also bring to it your intentions, decisions and actions, which themselves are shaped by your reasons for becoming a teacher and your professional values.

In this chapter we will consider what you should know about teaching, what questions about teaching you should ask as you get better at teaching and how you can evaluate what others have to say about how you should teach.

What is Teaching?

Teaching can be understood as two key processes. The first is that teaching is a process of assistance, where you support your pupils' learning by adjusting, clarifying, checking for understanding and adapting your teaching. The second is that teaching is a process of instruction, where you offer explanations and input to your pupils about what it is they need to learn.

In order to understand it better, research into teaching has taken two broad approaches. First, teaching has been investigated in order to describe what teachers do, and second, teaching has been investigated in terms of its effectiveness, i.e. how successful it is in terms of achieving prescribed outcomes. In this way, research into teaching has developed to understand teaching as an art or craft or science, and in terms of the knowledge and skills of the teacher, i.e. the teaching of the individual teacher. But it has also been developed to understand which forms of teaching might have the biggest impact on pupils' outcomes when measured in a particular school, area or country.

In general terms, research, evidence and theory into teaching have attempted to help us understand teaching in three ways:

1 To find ways to teach better, in terms of practice and also what impact teaching can have on outcomes.
2 To understand the complexity of teaching and the context in which it happens.
3 To understand teaching in the light of what we know about learning.

As a new teacher, when you interpret research, evidence and theory about teaching and then integrate it with your existing knowledge, it becomes part of your syntactic knowledge, i.e. you become able 'to think like a teacher'. The next section explains how we have come to understand teaching through these different research traditions.

Effective Teaching: A Research Timeline

Research into teaching effectiveness adopts a specific inquiry approach: it investigates which teaching strategies achieve certain outcomes. The following section takes the form of a timeline in two phases: 1979–1999 and 2000–2020.

1979–1999

The first stage of the timeline summarises three seminal studies. These studies form the basis of teaching effectiveness research in England as it evolved. From this research approach, important ideas emerged that have shaped teaching as we know it today.

1979 – 15,000 Hours Secondary Schools and Their Effects on Children (Rutter et al.)

Rutter, M, Maughan, B, Mortimore, P, and Ouston, J (1979) *15,000 Hours: Secondary Schools and Their Effects on Children*. London: Open Books

Key Idea: Schools and Teachers Have an Effect

This was a study of 2000 secondary school pupils from 12 secondary schools which took place over three years. It is regarded as the seminal study on the impact schools have on pupils and takes its title from the number of hours that pupils spend in schools. It gave rise to the school and teacher effectiveness and improvement movements (although the original authors may not always approve of some of the strategies that subsequently arose from their original research).

Before this study, it was assumed that the home and a fixed view of intelligence were the only factors that impacted attainment and achievement. However, two significant ideas arose from this work. The first idea is that there 'is a causal relationship between school processes and children's progress' (1979: 180). The second is that different schools can have different levels of impact, with teachers being an important element in such variability. They noted too that good teaching contributes to ethos, but also that ethos provides 'the optimal setting to bring out their teaching skills' (1979: 140).

1995 – Key Characteristics of Effective Schools: A Review of School Effectiveness Research (Sammons et al.)

Sammons, P, Hillman, J, and Mortimore, P (1995) *Key Characteristics of Effective Schools: A Review of School Effectiveness Research*. London: Institute of Education: International School Effectiveness and Improvement Centre

Key Idea: Value-Added Structured Teaching

This influential report, comprising a meta-analysis of 160 research papers, was written for Ofsted by the Institute of Education, University of London. Its aim was to summarise the School Effectiveness (SE) research to date and to identify the impact of school when considering the differences between schools in terms of their intakes. It meant that schools could be compared on a 'like for like' basis, so this study introduced the key idea of 'added value' to English schools. 'Added value' is a measure of the progress pupils make over time. It considers how much progress a child has made since their starting point, relative to the progress made by similar pupils (however, the term used in education is value-added). This study argued that educationally and statistically significant school effects could be determined (they cite the difference as 6 Grade 7s instead of 6 Grade 4s) and that this was particularly significant for disadvantaged groups.

The authors identified 11 factors (or correlates) of effectiveness, which they thought could be used as a tool for school self-evaluation, rather than as a checklist of independent items to be actioned or copied, which was largely how it came to be used. They were also clear that it should not be said that because a school might lack any of these features, it was ineffective.

That specific research had not yet taken place. Rather, they stated that an ineffective school might be driven by factors as yet unexplained.

The 11 factors for effective schools were:

1. Professional leadership.
2. A shared vision and goals.
3. A learning environment.
4. A concentration on teaching and learning.
5. Purposeful teaching.
6. High expectations.
7. Positive reinforcement.
8. Monitoring progress.
9. Ensuring pupils' rights and responsibilities.
10. Creating a home–school partnership.
11. Creating a learning organisation.

The authors recognised that quality teaching is 'at the heart of effective schools' (1995: 15), and while they acknowledged that there are 'problems in drawing general conclusions on effective teaching practices' (1995: 19), they also identified teaching practices in effective schools that they termed 'purposeful teaching'. The aspects of purposeful teaching are set out in Table 2.1.

Table 2.1 Purposeful teaching in terms of school effectiveness research

Efficient organisation	• being well organised in advance of a lesson • being absolutely clear about objectives • pacing a lesson so that objectives were achieved
Clarity of purpose	• pupils are aware of the purpose of the content of the lesson • objectives of the lesson are clearly explained at the start • lesson objectives should be referred to throughout the lesson • objectives should relate to both previous work and be personally relevant to pupils • the lesson should be structured by an overview at the start, with transitions clearly signalled • the main idea of the lesson should be reviewed at the end
Structured lessons	• questions should focus attention on key elements of the lesson • open-ended questions should be asked, followed by pupil answer and then teacher feedback • more time should be spent asking questions in primary schools, the room should be well organised and there should be lots for pupils to do; there should be a limited focus in each session; pupils' responsibility and independence should be promoted, with pupils being encouraged to manage their own work • in secondary schools, there should be an even greater stress on pupil independence and responsibility
Adaptive practice	• School Effectiveness research showed that using mandated curriculum materials and teaching procedures does not often bring about gains in achievement • Pupil progress is enhanced when teachers identify, modify and adapt teaching strategies which are sensitive to the needs of their pupils

These authors made modest claims for their work. Their hope was that it would stimulate debate for headteachers and teachers as they evaluated their schools. However, SE research was embraced by policymakers and this work led to the creation of the Standards and Effectiveness Unit and the National Strategies programmes by the Department for Education and Employment (DfEE). These policies led to many developments in teaching, including the three- or five-part lesson structure – a lesson structure of starter activity, main activity and plenary). The research also led to questions about how much effect an individual teacher might have and how the variable impacts between different teachers might be measured.

Suggested Activity

Use these questions, which have been developed from teacher effectiveness research, to consider your own practice and how you may ensure more effective learning:

- How often do I encourage pupils to think for themselves and try out new ideas?
- What techniques do I use to help pupils be more aware of how best they learn and why?
- What assumptions do I make about the individual pupil when I teach?
- On what are these assumptions based?
- How would I describe the climate I am trying to establish in the classroom?
- What do I say and do to establish this climate?

1998 – School Matters: The Junior Years (Mortimore et al.)

Mortimore, P, Sammons, P, Stoll, L, Lewis D, and Ecob, R (1998) *School Matters: The Junior Years*. London: Open Books

Key Idea: Schools Have an Effect on Disadvantaged Groups

This was a study of 2000 7–11-year-olds in 50 schools that took place over four years. It was a follow-up study to *15000 Hours* (Rutter et al., 1979), but set in primary schools instead of secondary schools. The authors had three research questions:

1. Are some schools or classes more effective than others when variations in the intakes of pupils are taken into account?
2. Are some schools or classes more effective for particular groups of children?
3. If some schools or classes are more effective than others, what factors contribute to these positive effects? (1998: 3)

The authors identified 12 key factors that point to effective primary schools:

1. Purposeful leadership of the staff by the head teacher.
2. The involvement of the deputy head.
3. The involvement of teachers.
4. Consistency among teachers.
5. Structured sessions.
6. Intellectually challenging teaching.
7. A work-centred environment.
8. Limited focus within sessions.
9. Maximum communication between teachers and pupils.
10. Record keeping.
11. Parental involvement.
12. Positive climate (1998: 250–261).

The authors established that the most effective primary school teachers:

> provided a structured learning situation for their pupils but gave them freedom within this framework. By being flexible in their use of whole class, group, and individual contacts, they maximise communications with each pupil. Furthermore, through limiting their focus within sessions, their attention is less fragmented. Hence the opportunities for developing a work centred environment and for presenting challenging work to pupils is increased. (1998: 261)

Further, they found that while all children benefitted from being in an effective school, 'disadvantaged children in the most effective schools can end up with higher achievements than their advantaged peers in the less effective schools' (1998: 217).

2000–2020

The second phase of the timeline summarises six important studies on the teacher effect and the impact of a good teacher. These six studies marked a shift of focus from the earlier research into what makes an effective school to identifying the specific elements of good teachers and teaching that impact pupils' achievement. In doing so, they sought to measure the effect of good teaching on pupils' achievement. Furthermore, research into effective teachers over these six studies moved beyond only looking at what kind of teaching achieved the best test outcomes. By 2014 research also begins to identify social and affective indictors of good teaching.

2000 – Research Into Teacher Effectiveness: A Model of Teacher Effectiveness (Hay McBer)

Hay McBer (2000) *Research into Teacher Effectiveness: A Model of Teacher Effectiveness*. Norwich: HMSO

Key Ideas: Teaching as Performance and Pupil Progress

This research was produced for the DfEE by Hay McBer (an international consultancy firm) to provide a framework to describe effective teaching. It involved analysing a range of data on 126 teachers from 80 schools against pupil progress data (i.e. academic achievement data collected at the beginning and end of a school year). It mapped 35 micro-behaviours (the behaviours teachers constantly exhibit when teaching a class), selected from previous research undertaken by David Reynolds (1989), who was the research lead for this study. These micro-behaviours, which included 'involving all pupils in the lesson', were clustered under the seven Ofsted inspection headings in use at the time (all in terms of time on task and lesson flow). The Ofsted headings were: high expectations, planning, methods and strategies, pupil management and discipline, time and resource management, assessment, and homework.

The aim was to identify those teachers who 'delivered value-added teaching' (Hay McBer, 2000: 3). They concluded that their framework predicted good teachers achieve 'well over 30% variance in pupil progress' (2000: 6) and that their model would be useful to assess how teachers achieve results and to identify how they might improve. They identified three main factors within a teachers' control that significantly influenced pupil progress:

- Teaching skills
- Professional characteristics
- Classroom climate

Teaching skills and professional characteristics are what a teacher brings to their job. Teaching skills can be learned but are sustained and deepened over time by professional characteristics. Classroom climate is what a teacher does: 'it allows teachers to understand how the pupils in their class feel about 9 dimensions of climate created by the teacher that influenced their motivation to learn' (2000: 4).

This study was adopted by the DfEE as the basis for teacher appraisal where performance-related pay was based on pupil progress.

2011 – Improving the Impact of Teachers on Pupil Achievement in the UK – Interim Findings (The Sutton Trust)

The Sutton Trust (2012) Improving the Impact of Teachers on Pupil Achievement in the UK – Interim Findings. London: The Sutton Trust. https://www.suttontrust.com/our-research/improving-impact-teachers-pupil-achievement-uk-interim-findings/

Key Idea: The Difference Between a Very Effective Teacher and a Poorly Performing Teacher is Large

This report was commissioned by The Sutton Trust, a charity founded in 1997 by Sir Peter Lampl to address social mobility and the links between a child's educational opportunities and life chances and their parent's socio-economic background. It was devised as a literature review and to suggest findings that could shape educational policies related to teaching. It was led by three education economists (who estimate the costs and benefits to society of different aspects of education) because value-added teacher performance and performance-related pay were now deemed problematic, unstable, and showed little impact on learning outcomes.

The authors of the report defined a very effective teacher as being in the 84th percentile in value-added scores (one standard deviation above the mean). They estimated that one in six teachers are at or above this level. A poorly performing teacher is in the 16th percentile (again, one standard deviation above the mean), with one in six teachers estimated to be at or below this level.

The Sutton Trust report made a claim about the impact of teachers that became highly influential:

> The effects of high-quality teaching are especially significant for pupils from disadvantaged backgrounds: over a school year, these pupils gain 1.5 years' worth of learning with very effective teachers, compared with 0.5 years with poorly performing teachers. In other words, for poor pupils the difference between a good teacher and a bad teacher is a whole year's learning. (2011: 2)

The report suggested several policies that could be adopted (and which later were), for example, further changes to performance-related pay, a fast-track route into teaching, changes to initial teacher education and changes to teacher dismissal processes.

In the same year (2012), The Sutton Trust, with the Department for Education (DfE), funded the creation of the Education Endowment Foundation (EEF) to 'make better use of evidence'. The EEF has received funding from the DfE to continue until 2032.

2011 – Effective Teaching: Evidence and Practice (Muijs and Reynolds)

Muijs, D and Reynolds, D (2011) *Effective Teaching: Evidence and Practice*. London: Sage

Key Idea: Research Into Effective Teaching Can Generate Ideas About Best Practice

This significant book was written by Daniel Muijs, who later held the post of Head of Research at Ofsted, and David Reynolds, both professors of education. In it they review research in effective teaching to summarise the most effective ways that teachers can teach. The book is divided into four parts: teaching and learning, creating a framework for learning, teaching for specific purposes and teaching specific subjects.

The book was influential in shaping the later emphases of educational policy and Ofsted in terms of what teachers should focus on when teaching. In particular, the book suggests that direct instruction is the best way to teach basic skills (chapter 2) and that interactive teaching is an essential component of all effective teaching methods (chapter 3). The authors summarise the recommendations for practice from research for group work, avoiding disruption and creating a pleasant classroom climate, and also address the importance of the values and expectations of teachers. They summarise how to teach phonics, numeracy, early years, and children with SEND, as well as teaching through cross-curricular and topic-based approaches. As such, this book laid the foundation for how teachers are expected to teach for the years that followed. However, Muijs and Reynolds (2011) also highlighted what they did not yet know in full at the time. They suggested that there was much yet to be learned about how to maximise teaching in terms of the newly developing research disciplines about learning, especially cognitive learning and brain science. As we saw in Chapter 1, they predicted this development very accurately and theories of learning are now clearly linked into those of teaching.

2013 – Effective Teaching: A Review of Research and Evidence (Ko and Sammons)

Ko, J, Sammons, P, and Centre for British Teachers (CfBT) (2013) *Effective Teaching: A Review of Research and Evidence*. Reading: CfBT/Education Development Trust

Key Ideas: Defining Teacher Effectiveness is Not a Simple Matter; Teacher Effects Are Not Stable but Vary and Fluctuate

Drawing on both research evidence and the views of stakeholders, this report sought to define teacher effectiveness and what makes an effective teacher. It identified and summarised the key characteristics and processes of classroom strategies that lead to better pupil outcomes.

The research evidence of this review suggested that effective teachers:

- are clear about teaching goals
- are knowledgeable about curriculum content and the strategies for teaching it
- communicate to their pupils what is expected of them, and why
- make expert use of existing teaching materials in order to devote more time to practices that enrich and clarify the content
- are knowledgeable about their pupils, adapting instruction to their needs and anticipating misconceptions in their existing knowledge
- teach students meta-cognitive strategies and give them opportunities to master them
- address higher-level as well as lower-level cognitive objectives
- monitor pupils' understanding by offering regular appropriate feedback
- integrate their teaching with that in other subject areas
- accept responsibility for pupil outcomes

In order to achieve good teaching, the review identified three teaching strategies, based on the foundation of the teacher's good subject knowledge:

1 The skilful use of well-chosen questions to engage and challenge pupils.
2 The skilful use of well-chosen questions to consolidate understanding.
3 The effective use of assessment for learning.

2014 – Effective Classroom Practice (Kington et al.)

Kington, A, Sammons, P, Regan, E, Brown, E, Ko, J, and Buckler, S (2014) *Effective Classroom Practice*. Maidenhead: Open University Press

Key Ideas: Teacher Effectiveness is Complex; Effective Teachers are Best Developed by Building and Sustaining a Positive Professional Identity as Autonomous and Reflective Practitioners

This book drew on the results of a national research project, 'Effective Classroom Practice' (ECP), which was based on 45 primary school teachers from 22 schools and 36 teachers from 11 secondary schools, plus the views of 1250 pupils from those 58 schools. All teacher participants were judged to be effective and more effective for a sustained period of at least three consecutive years in terms of their pupils' measured progress and attainment. The ECP was a follow-up project to the 2007 study 'Variations in Teachers Work, Lives and their Effects on Pupils' (VITAE), which was a four-year, large-scale, mixed methods project involving 300 teachers in 100 primary and secondary schools in seven local authorities (Day et al., 2007).

The authors suggested that defining teaching only in terms of test results was a partial indicator of teacher effectiveness. They identified ten key features of an effective teacher and developed a model of an effective teacher by analysing previous research, discussion and observation with teacher participants. The model had three inter-related dimensions:

1 Teacher–pupil relationships.
2 Praise and feedback.
3 High expectations.

The model was linked to values that the effective teachers described as being important to good teaching. These are:

- being fair and consistent
- being demanding and supportive
- being positive and open

They set out the ten key features of an effective teacher as:

1. Being highly motivated and committed to their pupils.
2. Valuing professional development and looking for opportunities to improve their subject knowledge and teaching practice.
3. Building strong relationships with their pupils and ensuring they know them well so that they can understand their needs.
4. Being firm but fair, positive, open and supportive.
5. Communicating clearly with pupils, particularly in terms of expectations and feedback.
6. Having high expectations of their pupils.
7. Giving positive praise and feedback to pupils, which is carefully adapted to the individual's needs.
8. Being flexible with lesson plans and being able to adapt and enrich lessons in ways appropriate for their pupils.
9. Planning creative, enjoyable and stimulating lessons to engage pupils in learning.
10. Encouraging pupils to take control of their own learning and asking questions to guide their own intellectual enquiry.

2020 – Great Teaching Toolkit: Evidence Review (Coe et al.)

Coe, R, Rauch, CJ, Kime, S, and Singleton, D (2020) *Great Teaching Toolkit: Evidence Review.* Cambridge: Evidence Based Education and Cambridge Assessment International Education. https://www.cambridgeinternational.org/great-teaching-toolkit/

Key Idea: What Can I Best Focus on to Improve as a Teacher?

The *Great Teaching Toolkit* is intended to be a long-term project with the aim of developing professional learning programmes, systems and instruments, and networks to support teachers to develop their effectiveness. This systematic review of eight research studies and five teaching frameworks was undertaken in order to develop a model for teaching as the basis of the toolkit.

The review identified four priorities for teachers who want to help their pupils to learn more:

1. To understand the content they are teaching and how it is learnt.
2. To create a supportive environment for learning.
3. To manage the classroom to maximise the opportunity to learn.
4. To present content, activities and interactions that activate their pupils' thinking.

From these four dimensions of teaching, 17 sub-elements, comprising a specific competency, skill or knowledge a teacher should aim to get better at, or the means by which to improve the learning environment, were developed (Table 2.2). Their aim was not to describe teaching, but to indicate how a teacher can improve their effectiveness.

Table 2.2 Elements to focus on to become a more effective teacher

Priority for effectiveness	Element	Element	Element	Element
To understand the content you are teaching and how it is learnt	Deep knowledge and flexible understanding of the subject matter of the curriculum	Knowledge of how the curriculum is sequenced and how the content relates to other ideas across the curriculum	Knowledge of relevant tasks by which the curriculum can be taught and knowledge of multiple and varied explanations and examples	Knowledge of common pupil strategies, misconceptions, and sticking points in relation to what you're teaching
To create a supportive environment for learning	Promote interactions based on mutual respect, care, empathy and warmth; avoid negative interactions; be sensitive to individual needs	Promote pupil-to-pupil relationships based on respect, care, cooperation and trust	Motivate pupils to learn by developing their feelings of being competent, autonomous and part of a learning group	Create an atmosphere where pupils feel okay to participate and where they feel they can address failure and improve success
To manage the classroom to maximise the opportunity to learn	Manage resources so that time is not wasted, particularly at the start of activities and in transitions between different activities; give crystal clear instructions and explanations; develop routines for smooth transitions	Explain and apply consistently clear rules, expectations and consequences for behaviour	Anticipate and respond to incidents which may disrupt learning; reinforce good behaviour; show that you are aware of potentially disruptive behaviour and respond so that it does not occur or escalate	
To present content, activities and interactions that activate your pupils' thinking	Structuring: sequence tasks; explain learning objectives and update their development through the lesson; use skilful scaffolding	Explaining: present ideas clearly; connect new ideas to previous learning; use examples; model new skills and procedures; use worked or part-worked examples	Questioning: use questions to promote elaboration and connected thinking, to elicit thinking, to evidence learning and to check your assessment evidence	Interacting: respond to what people say about what they think they know and understand; give feedback to develop their learning
	Embedding: create tasks to embed and reinforce learning; create tasks that enable practice to secure learning; create tasks to review or revisit previous learning	Activating: create tasks that move pupils from structured to independent learning; create tasks that require pupils to apply previous learning in a new situation; create tasks so that pupils have to plan for themselves how to complete the task successfully		

Key Takeaways

- The eight important studies summarised above in the two phases of the timeline (1979–1999 and 2000–2020) are all systematic reviews.
- A systematic review is a synthesis and appraisal of primary research. A clear and specific methodology is adopted to search for and to find all existing research on a given topic in order to minimise bias. The findings of those sources are synthesised to determine what evidence there is for the value of certain educational or teaching practices. In this way, evidence has been developed from research.
- Teacher effectiveness research developed from earlier research into school effectiveness.
- The term 'effective' in education means what can reasonably be expected to achieve a given result. It is used, in particular, in terms of pupils' outcomes, and what can narrow the 'gap' – which is the association of disadvantage with diminished outcomes. It is sometimes thought of as 'what works'.
- Teacher effectiveness research seeks to demonstrate whether and in what ways teachers can make a difference to pupils' outcomes, which are measured in terms of attainment (summative grades) and achievement (how far pupils have progressed from their starting points).
- Teacher effect is the measurement of the impact of the effectiveness of a teacher on pupil outcomes.
- Teacher effectiveness research has been very influential on educational policy because its findings are quantitative (i.e. they can be counted, measured and compared). In this way, evidence is seen to be linked to policy.

Significant Sources: Evidence-Based Teaching

As we have seen in the previous section, during the last 40 years research has been developed to provide evidence of and for effective teaching. This evidence base has shaped what teachers and schools have focused on in terms of the processes and purposes of teaching: academic outcomes that can be measured.

This section summarises two further highly influential sources of evidence about teaching. These sources are not systematic reviews, but instead have developed evidence about teaching from two different research approaches: a longitudinal study and a meta-analysis.

The Effective Teaching

The Effective Provision of Pre-school, Primary and Secondary Education (EPPSE) research study was a large-scale, longitudinal, mixed methods UK study from 1997 to 2014 (and the first of its type in Europe), funded by the Department for Education. It followed the education of 3000 children in 850 primary schools from their early years until their 16th birthdays. It was originally funded to examine the impact of pre-school (the experiences of children aged 3–5) but was expanded to follow those same children through primary school (ages 5–11) and then secondary school (ages 11–16). Of the sample, 2800 children had attended pre-school and a further sample of 300 had not attended pre-school. The study looked to identify the precise educational processes that create better outcomes for pupils, and to understand exactly how effective teachers promote sustained and successful learning.

It adopted a value-added approach, assessing the extent to which children's progress in schools exceeds that which might be predicted by defined starting points, such as family background or characteristics. It analysed the extra value or extra boost that teachers give to their pupils' progress above and beyond the non-school influences. But this study also controlled their analysis Contextual Value-added (CVA) for a range of influences related to the child, family and neighbourhood characteristics, so that the impact of teachers on learning and development could be compared.

EPPSE produced over 200 reports and sub-studies, one of which sought to identify differences between poor, good and excellent teaching: *Effective Primary Pedagogical Strategies in English and Mathematics in Key Stage 2: A Study of Year 5 Classroom Practice from EPPE 3-16 Longitudinal Study* (EPPSEM) (Siraj-Blatchford et al., 2011). They identified markers of excellent teaching that they summarised as 11 strategies that make a real difference to pupils' academic and socio-behavioural outcomes. Table 2.3 summarises these strategies.

Visible Learning

Hattie developed (from a version of his PhD taken in 1981 at the University of Toronto) a synthesis of 800+meta-analyses of the effects of various influences and interventions on pupil achievement. His book *Visible Learning: A Synthesis of over 800 Meta-analyses relating to Achievement* (2009) and the subsequent related publications (including Hattie, 2023) have acquired global influence. A meta-analysis is similar to a systematic review in that it gathers together current empirical research. It must have a clear set of criteria, a methodology and methods that set out which articles to include and how the data are handled. A meta-analysis combines the results of a number of previously published research studies in order to provide a more statistically significant result that can be applied more generally. However, it is important to note that the methods, methodologies and sample sizes used by the articles in the meta-analysis may vary.

Hattie's (2009) meta-analysis of educational interventions synthesises over 800 meta-analyses (sometimes his work is referred to as a meta-meta-analysis) of educational interventions and ascribes to them an 'effect size'. An effect size is a statistical measure of the strength of the relationship between different predictors and pupils' outcomes. It is generally recognised that in educational research effect sizes are typically small to moderate. This does not mean that they are unimportant. Hattie's effect sizes generated a visual and numeric indication of how much of an effect any particular intervention will have on a child's attainment.

Table 2.3 Strategies of excellent teaching (adapted from Siraj et al., 2019)

Strategy	Excellent teachers
Organisation	• organise lessons, materials and teaching time particularly well • plan lessons very carefully using time most productively • the quickness of pace left no time for pupils to slack off • there was a sense of urgency about the learning taking place • there was also an atmosphere of liveliness and sometimes fun • pupils tended to be more self-reliant (perhaps because classrooms and resources were well organised)
Classroom climate	• classrooms were happy places where everyone demonstrated mutual respect and common purpose • pupils felt safe enough to take risks with their learning • teachers were sensitive to the needs of individuals • children demonstrated high levels of liking and respect for their fellow pupils
Clear objectives, shared goals	• are particularly good at making certain that their lesson's learning intentions and activities are clear to all of their pupils • ensure that all of their pupils understand the ideas and concepts associated with the activity • used a plenary to recap and consolidate the objectives and how they had been met
Behaviour management	• manage pupil behaviour with humour and sensitivity by engaging them in their learning • breaches of rules were dealt with privately and informally
Collaborative learning	• while genuine collaborative learning is not common in most classrooms, pupils spent slightly more time working in groups • in groups they were encouraged: o to provide feedback to each other o to work together on a complex problem o to support each other's learning through peer tutoring and response partners
Personalised learning	• were sensitive to their pupils' personal needs • worked hard to meet their pupils' individual needs • provided social support for their pupils' learning • provided adapted tasks and activities • teaching was tailored to the individual interests, skills and abilities of pupils
Dialogic teaching and learning	• used discussion and dialogue • ensured they engage with their pupils at every level • arranged their classrooms, routines and resources so that pupils could be self-reliant • modelled and encouraged good relationships • because pupils knew their opinions and contributions were respected and valued, they engaged confidently in dialogue with each other and the teacher • because they learned in a particularly positive and supportive environment, they were able to attempt new challenges more easily
Assessment for learning	• assessment for learning was a natural part of the ongoing dialogue between teachers and pupils • teachers provided lots of evaluative feedback and opportunities for their pupils to reflect on their learning

(*Continued*)

Table 2.3 Strategies of excellent teaching (adapted from Siraj et al., 2019) (*Continued*)

Strategy	Excellent teachers
The plenary	• placed great emphasis on a plenary session in their lessons • they were not just a short session at the end to check on answers, but offered a real opportunity for pupils to reflect on, and consolidate, their learning, to deepen their understanding and to extend their thinking
Making clear links	• linked their immediate lesson with other areas of the curriculum and the world outside the classroom • found opportunities to link what the pupils were learning with their outside interests because they were aware of what they were • looked to spot lesson links when they occurred to make them clear to their pupils
Homework	• set homework in a variety of forms • set homework directly linked to what the pupils have been learning in the immediate lesson

Hattie wanted to add to the body of knowledge about how teachers can maximise learning by offering a list of evidence-informed strategies. This was because, in his view, a teacher can make between 7% and 21% difference to the achievement gains of pupils and that teachers are the biggest in-school factor to affect pupils. His goal was to ensure that each child made a year's growth in their learning for each year's input of teaching. There are some differences of approach developed between his work in 2009 and his book, *Visible Learning: The Sequel* (Hattie, 2023), which are set out below.

Visible Learning (2009)

Hattie's major message in *Visible Learning* (2009) is that what teachers do matters. His argument is that what some teachers do is more effective than others. He suggests that the most effective teachers teach in a deliberate and visible manner. Such teachers intervene in calculated and meaningful ways to ensure that learning attains shared, specific and challenging goals. Such teachers are aware of which of their teaching strategies are working or not. They are prepared to understand and adapt to their pupils and the situation, context and prior learning, and to share the experience of learning in this manner with their pupils.

Hattie adopts a particular view of learning. He argues that teaching and learning are visible in the classrooms of successful teachers because passion for learning and the knowledge and skill of the teacher and the pupil are required. Central to his argument is that 'what is most important is that teaching is visible to the pupil, and that the learning is visible to the teacher' (Hattie, 2009: 25). In this way, the teacher focuses on what they say and do and what their pupils say and do (i.e. the visible behaviours of teaching and learning) because that is within their control and can be attempted in a deliberate manner. Hattie describes information and understanding at a 'surface' level and a 'deep' level. Surface information or understanding is knowing or understanding ideas and facts, and 'deep' knowledge and understanding is relational – requiring integration of at least two pieces of information – and elaborative – when a pupil goes beyond the given information and is able to deduce a more general rule. Hattie defines learning as when pupils 'can move from idea to ideas and then relate and elaborate on them' (2009: 29).

From his synthesis, Hattie identifies six factors that contribute to pupil achievement:

1 The child.
2 The home.
3 The school.
4 The curricula.
5 The teacher.
6 Approaches to teaching.

Teacher contributions to pupil learning include:

- the quality of teaching, as perceived by the pupils
- the teacher's expectations
- the teacher's conceptions of teaching, learning, assessment and the pupils (do teachers believe all pupils can make progress? Is achievement changeable or fixed? And is the teacher able to understand and articulate progress?)
- the teacher's openness
- a warm socio-emotional classroom climate where errors are welcomed
- being clear in articulating success criteria and achievement
- being able to foster effort
- being able to engage all of the pupils

The aspects of teaching approaches that have an impact on pupil learning include:

- paying deliberate attention to learning intentions and success criteria
- setting challenging tasks
- providing multiple opportunities for deliberative practice
- understanding the critical role of teaching appropriate learning strategies
- planning and talking about teaching
- constantly seeking feedback information as to the success of their teaching on the pupils

Hattie's 2009 book includes two appendices: Appendix A lists the meta-analyses by topic and Appendix B lists the meta-analyses by rank order. In the top ten of his rank order by meta-analyses, four are attributed to the domain of teaching; two are attributed to the teacher; two to the pupil, and two to the school. The 2009 book by Hattie is widely cited and reviewed, and although his approach has been criticised, including his use of effect sizes, his work has provided a substantial body of analysis of educational interventions. However, Hattie continued to review his work, update the synthesis, respond to criticism and develop his ideas about teaching and learning. As a consequence, in 2023, he published the sequel to the 2009 book.

Visible Learning: The Sequel (2023)

There were three main areas of criticism about Hattie's work of 2009. First, there were criticisms about meta-analyses, their synthesis and effect sizes as a research approach in itself.

Second, there was criticism about how Hattie interpreted the data to come up with his views on teaching. But most of the criticism was linked to his Appendix B and the rank order of meta-analyses. This was because it was seen as a league table with the things teachers should do at the top and the things they should not do at the bottom. Hattie feels that others misinterpreted his work, but nevertheless he stopped using this rank order from 2018 and it is not included in the 2023 sequel.

In his 2023 book, Hattie now takes the view that rather than looking at teaching strategies in isolation and focusing on how teachers teach using them (e.g. whether a teacher uses feedback, open questions, scaffolds and success criteria), it is more important to consider the impact of teaching on how pupils think, know and solve. In other words, how the teacher pays attention to and responds to the learning of their pupils is more important than mastering and performing teaching techniques in isolation. Hattie argues that understanding teaching is more about understanding the pedagogical decisions and evaluations made in the moment.

Hattie describes his Visible Learning model of teaching as being based on five premises:

1 The why: being clear about the purpose of teaching (teachers see learning through the eyes of their pupils, pupils become their own teachers, and teachers become students of teaching).
2 The how: how teachers and pupils think.
3 The what: intentionally aligning decisions about the know-that, know-how, know-with aspects of the curriculum, and thinking of tasks in terms of cognition, the best teaching strategies and how to evaluate.
4 The doing – knowing pupils and their prior learning, backwards planning, evaluating through listening and feedback and reteaching as needed.
5 Evaluating – being an evaluative thinker.

In chapter 9 of *Visible Learning: The Sequel* (2023), Hattie outlines the attributes of a teacher that account for teacher effect. These attributes were developed from 2238 studies synthesised into 47 meta-analyses. They include: personality, verbal ability, expectations, not labelling pupils, accurate assessment of achievement, credibility, and clarity. In chapter 11, Hattie establishes his main claim, which is that teaching needs to be intentional, i.e. a teacher must intentionally align the various elements of a lesson: success criteria, feedback, learning strategies, teaching methods, activities and assessments. He outlines the deep understanding a teacher needs to have in order to be able to teach intentionally:

1 An understanding of the curriculum, learning progression, knowledge of what success looks like and learning intention.
2 Cognitive task analysis, which involves analysing the steps required to complete a cognitive task. This includes understanding the nature of the knowledge to be taught and the associated learning strategies required for success.

3. Pupils' current levels of attainment, prior attainment and the trajectories of their learning.
4. An understanding of teaching strategies and feedback that can reduce the gap between current pupil knowledge and understanding and desired pupil knowledge and understanding.
5. How to monitor how well you are teaching in terms of the impact on your pupils during and at the end of a lesson.

Hattie concludes that it is important for teachers to move away from seeing their lessons as a series of activities, which can be exacerbated by seeing the lesson in terms of stages, parts or phases that have to be completed by the pupils. Instead, his view is that teaching should provide pupils with multiple opportunities to engage in the learning required to meet the success criteria and for the teacher to be acutely aware of the levels of challenge each pupil is able to meet.

Key Takeaways

- As a new teacher you are expected to engage with up-to-date and pertinent research findings.
- You are expected to study research from high-quality systematic reviews.
- You should be able to consider research in terms of the appropriateness of method, quality of study, nature of results and relevance of research. and consider causal claims in terms of comparison groups.
- You should be able to assess the appropriateness and value of teaching approaches by considering the validity and reliability of the research approach, the professional context in which research is debated and applied, and relate it to your teaching experience.
- You are expected to be able to interpret research for your teaching. For example, does evaluative research explain how teaching is implemented but not consider its impact? And, conversely, might a controlled trial explain the impact of a teaching strategy, but not how to implement it?
- You are expected to be able to apply research when making professional decisions and to use evidence to critique your teaching.
- An intervention implies pre- and post-testing of attainment, and often has the aim to close an attainment gap.
- Interventions are designed to tackle weaknesses in how pupils do something.
- A teaching strategy is a way to achieve something (in either a single classroom or across a school).
- A teaching technique is the performance of a teaching procedure by the teacher (the teacher's know-how or skill).
- Consider focusing less on perfecting specific teaching techniques and more on the impact of your teaching on your pupils.

How Ofsted Has Shaped the Way Teachers in England Understand Teaching

This section will address how the Office for Standards in Education (Ofsted) has influenced recent understandings of teaching. It is important to know this as a new teacher because Ofsted regulate and judge standards in schools and consequently many schools adopt their definitions and approaches.

Ofsted was founded in 1992, and from then until 2005 a school inspection would spend 60% of its time in a school observing lessons (typically for a period of five days with between 10 and 15 inspectors). Each teacher would be graded, and those grades shared with the headteacher. At this time (1995–2005), inspectors gathered evidence on teacher behaviours and pupil interactions under the following headings:

- secure knowledge and understanding of the subjects taught
- setting high expectations to challenge and deepen pupils' knowledge and understanding
- plan effectively
- employ teaching methods and organisational strategies which match curricular objectives and the needs of all pupils
- manage pupils well and achieve high standards of discipline
- use of time and resources
- assess pupils work thoroughly and constructively to inform teaching (when teaching by listening and responding to pupils in the lesson)
- use homework to reinforce and extend what is learned in school

The framework changed in 2015 and individual teachers were no longer graded, nor was the teaching quality of individual teachers judged. Rather, the focus was on the teaching across the whole school. There was a focus on pupil learning over time and so inspectors also scrutinised work and spoke with groups of pupils. All of this evidence was set against lesson observations, where inspectors evaluated the impact of teaching on pupils' progress. From 2015, good teaching was described in the Ofsted framework as:

- The Teachers' Standards are met
- Teachers have consistently high expectations of what each pupil can achieve, including disadvantaged pupils and the most able
- Teachers have secure understanding of the age group they are working with and relevant subject knowledge that is detailed and communicated well to pupils. Pupils' assessment information is gathered from looking at what pupils already know, understand and can do
- assessment information is used to plan appropriate teaching and learning strategies, including to identify pupils who are falling behind in their learning or who need additional support, enabling all pupils to make good progress and achieve well

- Pupils understand how to improve as a result of useful feedback, written or oral, from teachers
- Equality of opportunity and recognition of diversity are promoted through teaching and learning
- English, maths, and the skills necessary to function as an economically active member of British society, are promoted through teaching and learning

From 2019, a new framework was introduced with a more qualitative approach that focused strongly on pupils' knowledge. This change aligned closely with the 2014 National Curriculum, whose intent was to equip more children to participate in the future knowledge economy. As part of the development of this framework, Ofsted (2019) published an overview of the research underpinning the framework. In its section on the research into teaching that underpins the framework, Ofsted drew on teacher effectiveness research and the view that: 'classroom practice, and in particular teaching effectiveness, is the single most important factor in school effectiveness. Teaching effectiveness is a strong predictor of pupils' progress throughout school, and having a succession of strong or weak teachers can have lasting effects' (Ofsted, 2019: 13). The key research findings that have shaped how Ofsted interpret teaching identify what teachers do that impacts on pupils' attainment. They identified the three most important factors as:

1 The amount and pacing of teaching.
2 The amount of content taught to pupils.
3 Time on task (the amount of time that pupils are actively engaged in learning in a lesson).

They further set out how teachers go about teaching the curriculum content so that it maximises pupils' achievement. Teachers:

- provide overviews and reviews of learning objectives
- outline the content that will be covered and signal transitions between the different parts of the lesson where the different elements of the content are being covered
- emphasise the main ideas being covered
- review and repeat the main ideas being covered
- explain ideas, activities and expectations clearly and directly to pupils so that they are not pitched beyond their current level of understanding
- use questions to provide feedback to pupils in relation to their understanding of the content to be covered; use a mixture of recall and higher-order questions; ask questions which require a single response and those which ask for explanations from pupils
- structure and prepare pupils to participate in pair and group tasks so that they contribute to pupils' learning
- provide focused support to pupils who are not making progress

In the 2019 Education Inspection Framework (Ofsted, 2019), the quality of teaching is described as the implementation of education, which requires teachers to be able to do the following:

- have good subject knowledge
- present subject-matter clearly
- promote appropriate discussion about the subject-matter
- check understanding systematically
- identify misconceptions accurately
- provide clear, direct feedback
- respond and adapt teaching (without unnecessarily elaborate or differentiated approaches)
- plan teaching so that pupils are helped to remember in the long term the content they have been taught and to integrate new knowledge into larger concepts
- use assessment to help pupils embed and use their knowledge
- use assessment to check understanding and inform teaching
- create a learning-focused environment
- select resources that reflect the ambition and sequencing of curriculum
- teach reading rigorously to promote confidence and enjoyment

Key Takeaways

- 1995 and 2005: Ofsted focused on teaching in terms of the performance of behaviours by teachers and how well pupils interacted with each other.
- 2015–2019: Ofsted focused on the use of assessment data and pupil progress.
- 2019: Ofsted focused on teaching being designed to help pupils to remember in the long term the content they have been taught and to integrate new knowledge into larger concepts.

What the Core Content Framework Says About Teaching

Two sections of the *Core Content Framework* (CCF) relate directly to teaching (DfE, 2019). The first section on High Expectations sets out the knowledge that new teachers are expected to learn about the impact of teachers:

1 Teachers have the **ability to affect and improve** the well-being, motivation, and behaviour of their pupils.

2 Teachers are **role models**, who can influence the attitudes, values, and behaviours of their pupils.

3 Teacher **expectations can affect pupil outcomes**; setting goals that challenge and stretch pupils is essential. (DfE, 2019: 9)

The fourth section of the CCF, Classroom Practice, sets out what new teachers are expected to learn and be able to do in order to plan and teach. New teachers are expected to know the following *about* teaching:

1. Teaching transforms pupils' knowledge, capabilities and their beliefs about learning.
2. New material is introduced in steps linked to previous learning.
3. Modelling by teachers makes abstract ideas concrete and accessible and helps pupils understand new processes and ideas.
4. Worked examples and scaffolds help pupils apply what they have learned.
5. Teaching pupils how to plan, monitor and evaluate their own work explicitly develops independence.
6. Questioning is a key tool which can be used for a variety of different reasons.
7. Talk helps pupils to articulate ideas, consolidate their understanding and extend their vocabulary.
8. Teachers create repeated opportunities for practice.
9. Pupils need help to be able to work together successfully.
10. Pupil groupings should be monitored for effectiveness.
11. Quality of homework is more important than quantity of homework.

Furthermore, learning how to teach is set out in the CCF as a series of four learning processes (see Table 2.4):

1. Observing how other teachers 'do' an aspect of teaching.
2. Practising, getting feedback and thus improving.
3. Discussing and analysing.
4. Being explicitly taught how to do something by a more experienced teacher or teacher educator.

Table 2.4 Learning processes in the CCF

Learning processes			
Observe how other teachers do an aspect of teaching	**Practise a teaching skill, receiving feedback, and thus improving**	**Discuss and analyse...**	**Be explicitly taught by a more experienced teacher or teacher educator...**
Break tasks down into smaller steps	Use modelling explanations and scaffolds	how to use concrete representations of abstract ideas	how to provide scaffolds to make sure that pupil talk is of high quality
	Ensure content knowledge is secure before introducing problem solving and critical thinking	how to make the steps in a process memorable and check that pupils can remember them	

(*Continued*)

Table 2.4 Learning processes in the CCF (*Continued*)

Learning processes			
Observe how other teachers do an aspect of teaching	**Practise a teaching skill, receiving feedback, and thus improving**	**Discuss and analyse...**	**Be explicitly taught by a more experienced teacher or teacher educator...**
	Know when to reduce scaffolding	how to make sure that pair or group work is effective	
	Make sure enough time is spent on creating opportunities for pupils to consolidate and practise applying their new knowledge and skills		
	Pitch explanations at the right level		
	Combine representations of ideas and process with verbal explanations		
	Use the think aloud process when modelling		
	Show pupils how things can go wrong and explain to them how to avoid this		
	Plan lesson activities that will cause pupils to think hard		
	Use questions to help pupils think hard		
	Use wait time after you have asked a question		

In this way, the foundational approaches the CCF suggests you first focus on as a new teacher learning how to teach are:

- breaking down what pupils are learning into smaller steps
- providing assistance so that pupils can remember new knowledge, connect it with their previous knowledge and then apply it in new contexts

As such, these approaches to teaching align with the theories of learning outlined in Chapter 1.

Suggested Activities to Develop Your Practice

Discuss With a More Experienced Teacher

1 Talk through how you have planned a lesson before you teach it (perhaps record this conversation on your phone). After the lesson, record the decisions and evaluative

decisions you made in the moment while you were teaching. Then discuss with a more experienced teacher what you did and why, so that together you can think aloud and develop a dialogue to critique your teaching. In this way, you will develop a clearer understanding about how to keep getting better.

For You to Think About After A Lesson

1 Would your pupils have considered you caring, understanding and responsive?
2 What are the ways in which you demonstrate those characteristics during a lesson?
3 Which pupils did not engage with you during the lesson? Ask yourself why might they have wanted to be silent, or were they confused by the lesson?
4 Analyse the tasks and activities you designed: check their cognitive complexity.

For You to Do

1 Survey your pupils by asking the following questions:
   - What expectations do you (the pupils) have?
   - Do you like challenge?
   - How you deal with distraction?
   - Are you prepared to seek help from your teachers?
   - What is your perception of teachers' enthusiasm?
   - How do you feel when you make an error? (Is it an opportunity?)
   - Are the rules within the class applied fairly?
   - Do you feel like you belong?
   - Do you feel as though you are invited to learn?

Then consider your pupils' responses and what this tells you about the culture and environment for learning you have created. Can you think of any improvements to make it even more conducive for learning and to enable teaching activities to take place successfully?

Deepening Your knowledge

The EPPSE study produced over 200 reports and sub-studies analysing their findings in the following topics: effective provision at pre-school, primary, early years and end of secondary school, post-16; aspects of pedagogy; successful transition, SEN and social equality). These reports can be downloaded from: www.ucl.ac.uk/ioe/research/featured-research/eppse-publications

Pupil Premium funds were introduced by the Coalition Government in 2010 to provide ring-fenced funds to improve the performance of the poorest pupils. In 2011, The Sutton Trust charity developed a Pupil Premium Toolkit. It was an accessible guide to the best ways to improve pupils' attainment and was designed to emphasise that some ways in which schools used Pupil Premium Funds were more likely to improve pupil progress directly. It was a 20-page report collating findings from thousands of studies, consolidated into an evidence summary of 20 teaching approaches aimed at improving learning. The report was adopted by the Educational Endowment Foundation, which was launched in 2010 by the government to promote the use of evidence in schools and to fund randomised control trials (RCTs) assessing different approaches and programmes in English schools. The EEF has been funded until 2032. The Pupil Premium Toolkit, evidence summaries and the new evidence developed through its work with schools and universities in the form of case studies and RCTs can be found on the EEF website: https://educationendowmentfoundation.org.uk/about-us/how-we-work

'Learning from Research', Chapter 3 of Wiliam's 2016 book, offers a very clear explanation of how to make the most of educational research as a teacher. Wiliam, a world-famous professor of education, explains different types of educational research (lesson study, educational neuroscience, systematic reviews, meta-analysis) and some of the issues with their methodology. In particular, he discusses some of the limitations of effect sizes and critiques the 'what works' approach to teacher effectiveness research. In the remainder of the book, he argues for the importance of formative assessment to the quality of teaching (i.e. all and any activities undertaken by the teacher to provide information to be used as feedback, by which to adapt teaching and learning activities).

Following the publication of *Improving the Impact of Teachers on Pupil Achievement in the UK – Interim Findings* (The Sutton Trust, 2012), the phrase 'the difference between a good teacher and a poor teacher is a whole year's learning' has been ubiquitous, cited widely as evidence of the significance of an individual teacher. This is because the report appeared to provide definitive evidence of the impact a good teacher (as opposed to a poor teacher) has on the outcomes of pupils. However, Shire's article analyses the research basis for this claim. The paper suggests that this is an unsubstantiated claim because the original research study was devised to measure the cost-effectiveness of universal welfare benefit in the USA in the early 1970s and was ultimately unpublished because of its many methodological weaknesses.

Reflection on important questions

Teaching can be understood through two different, but related, lenses. Teaching is an activity by the teacher that operates as a form of assistance to their pupils, but it is also based on sets of beliefs about how children (and society) might benefit from learning, and specifically benefit from learning the content of a curriculum. What makes improving as a teacher rather different from simply acquiring more knowledge about teaching or becoming more skilful in the doing of teaching is that teaching has a dual focus at all times: teaching the pupils in the class the subject-matter of the curriculum.

Good teaching draws from learning-focused teaching strategies that respect the role of the pupil as a learner. Good teaching takes place in an environment (shaped by the teacher, the school and by wider society) that brings out the best in the teacher and in their pupils, and as such is shaped by the values of the teacher and of the education system.

Research over time points to a consensus about what teachers may do when they teach. More recently, evidence has considered theoretical understandings of how children learn and the nature of the curriculum. As a new teacher, you are expected to:

- understand and be interested in educational research
- use research evidence to inform your teaching
- be able to translate research into your own teaching, avoiding what are known as 'lethal mutations', where a helpful approach is mistranslated or mis-implemented to the point where it becomes unhelpful
- take decisions about how you teach on the basis of your knowledge of your own context

Conclusion

There are two final important points to make about teaching and about learning how to teach. First, many research studies and summaries of research list aspects of teaching in the form of checklists of dimensions or activities. However, one cannot get better at something as cognitively complex as teaching by simply attempting to copy a listed behaviour. This is because teaching turns on social understanding (the ability to interpret social interactions), which is built over time in the following forms of teacher knowledge:

- Pedagogical content knowledge – the ability to make the content of the curriculum teachable
- Professional judgement – doing the right thing at the right time in the right way for the right reason
- Syntactic knowledge – being able to 'think like a teacher'
- Know-why (i.e. higher order procedural knowledge) – knowing why things work at a specific level, which is drawn first from principles and concepts

Second, the 'what works' approach to effective teaching ignores the fact that everything can work somewhere, and nothing works everywhere. Instead, the question for teachers is 'under what conditions does an aspect of teaching work best?'

References

Coe, R, Rauch, CJ, Kime, S, and Singleton, D (2020) *Great Teaching Toolkit: Evidence Review*. Cambridge: Evidence Based Education and Cambridge Assessment International Education

Day, C, Stobart, G, Simmons, P, Kington, A, Gu, Q, Smees, R and Mujtaba, T (2007) Variations in Teachers' Work, Lives and Effectiveness Research report RR743 DfES

DfE (2019) *ITT Core Content Framework*. London: HMSO

Hattie, J (2009) *Visible Learning: A Synthesis of over 800 Meta-analyses relating to Achievement.* Abingdon, UK: Routledge

Hattie, J (2023) *Visible Learning: The Sequel. A Synthesis of over 2 100 Meta-analyses relating to Achievement.* Abingdon, UK: Routledge

Hay McBer (2000) *Research into Teacher Effectiveness: A Model of Teacher Effectiveness.* Norwich: HMSO

Kington, A, Sammons, P, Regan, E Brown, E, Ko, J, and Buckler, S (2014) *Effective Classroom Practice.* Maidenhead: Open University Press

Ko, J, Sammons, P, and Centre for British Teachers (CfBT) (2013) *Effective Teaching: A Review of Research and Evidence.* Reading: CfBT/Education Development Trust

Mortimore, P (2014) *Education under Siege.* Bristol: Policy Press

Mortimore, P, Sammons, P, Stoll, L, and Ecob, R (1998) *School Matters: The Junior Years.* London: Open Books

Muijs, D and Reynolds, D (2011) *Effective Teaching: Evidence and Practice.* London: Sage

Ofsted (2019) *Education Inspection Framework: Overview of Research.* London: Ofsted

Reynolds, D., Davie, R and Philips, D. (1989) The Cardiff programme – an effective school improvement programme based on school effectiveness research, in Creemers, B.P.M. and Scheerens, *J (Des) 'Developments in School Effectiveness Research (Special issue of the International Journal of Educational Research)* 3 (7), 800-814

Rutter, M, Maughan, B, Mortimore, P, and Ouston, J (1979) *15 000 Hours: Secondary Schools and Their Effects on Children.* London: Open Books

Sammons, P, Hillman, J, and Mortimore, P (1995) *Key Characteristics of Effective Schools: A Review of School Effectiveness Research.* London: Institute of London, ISEIC

Shires, L (2017) It's all about the teacher: Why that 'truth' might not be all that it seems. *Forum* 59(3), 477–482. https://journals.lwbooks.co.uk/forum/vol-59-issue-3/article-6380/

Siraj-Blatchford, I, Shepard, D-L, Melhuish, E, Taggart, B, Simmons, P and Sylva, K (2011) Effective primary pedagogical strategies in English and mathematics in key stage 2: a study of year 5 classroom practice for EPPSE 3-16 longitudinal study. Project Report. Department for Education, London

Siraj, I., Taggart, B., Sammons, P., Melhuish, E., Sylva, K., & Shepherd, D. L. (2019). Teaching in Effective Primary Schools: Research into Pedagogy and Children's Learning. Trentham Books.

The Sutton Trust (2011) *Improving the Impact of Teachers on Pupil Achievement in the UK – Interim Findings.* London: The Sutton Trust

Wiliam, D (2016) *Leadership for Teacher Learning: Creating a Culture Where All Teachers Improve so that All Students Succeed.* Palm Beach, FL: Learning Sciences

3
WHAT IS A CURRICULUM?

Important Questions

- What is a curriculum?
- Why is it important to be able to make sense of a curriculum?
- How should you make use of a curriculum?

Introduction

Having considered what a new primary school teacher needs to know, understand and be able to do in terms of learning and teaching in Chapter 1 and 2, this chapter examines what you have to teach to your pupils: the curriculum. Chapter 4 then addresses how you should use these ideas of teaching, learning and the curriculum to plan the lessons that you will teach to your pupils. Part 2 will set out how to put these theoretical concepts into action.

The curriculum is an important concept that can be defined in very specific or general terms (Moore, 2015). First, it is important to think carefully about the curriculum. This is because rather than assuming that a curriculum is 'obvious', 'common sense' or merely a 'thing' devised outside and transferred into a school, thinking hard about the nature of the curriculum you teach helps you to understand the complex processes of schooling in today's society and your role within it. Second, it is important to think carefully about the curriculum in terms of its various elements. This is because ideas about teaching and learning inform *how* you teach, but the curriculum is *what* you teach to your pupils. In other words, you need to be able to interpret the different character and forms of the knowledge, skills and understanding of the different subjects on the curriculum so that you can devise tasks and activities that work from conceptual understanding. Doing so supports your development of subject-specific pedagogy as you develop more generic teaching strategies. By the end of this chapter, you will understand how a curriculum is defined, the knowledge you need to have about the curriculum, and how you can use the curriculum as a key factor in your role as a teacher.

Why is a Curriculum an Important Tool for Teachers?

Stemming from the Latin verb 'currere', meaning to run, the noun *curriculum* literally translates as 'racecourse'. Historically, the word 'curriculum' was used to describe the subjects taught during the classical period of Greek civilisation. Today, numerous definitions exist for the 'curriculum'. Ralph Tyler (1949) first proposed that the curriculum should be seen as a means to an end rather than an end in itself. He identified four fundamental questions that must be answered in developing any curriculum:

1 What educational purposes should the school seek to attain?
2 What educational experiences can be provided that are likely to attain these purposes?
3 How can these educational experiences be effectively organised?
4 How can we determine whether these purposes are being attained?

One of his colleagues, Hilda Taba (1962), developed his work and defined a curriculum as a plan for learning. She proposed a seven-step model for curriculum development:

1 Diagnosing needs.
2 Formulating specific objectives.
3 Selecting content.
4 Organising content.
5 Selecting learning experiences.
6 Organising learning experiences.
7 Evaluating.

Taba's model (1962) recognised that the curriculum should connect with the learning needs of pupils. One way in which teachers can utilise this connection is through backwards planning (see Chapter 4). She also recognised that curriculum content is linked to pedagogy: 'the way in which learning experiences are planned and conducted in the classroom' (Taba, 1967: 11).

Defining the curriculum as a plan for learning has subsequently been taken up in terms of two approaches to curriculum theory:

1 What knowledge is to be acquired over time? (The content and subjects to be studied.)
2 What types of learners and citizens does society want or need? (The aims, values and purposes of being educated and of becoming an effective learner.)

For your pupils to achieve academic success, you need to draw on your understandings of teaching, planning and the curriculum in terms of the question that each of these forms of teacher knowledge have in common: what is to be learnt?

To be academically successful, a pupil has to 'grasp an area of knowledge' (Edwards, 2015: 14) and have developed the capacity to be in control of their own learning. It was Schwab (1978), a Chicago-based science educator, who first made a useful distinction between the forms of knowledge that make up a subject. He termed these forms of knowledge as substantive and syntactic. Substantive knowledge is made up of the key concepts in a subject and their relation to each other in that subject, i.e. what you need to know in order to 'do' the subject. For example, in history, these might include empire and being a nation. Syntactic knowledge is seen as the ways of thinking and using those key concepts like an expert in the subject does, i.e. through ways of demonstrating the validity of ideas using, for example, inference, causality and evidence-based argument. The content and the form of the subject are necessarily intertwined so that pupils can represent the knowledge of the subject and construct their own understandings of it. Schwab's (1978) argument that a teacher needs to be aware of the forms of knowledge that make up the subject they are teaching has been extremely influential. This is because the concepts of substantive and syntactic knowledge help us to understand what a teacher needs to know about the curriculum when working with it to plan and teach. His ideas have been taken up by subsequent curriculum theorists, especially Christine Counsell (see below).

The second aspect of academic success relates to the pupil as a learner, i.e. learning how to be effective when learning and applying the curriculum content. This is important because a goal of teachers is for their pupils to be able to function independently of their teacher and to self-regulate their actions when learning. This can be thought of as the strategies a learner uses 'to shape their own pathways through classroom tasks' (Edwards, 2015: 15). Nisbet and Shucksmith (1986) summarised these strategies as:

- asking questions: defining hypothesis, relating to previous work
- planning: deciding on tactics and timetables, identifying what materials and skills are needed
- monitoring: making continuous attempts to match progress to initial questions or purposes
- checking: assessing preliminary results and performance
- revising: in the light of evidence
- self-testing final assessments of results and performance

Claxton (2007) developed a metaphor to explain the way in which teachers address the dual focus of their work, i.e. the curriculum and the development of their pupils as learners: split-screen thinking. He describes it as: 'On one "screen" inside their heads teachers are thinking about how to help students grasp the content. On the other, at the same time, they are thinking about how to help students develop their learning capacity' in relation to the curriculum content and the broader aims and values of the curriculum (Claxton, 2007: 125). Discussing explicitly (in the form of a meta-commentary) the forms of the knowledge that make up the curriculum (in age-appropriate ways) and the learning strategies listed above can help teachers to motivate pupils. The teacher's meta-commentary enables pupils to develop awareness of what the learning is meant to achieve and gives them a greater sense of control over their own learning, leading to both independence and agency as learners (Shires, 2022).

The next section summarises the work of three significant curriculum theorists (Basil Bernstein, Michael Young and Christine Counsell), whose ideas about and explanations of the curriculum have shaped the way in which classroom teachers today are required to interpret their role.

Key Curriculum Theorists and Their Ideas

Basil Bernstein (1924-2000): Recontextualisation

Bernstein was a sociologist of education. His major interest was in the internal features of pedagogy that structure the content of the curriculum and how that differs between social groups. Bernstein wanted to bring our attention to the relationship between everyday knowledge and the knowledge transmitted in school by teachers to their pupils through their pedagogy. His theory was that knowledge is shaped as it is taken from the external world into a school. He termed the process by which pupils access this knowledge via the pedagogy of their teachers *recontextualisation* (Bernstein, 2000). Recontextualisation of knowledge for the school curriculum explains the process by which the subjects on the school curriculum are created in relation to the broader discipline in universities. In other words, he was concerned less with the curriculum as an entity, and more with the pedagogic device, which he defined as the rules and procedures by which knowledge is converted into the school curriculum.

Thinking hard about the process of recontextualisation can clarify the differences and relations between school subjects and their disciplinary knowledge as it exists in universities, industry, etc. In universities, disciplines mark the separations and specialisations of knowledge, where the priority is to discover new knowledge. In schools, specialisation is subject-based (and subjects are drawn from disciplines). Whereas disciplines are oriented towards the discovery of new knowledge, school subjects are oriented towards the transmission of knowledge, and consider the age and stage of the development of pupils and the knowledge they bring to school. It follows, then, that in order to understand the subjects on the school curriculum that you are asked to teach, you must develop an awareness of the disciplines to which they relate. In other words, you need to have an awareness of what a particular subject 'is all about' and what the 'point' of a particular subject is. In this way, you will be better able to discuss the curriculum effectively. For example, you will be clearer about how to make the subject appropriate for your pupils, while keeping in mind the knowledge and nature of the subject as a discipline. In other words, you will be able to discuss the subject on the curriculum in terms of its structure of knowledge and progression. For example, structuring knowledge and planning for progression looks quite different in chemistry compared with art. As a teacher, you need to understand both the disciplinary and substantive knowledge that underpins a subject on a school curriculum in order to do this well. Disciplinary knowledge is knowledge of how a discipline generates knowledge or meaning in the world, and substantive knowledge is knowledge of the claims about the world put into the world by a discipline. As such, Bernstein's concept of recontextualisation is a way for you to think about the subjects you teach and how to teach them. It will help you to think through the disciplinary and substantive knowledge of the subjects you teach.

Michael Young: Powerful Knowledge

Michael Young is a sociologist whose work considers the purpose of schools in terms of the knowledge that schools can offer all pupils. He argues that a school curriculum does not replace the knowledge pupils bring to school, but ought to challenge it to enable pupils to transform and extend their everyday knowledge by engaging with new ideas.

The knowledge related to a pupil's experience of growing up is not acquired as a specific act of learning, but is incidental to growing up in a particular community. In other words, the curriculum is an opportunity to think about the world beyond a pupil's everyday experience. A school curriculum, and the knowledge that it gives access to, is different from the knowledge that pupils acquire from their experience of being in a family and community. By contrast, a pupil going to school is confronted with knowledge that is not based on their experience, and which requires their conscious involvement if they are to acquire it. For example, pupils encounter new ways of thinking why plants grow or why a particular period of history was dominated by religious wars. Thus, a school curriculum is distinct because it organises concepts not according to pupil experience, but according to principles established by specialists, which are ordered into subjects in ways which are different from most children's everyday experience.

A curriculum organises knowledge for the purpose of making it accessible in a coherent and sequenced way. The curriculum is designed so that pupils can test their new knowledge against what they know about the world. On becoming pupils, children are encouraged to extend their knowledge with ideas that take them beyond their experience and to begin to ask and answer questions about why the world is as it is. In other words, acquiring different types of knowledge (via school subjects) empowers pupils because they are able to generalise, predict, question, imagine and explore alternatives. However, the extent to which this happens depends on you, as their teacher, having adequate knowledge of both the subject in question and how best to engage your pupils.

Young's writing (2008a, 2008b) developed from his work in South Africa after the apartheid era. In 2010, he wrote a paper with Johan Muller (Young and Muller, 2010) where they analysed the different types of knowledge that were valued and taught at different times in history. They identified two historical periods and analysed their assumptions about knowledge and how it was taken up by the school curriculum of each time period. They called these periods Future 1 and Future 2 and they are explained in Table 3.1.

As a consequence of their analysis, Muller and Young (2010) developed an alternative model for the curriculum based on the concept of 'powerful knowledge'. They called it Future 3 and it has shaped current approaches to curriculum design. For Young and Muller, 'powerful knowledge' is to distinguish thinking about the curriculum in terms of the ideas *of* the powerful (i.e. a list of knowledge to be transmitted by the teacher). Their concept of powerful knowledge emphasises particular features of knowledge, our relationship to that knowledge, and what it can do for those who have access to it. Powerful knowledge is a way of seeing knowledge in terms of its creation and purpose. Thinking about the curriculum in terms of powerful knowledge should lead teachers to consider the nature of knowledge in their subject, about what they want to teach and why.

Table 3.1 An explanation of a Future 1 and Future 2 Curriculum (Young and Muller, 2010)

Future	Historical period	Assumptions about knowledge	Pedagogy based on	Subjects	How seen in terms of current pressures on schools
1	The beginning of mass education in the 19th century	The elite are educated and knowledge is treated as given Knowledge is stable and rigid Knowledge presented as the finished article	Pupils are required to be compliant	School subjects emerge at the end of the 19th century	An overemphasis on exam results
2	After World War 2	No theory of knowledge Knowledge is constructed and democratic Emphasis is placed on generic outcomes and learner-directed trends Social base of knowledge is over exaggerated	Children cannot see how to get better because the removal of subject boundaries also removes the models of progression	Subject boundaries are weakened	A response by schools when they struggle with disaffected pupils and have a shortage of staff with specialist subject knowledge

A Future 3 curriculum links a subject's concepts, contents and activities. Knowledge, which is powerful, takes pupils beyond the everyday, and describes both the objects of a discipline and its ways of working, rather than being the knowledge of those who are powerful. In other words, powerful knowledge is a way of looking at curriculum. In terms of powerful knowledge, the curriculum has the following three aims:

- To provide ambitious and well-chosen knowledge to pupils so that they may be inducted into the subject disciplines and appreciate the meaning-making that human intellect has developed through these disciplines
- To provide the curricular basis for a rigorous education that brings opportunities
- To enable pupils to learn not only the great claims and contributions of the subject disciplines, but also how disciplines operate so that pupils regard knowledge and meaning as the products of ongoing discourses – discourses that they are empowered to join, participate in and challenge as educated people

Christine Counsell: Disciplinary and Substantive Knowledge

Christine Counsell is a teacher educator and educational leader whose work, which is related to the teaching of history and the history curriculum, has influenced recent educational policy in England. Her approach to the curriculum has developed from extensive innovation and debate about the relationship between curriculum and pedagogy, with a particular focus on teaching based on a disciplinary curriculum. Counsell regards the subjects of the curriculum not as bodies of information, but as distinctively structured fields of knowledge or different systems of meaning. She developed her work from that of Schwab (1978). She adopts his term and definition of 'substantive' to represent the forms of knowledge that emerged from subject debates about the structure, status and origin of knowledge. However, rather than use Schwab's term 'syntactic knowledge', she refers to 'disciplinary knowledge'. Disciplinary knowledge, as Counsell defines it, overlaps with syntactic knowledge but is a broader conception because it includes knowing about the origins and social production of knowledge, not just its processes, structures, rules and conventions. In this way, Counsell's approach to the curriculum incorporates Young's concept of powerful knowledge and the perspective that knowledge is provisional and revisable, not a fixed cannon of facts. Table 3.2 summarises the ways in which you can interpret substantive and disciplinary knowledge as curricular terms, i.e. as they relate to the subjects on the school curriculum.

It is important to be able to analyse the subject you teach, using these curricular concepts to interpret the nature of the knowledge, because having that level of understanding as a classroom teacher enables you to plan your teaching for learning more precisely and accurately. It allows you to pay attention to the nature of what your pupils are to remember and its role in their subsequent learning.

Table 3.2 Ways to understand substantive and disciplinary knowledge as a classroom teacher

Substantive knowledge	Disciplinary knowledge
Knowledge of claims about the world are subject content	How subject investigates substantive knowledge and constructs subject's claims, arguments and accounts
Shaped by disciplinary approaches (subject knowledge of)	How a subject distinctly pursues its own truth (e.g. beauty in art, testing in science, logic in maths)
The content that you teach as established fact. You treat the material presented as a given	Has a purpose if related to the problems of the subject so that pupils can reason, debate and infer (drawing on substantive knowledge)
	What pupils learn about how knowledge was established, its certainty and how it is being revised by schools, artists or professional practice
	What is taught in school is not all that there is to the subject – and not relevant to all subjects (i.e. school-level languages) but it is expressed differently in different subjects

In addition to being able to understand the forms of knowledge so that you are able to get better at teaching, Counsell's research into how teachers develop the disciplinary thinking of their pupils yielded the term 'second-order concepts'. These concepts enable teachers to talk about disciplinary knowledge and then to shape what they teach in ways which develop their pupils' disciplinary knowledge. In other words, second-order concepts are tools that allow teachers to grasp what it means to learn a particular subject and they shape the key questions asked in a subject and how the subject is structured. For example, much of the work of history teachers, curriculum developers and education researchers in the last 40 years has been devoted to trying to understand how to integrate first- and second-order dimensions of learning about history so that they develop together, and to enable knowing a subject to be meaningfully realised in and through the classroom. For example, Table 3.3 illustrates the main second-order concepts in history.

To learn history means that a pupil acquires knowledge and understanding of the past. This can be understood as substantive (or first-order) knowledge of the past and structural knowledge and understanding of how history works (second-order). Second-order concepts are tools for learning that generate first-order (or substantive) knowledge and organise and structure it so that it can be used by the learner. Second-order, then, does not mean secondary, in the sense of being supplementary to primary factual knowledge. Second-order knowledge:

> is better understood as *meta*historical knowledge and understanding – as knowledge and understanding *about* historical knowledge and understanding. Second-order knowledge and understanding [are] fundamental to the development of substantive knowledge in history above the level of isolated or aggregated facts: [they] help[s] both to form substantive knowledge and [to] give substantive knowledge form. (Chapman, 2016: 228)

Christine Counsell holds the view that teachers who enable all the children in their class to learn subjects though both substantive and disciplinary knowledge are Future 3 curriculum 'pioneers' (Counsell, 2016: 215).

Table 3.3 Second-order concepts used by teachers develop pupils' disciplinary knowledge in history

Used by teachers to classify types of historical argument taught to pupils	The processes by which evidence is established and accounts are constructed
Cause	Sources and evidence
Consequence	Historical interpretations
Change and continuity	
Similarity and difference	
Historical significance	

Key Takeaways

- As a teacher, you are a curriculum maker. It is a mistake to think that just because there is a National Curriculum or centralised planning in your school that you do not need to know and understand curriculum theory. Knowing about the knowledge that makes up the subjects on the curriculum is an important aspect of your role and informs your decisions and actions to bring about learning from your teaching.
- One helpful way to identify an ambitious curriculum is to think about it in terms of powerful knowledge and that knowledge is generative: knowledge helps pupils secure more knowledge.
- Progression can be understood as learning more of the curriculum by getting better at the particular subject.
- Current approaches to pupils getting better at a subject prioritise the teacher focussing their teaching on the curriculum, rather than testing pupils to assess their progress. From a curriculum knowledge is learned, whereas assessment samples and measures to infer the learning that has taken place.
- Teachers sequence the curriculum because they work with teaching the curriculum over time. To sequence a curriculum, you need to draw on your knowledge of the nature, structure and components of the subject you are teaching, and which activities will help your pupils to be successful at learning them.
- It is important to understand the difference between the final endpoint in the subject you are teaching and the steps along the way that develop pupils to reach this final endpoint. A curriculum is not just one thing after another, but a mixture of a journey, narrative and conversation between the subject-matter of the curriculum and your pupils.

What the Core Content Framework Says About Knowing and Working With the Curriculum

The Core Content Framework (CCF) (DfE, 2019) has a section devoted to what you should know about and be able to do with the subject and curriculum in terms of what you teach. First, it states what you should know about the role of a curriculum: that it enables a school to set out its vision for the knowledge, skills and values that its pupils will learn. You should also know that the school curriculum encompasses the national curriculum within a wider and coherent vision of how a school defines successful learning. Second, the CCF requires you to understand the role of your subject knowledge in three ways. Subject knowledge enables you:

- to teach better
- to identify the role of foundational concepts as part of the subject
- to anticipate misconceptions

Third, you should aim to teach the knowledge and skills within each subject explicitly and you should also explicitly teach reading, writing, speaking and listening in terms of each subject as part of your professional responsibility for your pupils' literacy. Finally, you are expected to think about the curriculum in terms of how your pupils will learn:

- That pupils need to have secured knowledge before they apply it in critical thinking activities
- That you need to structure the sequence of your teaching bearing in mind that pupils learn new ideas by linking them to what they already know
- That you should not assume that your pupils can transfer knowledge and skills to a new subject
- The importance of early literacy

You are expected to master the following three skills in terms of what you teach:

1 To be able to deliver a carefully sequenced and coherent curriculum.
2 To be able to support pupils to build increasingly complex mental models.
3 To develop pupils' literacy.

Table 3.4 sets out how the CCF (DfE, 2019) suggests you should secure teacher knowledge about the curriculum and master these teaching skills related to teaching the content of the curriculum.

Key Takeaways

- Teacher knowledge that draws on an understanding of curriculum theory can be defined as:

1 Content knowledge – knowledge of the subject.
2 Pedagogical knowledge – knowledge of general effective teaching strategies.
3 Pedagogical content knowledge – knowledge of how to teach a subject effectively.

- It is important that you develop good subject knowledge of all the subjects you teach so that you can:
  - present information clearly
  - promote pupil discussion
  - check understanding systematically
  - identify misconceptions accurately
  - provide clear, direct feedback
  - respond and adapt (not differentiate)
  - teach reading well
  - enable pupils over time to remember new content and integrate it into larger concepts

Table 3.4 Ways in which you can secure your subject knowledge

Practise...	Observe how other teachers...	Discuss and analyse...	Being mentored in...
1 teaching so that all pupils learn and master essential concepts, knowledge, skills and principles 2 accumulating your PCK (analogies, illustrations, examples, explanations, demonstrations) 3 using resources, the materials designed by someone else 4 being aware of misconceptions 5 linking your content to concepts in the subject 6 providing tools to support learning of key ideas 7 ensuring knowledge is secure before thinking critically 8 teaching unfamiliar vocabulary 9 modelling and requiring high-quality language	1 ensure thinking is focused on the key ideas of this subject 2 use retrieval and spaced practice to build recall of key knowledge 3 interleave concrete and abstract examples and slowly withdraw the concrete examples 4 ensure pupils understand their phonics sessions	1 the rationale for curriculum choices, how these were arrived at and how to use them in lesson plans 2 how to revisit the big ideas of the subject over time and via examples 3 how to balance exposition, repetition, practice of skills and knowledge 4 how to support fluency in reading and writing	1 how to identify essential concepts, knowledge, skills and principles 2 how to model reading comprehension by asking questions, summarising and making predictions 3 promoting reading for pleasure

Suggested Activities to Develop Your Understanding of the Curriculum

Discuss With a More Experienced Teacher

Ask a more experienced teacher what they use as second-order concepts when teaching the range of subjects across the curriculum (e.g. for art: line, shape, tone, texture; for music: melody, harmony, tempo, timbre). Collect these so you can refer to them as you plan for pupils to learn substantive and disciplinary knowledge in your lessons and as they complete the lesson's activities.

For You to Think About Before a Lesson

- What should your pupils know about the subject?
- What should your pupils be able to do in the subject?
- What sort of questions should they be able to answer about the subject?
- How should they be able to see and interpret the world in terms of the ideas of the subject?
- What should your pupils be able to take with them from your lesson to prepare them for the next stage in their learning of the subject?

For You to Do

As a curriculum maker, when you are devising an activity or task for your pupils, think hard about the following:

- What is thinking in the subject (e.g. thinking geographically, thinking scientifically, etc.)?
- Does the activity or task take the pupil beyond what they already know?
- What key concepts from the subject underpin the activity or task?

Deepening Your Knowledge

If you are interested in learning more about how to develop your pupils as effective learners, then this evidence report by the Education Endowment Foundation (EEF) reviews the best available research to offer practical advice on how to develop your pupils' metacognitive skills and knowledge. The report has recommendations in seven areas and 'myth busts' common misconceptions teachers have about metacognition.

Education Endowment Foundation (EEF) (2018) *Metacognition and Self-regulated Learning: Guidance Report*. London: EEF. Available at: https://d2tic4wvo1iusb.cloudfront.net/eef-guidance-reports/metacognition/EEF_Metacognition_and_self-regulated_learning.pdf?v=1683809002

Reflection on Important Questions

A curriculum can be seen as a framework that sets out the aims of a school in terms of:

- the knowledge and skills to be gained by pupils at each stage of their schooling
- a structure and narrative that is developed over time
- a basis for evaluating what knowledge and skills have been gained against the expectations set out by the school

The curriculum defines:

- what pupils know and are able to do by the time they have finished a stage of education
- the knowledge and experiences pupils will gain *beyond those from their home and everyday life* (this links to the aims for learning explained by learning theories)

As a teacher, you will both make sense of and use a curriculum in the following ways:

- to understand the character of knowledge to be acquired
- to extend pupils' knowledge beyond their everyday knowledge
- to interpret the purpose of your pedagogy as to engage pupils with the curriculum based on your disciplinary knowledge

Conclusion

Much of the impetus for emphasising the importance of curriculum theory for teachers was initiated by Ofsted's (2019) own research into how much this knowledge was used in schools and by teachers to shape teaching and learning. Ofsted found that teachers had tended to conflate curriculum with the timetable and had generic understandings of the curriculum.

As a consequence, it is now seen to be very important for new teachers to have a good grasp of curriculum theory. This is because curriculum theory will help you to understand the relationship between the curriculum and pedagogy. It will also help you to acquire a deeper understanding of the different forms of teacher knowledge as well as the forms of knowledge that make up the different subjects on the curriculum. Curriculum theory provides a way of thinking about how to teach all the subjects on the primary school curriculum equally successfully so that your pupils develop conceptual understanding.

References

Bernstein, B (2000) *Pedagogy, Symbolic Control, and Identity: Theory, Research, and Critique.* New York: Rowan and Littlefield

Chapman, A (2016) Historical thinking/historical knowing: On the content of the form of history education. In Counsell, C, Burn, K, and Chapman, A (Eds.), *Masterclass in History Education: Transforming Teaching and Learning.* London: Bloomsbury

Claxton, G (2007) Expanding young people's capacity to learn. *British Journal of Educational Studies* 55(2), 115–134

Counsell, C (2016) History teachers' publication and the curricular 'what?': mobilising subject-specific professional knowledge in a culture of genericism. In Counsell, C, Burn, K, and Chapman, A (Eds.), *Masterclass in History Education: Transforming Teaching and Learning.* London: Bloomsbury

DfE (Department for Education) (2019) *Education Inspection Framework: An Overview of Research.* London: HMSO

Edwards, A (2015) Designing tasks which engage learners with knowledge. In Thompson, I (Ed.), *Designing Tasks in Secondary Education: Enhancing Subject Understanding and Student Engagement.* Abingdon: Routledge

Moore, A (2015) *Understanding the School Curriculum: Theory, Politics, and Principles.* Abingdon: Routledge

Nisbet, J and Shucksmith J (1986) *What are Learning Strategies?* London: Routledge Kegan Paul

Ofsted (2019) *Education Inspection Framework: An Overview of Research.* London: Ofsted

Schwab, J (1978) *Science, Curriculum, and Liberal Education: Selected Essays of Joseph Schwab.* Edited by I Westbury and N Wilkof. Chicago, IL: University of Chicago Press

Shires, L (2022) *Expert Teaching: What Matters to Expert Teachers? A Cultural-historical Perspective on Relational Expertise.* Oxford: Oxford Brookes University

Taba, H (1962) *Curriculum Development: Theory and Practice.* New York: Harcourt Brace Jovanovich

Tyler, RW (1949) *Basic Principles of Curriculum and Instruction.* Chicago, IL: University of Chicago Press

Young, M (2008a) Curriculum theory and the problem of knowledge: A personal project and an unfinished journey. In Waks, L and Short, E (Eds.), *Leaders in Curriculum Studies: Intellectual Self Portraits.* Rotterdam: SENSE Books

Young, M (2008b) From constructivism to realism in the sociology of the curriculum. In Kelly, G, Luke, A, and Green, J (Eds.), *What Counts as Knowledge in Educational Settings?* Washington, DC: American Educational Research Association

Young, M and Muller, J (2010) Three educational scenarios for the future: Lessons from the sociology of knowledge. *European Journal of Education* 45(1), 11–27

4
WHAT IS BACKWARDS PLANNING?

Important Questions

- Why is planning an important skill to master?
- What knowledge is the foundation for skilful planning?
- Why is backwards planning an important approach for teachers?

Introduction

This chapter will bring together the ideas in the three earlier chapters in this part of the book by looking closely at planning. Planning is often seen as problematic because it is work undertaken away from the classroom and in anticipation of the act of teaching itself. This means you have to have knowledge of what has happened in the past and where the pupils ought to be heading to plan their next steps in the coming lesson. You have to think through what both you and your pupils will do to cause the learning of a particular group of pupils at that moment in time. This chapter explains what planning is intended to achieve and how its elements are structured across the *Core Content Framework* (CCF) (DfE, 2019). It then looks at ideas about planning in terms of the type of knowledge a teacher needs to have in order to plan well, and outlines an approach to planning that focuses on pupils' understanding of the curriculum. By the end of this chapter, you will be clear about how to approach planning.

What is Planning?

Planning is when you set out your thinking about the forthcoming lesson or sequence of lessons. It is when you 'think like a teacher' – i.e. when you use your syntactic knowledge (the conceptual understanding that underpins the ways of thinking and representing that are expected of expert teachers). Planning is an opportunity for you as a new teacher to practise the skill of developing learner-focused teaching strategies. In the same way, the various lesson plan templates made available to you are scaffolds for your learning. However experienced and expert they are, good teachers continue to plan their lessons – it is not an activity just for new teachers. This is because planning draws on your knowledge of learning, teaching and the curriculum to shape the practical activity of teaching your pupils the subject-matter of the curriculum, and as such, it is both a professional process and core practice.

Why is Planning a Problem?

Many new teachers share common worries about lesson planning:

- Planning can be seen as 'admin' about teaching, rather than being essential to teaching well
- Planning templates can seem like boxes to fill
- There is a fear of not 'getting it right' or 'doing it wrong' in the eyes of your mentor
- Thinking up a variety of different tasks, questions, scaffolds and explanations that enable pupils to learn the subject-matter of the curriculum
- How much detail to include on a plan?
- How much time to spend on planning a lesson?

And there are yet more practical worries about how helpful planning is when teaching during a lesson:

- How can I actually use and refer to the plan when teaching?
- How will I recognise learning in terms the pupils getting better at the curriculum I am teaching – 'How will I know if the plan worked?'

What the Core Content Framework Says About Planning

Table 4.1 sets out how the Core Content Framework (CCF) (DfE, 2019) deconstructs what you need to think hard about as you plan. This table is useful because it deconstructs the elements of what a teacher does when they teach, and what needs to be planned ahead of the lesson. There are seven areas to consider: task design, sequence, modelling, scaffolding, explicit teaching, questioning and explanations. They draw on eight dimensions of a teacher's role: having high expectations, pupils' learning, teaching the subject-matter of a curriculum, classroom practice, adaptive teaching, assessment, managing behaviour and being professional. It is clear that in the CCF (DfE, 2019) a central focus of planning is the role the lesson will play in the schema formation of pupils – i.e. how to break down knowledge and skills into small steps and how to connect new knowledge with existing knowledge to extend it.

Table 4.1 What the CCF requires new teachers to know and be able to do when planning teaching

	What to think hard about when you plan a lesson						
CCF strand	**Task design**	**Sequence**	**Model**	**Scaffolds**	**Explicit teaching**	**Questions**	**Explanations**
High expectations	Set tasks that are achievable but challenging						
How pupils learn	Link what pupils already know to what is being taught Balance exposition, repetition, practice and retrieval of critical knowledge and skills Design practice and generation and retrieval tasks that provide enough support so that pupils experience a high success rate when attempting challenging work	Take prior knowledge into account when introducing new material Secure foundational content before more complex content Regularly review and practise key ideas and concepts over time	Worked examples that take pupils through each step of a new process	Break complex material into smaller steps Increase challenge with practice and retrieval as knowledge becomes secure (remove scaffold)	Identify misconceptions and prevent them from forming		
Subject and curriculum	Provide tasks that support pupils to learn key ideas securely	Ensure pupils master foundational concepts before moving on Learn new ideas by linking them to existing knowledge and moving on to increasingly complex mental models Revisit big ideas over time and teach key concepts through a range of concepts Use retrieval and spaced practice to build recall of knowledge		Interleave concrete and abstract examples, slowly withdrawing concrete examples and drawing attention to the underlying structure of problems	Explicitly teach subject knowledge and skills needed to succeed Draw explicit links between new content and the core concepts and principles in the subject Ensure pupils have relevant domain-specific knowledge, especially when asked to think critically within a subject		

(Continued)

Table 4.1 What the CCF requires new teachers to know and be able to do when planning teaching (*Continued*)

	What to think hard about when you plan a lesson						
CCF strand	**Task design**	**Sequence**	**Model**	**Scaffolds**	**Explicit teaching**	**Questions**	**Explanations**
Classroom practice	Independent practice via tasks broken down into components using metacognitive and procedural processes Ensure there are repeated opportunities to practise Talk to support pupils to articulate key ideas, consolidate understanding and to extend vocabulary Plan activities around what you want pupils to think hard about		To make abstract ideas concrete and accessible and to understand new processes and ideas Make each step memorable so that pupils can recall them	Used to help pupils apply new ideas but they are gradually removed when pupils have a high degree of success in applying previously taught material	Metacognitive strategies of how to plan, monitor and evaluate Guide, support and practise how to work together in pairs and group activities Narrate thought processes out loud to make thinking explicit	Use to check prior knowledge, assess understanding and break down problems Use a range of types of questions to extend and challenge pupils	Pitched at the point of current understanding, sometimes with a graphical representation
Adaptive teaching	Avoid setting distinct tasks for groups of pupils or having lower expectations for particular pupils Build in additional practice or remove unnecessary explanations Make use of well-designed resources Ensure all pupils have access to a rich curriculum	Connect new content with existing knowledge or pre-teach if pupils lack critical knowledge		Pupils learn at different rates and require different levels and types of support Pupils with SEND are likely to require additional or adapted support Identify pupils who need new content to be further broken down		Reframe questions to provide greater scaffolding or stretch	

Table 4.1 What the CCF requires new teachers to know and be able to do when planning teaching

	What to think hard about when you plan a lesson						
CCF strand	**Task design**	**Sequence**	**Model**	**Scaffolds**	**Explicit teaching**	**Questions**	**Explanations**
Assessment	Structure tasks to enable the identification of knowledge gaps and misconceptions		Share or model work with pupils that highlights key details so that pupils learn how to self-assess			Plan formative assessment tasks that are linked to lesson objectives and think ahead about what would indicate understanding Ask questions to identify knowledge gaps and misconceptions Prompt pupils to elaborate when responding to a question to check the correct answer stems from secure understanding	
Managing behaviour	Check understanding of instructions before a task begins				Use verbal feedback in the place of written feedback in lessons, where possible		Give manageable, specific and sequential instructions
Professional behaviours	Learn to extend subject and pedagogic knowledge as part of preparing the lesson Collaborate with colleagues to share the load of planning and make use of shared resources						

Table 4.1 can be used to identify what needs to be included in your thinking as you plan a lesson and how those elements range across the key areas of teaching in the CCF strands.

Pedagogical Content Knowledge: What Good Teachers Know

Pedagogical Content Knowledge (PCK) was first identified as the specialist knowledge of teachers by Lee Shulman, a professor of psychology at Stanford University in the USA (Shulman, 1986). PCK is an important idea for teachers to understand because it helps to explain what it is teachers do and the knowledge base that they draw on. It was a key idea when it emerged in the 1980s because it explained what makes teaching a profession, i.e. having a distinct body of knowledge. PCK has been heavily researched since then because it helps us to deconstruct and understand good teaching.

In 1986 and 1987, Shulman published two seminal papers where he defined PCK and analysed the knowledge base of teaching. Shulman delivered the Presidential address to the 1985 annual meeting of the American Research Association. It was published the following year in their journal, *Educational Researcher* with the title 'Those who understand: Knowledge growth in teaching' (Shulman, 1986). Shulman's talk revisited how teachers had been taught to teach in the recent past in the USA (by exams and with a focus on topics related to teaching, e.g. 'understanding youth'). He was concerned that the new reforms being proposed neglected the subject-matter of the curriculum as being essential knowledge for teachers. He argued that knowledge of content (what is taught) and pedagogy (how it is taught) is what teachers really need to understand. He suggested three categories of content knowledge:

1. Subject content knowledge (CK) – understanding the structures and detail of the subject you teach beyond its facts and concepts, but in terms of its substantive structures ('the variety of ways in which the basic concepts and principles of the discipline are organised to incorporate its facts') and its syntactic structures ('the set of ways in which truth or falsehood, validity, or invalidity, are established') (Shulman, 1986: 9).
2. Curricular knowledge – how to teach a subject at a particular level and all the resources available. Curricular knowledge is lateral (what subject is being taught at a point in the year and how it relates to other subjects) and vertical (what has been taught before and what will be taught later).
3. Pedagogical Content Knowledge (PCK) – knowing and understanding the subject-matter for teaching.

Shulman's message was that to be a good teacher, one needs both subject-matter knowledge and pedagogical content knowledge and that general knowledge about what is to be taught is insufficient for good teaching. This is because CK (the subject-matter in the mind of the experts) is different from PCK (the subject-matter as preparation for your pupils).

Shulman then wrote a second paper, which was published in *Harvard Educational Review*, called 'Knowledge and teaching: Foundations of the new reform', where he explained how a focus on the relationship between what teachers know and do is the basis for helping teachers get better at teaching (Shulman, 1987). This is an important idea because a lot of what goes on in teaching is invisible to an observer. He argued that to help work out how to get better at teaching requires making the nature of teacher knowledge explicit and systematic. This article addressed two central questions. First, what should teachers know? And second, what should they know how to do? He compared experienced and novice teachers to consider what allows experienced teachers to teach in the way that they do. He listed categories of knowledge that underpin teachers' understanding when they teach well: content knowledge, general pedagogical content knowledge, curriculum knowledge, PCK, knowledge of learners and their characteristics, knowledge of educational contexts, knowledge of educational ends, purposes and values, and their philosophical and historical grounds. He suggested that really successful teachers are engaged in processes of pedagogical reasoning where the teacher, 'reconstructs, re-enacts, and/or recaptures the events, emotions, and the accomplishments' (Shulman, 1987: 20), which leads to the development of their PCK: a deeper understanding of what is to be taught, its broader purposes and of the pupils themselves. His key idea is that being a really effective teacher means being knowledgeable about what you are teaching. You not only need to understand it, but you also need to be able to understand it in several ways. This knowledge gives you the confidence to explain the content in a clear and cohesive fashion, address any pupil misconceptions or questions as they arise, and be able to draw links and analogies with other knowledge that might illuminate pupil understanding or, as Shulman (1987: 16) puts it, 'understand how a given idea relates to other ideas within the same subject area and to ideas in other subjects as well'. You also need to be aware of 'the broader purposes of what you are doing to attend to the equality of opportunity and equity amongst pupils of different backgrounds and cultures' (Shulman, 1987: 15). Ultimately, he argued that knowledge of subject is not enough and that effective teaching lies 'at the intersection of content and pedagogy' (Shulman, 1987: 15).

PCK is a concrete example of thinking about the knowledge of teaching. It is the knowledge of the particular subject-matter, in a particular way, for a particular reason to enhance your pupils' learning. It is a very specialised form of knowledge where the relationship between teaching and the curriculum is the major focus. Shulman (1986: 9) further explained PCK as: 'The most regularly taught topics in one's subject area, the most useful forms of representation of those ideas, the most powerful analogies, illustrations, examples, explanations, and demonstrations – in a word, the ways of representing and formulating the subject that make it comprehensible to others.' PCK involves you knowing and being able to explain the dependencies and connections between different parts of the curriculum and, as a result, how to work out the best order (how to sequence) the curriculum for teaching.

Shulman's ground-breaking work led to decades of research in the subject areas of the school curriculum to work out what the most useful forms of representation might be. He also suggested that PCK 'includes an understanding of what makes the learning of specific topics easy or difficult: the conceptions and preconceptions that students of different ages and backgrounds bring with them to the learning of those most frequently taught topics and lessons' (Shulman, 1986: 9). Pedagogical Content Knowledge is more than just knowledge about the content itself; it is also the learning associated with that particular content. This means asking yourself:

1 What knowledge and skills your pupils must already have to enable new learning?
2 If a pupil is struggling with an idea or a technique, what kinds of gaps in underpinning knowledge might explain that?
3 For each new idea, what connections do your pupils need to make with previous knowledge?

This kind of teacher curriculum knowledge is what happens when you plan a lesson, a scheme of work or the overall curriculum because you are considering the best sequence for teaching and how to reactivate your pupils' prior knowledge. PCK is not using a teaching strategy because it has been said 'to work', nor is it breaking the subject-matter of the curriculum into manageable 'chunks'. Rather, it is the combination of knowledge of content and pedagogy together, each shaping and interacting with the other so that what is taught, and how it is constructed, is purposefully created to ensure that the content is better understood by the pupils in any particular lesson because of the way the teaching is organised, planned, analysed and presented.

Pedagogical Reasoning: What Good Teachers Do

PCK exists in a teacher's head and is evidenced in the teacher's pedagogical reasoning and actions. Shulman (1987: 15) defines it as the process of a teacher 'transforming subject matter knowledge into forms that are pedagogically powerful'. This is the process when teachers design and teach lessons that have been considered in terms of what their pupils will know, rather than just in terms of managing behaviour. Shulman (1987) found that transformation of knowledge has to take place before the teacher can teach it. He outlined six steps that teachers go through to reshape and adapt the subject-matter of the curriculum to make it teachable. These steps are:

1 Comprehension – you have to understand what it is you are to teach, and to understand it in several ways.
2 Transformation – the ideas that you understand have to be transformed in some manner so that they can be taught, i.e. you have to think about the subject-matter from the point of view of your pupils.
3 Instruction – this is the observable part of your teaching, i.e. how you explain and question.
4 Evaluation – this is when you check for understanding, misunderstanding and confusion as you teach.

5 Reflection – how you analyse your teaching after the lesson in terms of the pupils' learning rather than what you said or did.
6 New comprehensions – reflecting on what you have learned about how to teach well by considering your lesson, how it worked and what you would do differently if you were to teach the lesson again or what sections you need to reteach and return to in future lessons.

This model of how teachers think about what they want to achieve and then connect that with their teaching actions is not fixed and can occur in different orders. However, Shulman's (1987: 19) view was that the six steps provided new teachers with the knowledge and practical abilities to reason their way through the 'complete act of pedagogy'. Furthermore, as a new teacher, PCK and the steps of pedagogical reasoning can help you to talk with more experienced and expert teachers about how they teach so that their pupils learn. The importance of PCK can be most recognisable when you are teaching a subject outside your area of expertise. You may know general approaches to teaching, but 'issues associated with difficult aspects of the topic, pupils' alternative conceptions, important big ideas, conceptual hooks, triggers for learning and so on, are not well known or understood by the teacher when rich understandings of subject content are lacking' (Loughran et al., 2012: 7).

Key Takeaways

- A sound knowledge of what you are teaching is essential to becoming an expert teacher.
- It is not enough to know what you are teaching. You need to know it in several ways.
- Explaining and showing are essential elements of good teaching.
- You need to develop a repertoire of representational examples, analogies and connections to the other subjects that you teach.

What is Backwards Planning?

Backwards planning was first developed in 1998 from a body of work about planning how to teach called *Understanding by Design* by Grant Wiggins, who worked in educational reform in Vermont, USA, and Jay McTighe, who researched assessment in Maryland, USA. They developed this approach to planning based on work by Ralph Tyler (1949). Tyler first suggested that stating objectives about the intended learning for pupils helps to shape the way teaching activities are planned and developed.

Backwards planning begins with the end in mind and is a three-stage process of thinking about why to teach, what to teach and how to teach an element of the subject-matter of the curriculum. Backwards planning is a form of forward thinking. It is an approach that works as well for a lesson, a scheme of work or a yearly plan because it focuses on the big ideas and essential questions your pupils need to remember over time. Although backwards planning is not intended to be a rigid sequence, and is a way of thinking where you move backwards and forwards as you think through the impact of one stage on another, it does have three-stage logic (i.e. you do need to think about all three stages).

Stage 1: Begin With the End in Mind

Stage 1 is very important because it is in thinking this through that you begin to focus on understanding and content rather than thinking about activities and tasks for your pupils to do.

- Establish what you want your pupils to know, understand and be able to do
- Unpack the curriculum: what are the aims or purposes of the curriculum expectations?
- Identify a 'big idea' (a concept, point of view, theory, theme or principle), which can be turned into an 'essential question' (a doorway for exploring the big idea) that leads to the understanding you want for your pupils.

If you are planning for your pupils to learn how to do something, then the following four questions can help you to understand the four aspects of skills:

1 Underlying concepts: what makes this skill work?
2 The purpose: what larger goal will this skill help you accomplish?
3 Use of strategies: what strategies will help you learn this skill more efficiently and effectively?
4 Context: when should the skill or strategy be used?

Stage 2: What is the Evidence?

Stage 2 addresses the invisibility of learning and the importance of thinking through how you will use formative assessment when teaching to check for understanding. In Stage 2 you are thinking about how you will gather evidence that your pupils understand the big idea and are able to answer the essential questions you developed in Stage 1. In this stage, you are drawing on your PCK and your understanding of what it means to get better in the subject-matter you are teaching. Such evidence can be thought of in terms of the verbs that describe what pupils will be doing. For example, application of understanding might be demonstrated by calculating, examining, sketching or using. You may decide to focus on a task that your pupils will perform where they are asked to explain, interpret or apply what they have learned, or one where pupils will self-assess their understanding by considering what they have learned from a new perspective, with empathy for the subject-matter or by reflecting on the change in their learning through metacognitive activities (such as pre- and post-learning quizzes).

Stage 3: Planning Learning Activities, Tasks and Your Teaching Inputs

This approach to planning is called backwards because stage 3 (thinking up activities and tasks for pupils and planning your questions and explanations) is typically where planning often starts. In backwards planning, however, we have started by thinking about learning the content and we end by thinking about activities. It is in stage 3 that you can now think about what it is that you and your pupils will say and do in the lesson that will cause them to think hard about the subject-matter of the curriculum. By the time you get to thinking about your plan at stage 3, you will find that a 'golden thread' to the whole lesson has emerged (an idea that you will repeat as a vertical theme that links together everything that is said, done and thought about in the lesson).

Why Backwards Planning is Important?

Rather than planning being the creation of a list of activities or topics or facts, the iterative process of backwards planning ensures that the lesson has focused on learning rather than pupils being busy. Backwards planning addresses an important aspect of the CCF. In Assessment, the second 'Learn that…' states:

> Learn that good assessment helps teachers avoid being over-influenced by potentially misleading factors, such as how busy pupils appear. (DfE, 2019: 23)

Professor Robert Coe of Durham University, North Carolina, when speaking about his report *What Makes Great Teaching?* (Coe et al., 2014) at a conference in 2015, suggested that because learning is invisible, we use proxies for learning. He identified six proxies for learning that look like learning but are in fact activities that do not necessarily cause learning. These 'poor proxies for learning' are (Coe, 2015: 12):

1. Students are busy: lots of work is done (especially written work).
2. Students are engaged, interested, motivated.
3. Students are getting attention: feedback, explanations.
4. Classroom is ordered, calm, under control.
5. Curriculum has been covered (i.e. presented to students in some form).
6. (At least some) Students have supplied correct answers, even if they
   - have not really understood them
   - could not reproduce them independently
   - will have forgotten it by next week (tomorrow?)
   - Already knew how to do this anyway

Coe suggested that a better proxy for learning is that learning happens when people have to think hard. Backwards planning enables you to approach teaching with that theory of learning in mind.

CoRE: How to Backwards Plan

John Loughran, a professor of education at Monash University in Australia, researched PCK in terms of how teachers might use it as a process when planning. Getting better at teaching is different from getting better at other skills because teachers have a dual focus: the subject-matter of the curriculum and the learning of their pupils. Loughran investigated how teachers draw on their PCK to plan lessons that address how teachers want their pupils to relate to the curriculum, i.e. by learning it and incorporating new learning into how they see and are able to act in the world. His approach is useful when you are learning how to backwards plan because it supports you in identifying the big ideas or concepts that underpin the curriculum and it leads to enduring understanding and learning as a 'psychological event': a 'relatively permanent change in the way an action is achieved, as a result of prior experience' (Chaiklin, 2015: 94).

Loughran (2019) developed a series of prompts arising from the thinking of expert teachers when they backwards plan and use their PCK. He calls these prompts CoRE (Content Representation) and many teachers have found them useful because they make PCK explicit. New teachers find these prompts to be a useful scaffold for developing PCK. The prompts are:

1 What do you intend pupils to learn about this idea?
2 Why is it important for pupils to know this?
3 What else do you know about this idea (but that you do not intend pupils to know yet)?
4 What difficulties/limitations are connected with teaching this idea?
5 What knowledge about pupils' thinking influences your teaching of this idea?
6 What other factors influence your teaching of this idea?
7 What teaching strategies do you use (and what are the particular reasons for using them to engage with this idea)?
8 What specific approaches do you use to ascertain pupils understanding or confusion around this idea?

Typically, when learning how to teach, new teachers start with prompt 7 about teaching strategies, because it resonates with their understanding of their knowledge of teaching. Prompt 7 becomes a springboard to unpacking the other prompts in ways that help make knowledge about teaching for learning explicit and easier to access and repeat in the future.

Key Takeaways

- Teachers have a dual focus: the subject-matter of the curriculum and the learning of their pupils.
- Teachers cannot see learning as it is invisible, but they can think about learning as when their pupils are thinking hard.
- Pupils show they have learned when they can apply new knowledge, skills or understanding in a new context.
- When planning how to sequence learning, teachers unpack what is new learning, what needs to be scaffolded and what needs to be repeated.
- Teachers look for activities and resources that make the curriculum relevant to their pupils.
- Extending and updating your subject knowledge (CK) and your knowledge about how to teacher well (PCK) is a key professional behaviour.

Suggested Activities to Develop PCK and to Get Better at Backwards Planning

Discuss With a More Experienced Teacher

1 What does it mean to get better at the subject you plan to teach?
2 What are the key concepts and procedures pupils learn in the subject you plan to teach?
3 What kinds of things are pupils expected to learn and remember over time?

For You to Think About After a Lesson

1 What did you want pupils to learn?
2 Why did you decide to do a particular activity?
3 How did you make sure the pupils were thinking hard about the content of the lesson and not the activity in which they were participating?

For You to Do

1 Consider joining the subject association for the subjects in which you are most keen to practise your PCK and backwards planning. There are subject associations for every curriculum subject, and they provide excellent examples of teaching resources and teaching strategies, which you can use and which reflect the very best representations of the curriculum.

Deepening Your Knowledge

- Singh's (2002) article explores in detail one idea from the work of the very influential sociologist Basil Bernstein (2000). It looks at how knowledge is translated into communication that teaches. It describes the rules and procedures by which knowledge is changed into classroom talk and a curriculum. It explains Bernstein's concept of the pedagogic device – the principles by which knowledge is turned into something teachable – in terms of three rules, which have become very important for understanding what, how and why we teach: distribute, recontextualise and evaluate.

Singh, P (2002) Pedagogising knowledge: Bernstein's theory of the pedagogic device. *British Journal of the Sociology of Education* 23(4), 571–582

- Loughran's (2019) article argues that pedagogical reasoning underpins the decision-making, intents and actions of teachers: the strategies they use to make knowledge accessible and demonstrable. Loughran suggests that close examination of a teacher's pedagogical reasoning shines light on the sophisticated and complex how, what and why of teaching.

Loughran, J (2019) Pedagogical reasoning: The foundation of the professional knowledge of teaching. *Teachers and Teaching* 25(5), 523–535

Conclusion

Rather than plan your lessons in terms of what pupils will do, instead plan your lessons in terms of how pupils will think hard about the content of the lesson. It is important to think about how your pupils will acquire the knowledge, skills and understanding of the subject-matter of the curriculum. Backwards planning is a way of enabling your pupils to want to learn, and to feel positive about their progress in learning because the specific learning is so central to and valued in the lesson.

In Parts 2 and 3 that follow we go into detail about the different components of planning by looking at each one separately so that you can understand what it is, why it is important and how to use each idea so that you can teach successfully. In the conclusion that ends the book, we address how you can bring all your knowledge together to ensure that you think not only about your teaching as something that you do, but also about the impact of your teaching on the learning of your pupils.

References

Bernstein, B (2000) *Pedagogy, Symbolic Control, and Identity: Theory, Research, and Critique.* New York: Rowan and Littlefield

Chaiklin, S (2015) The concept of learning in a cultural-historical perspective. In Scott, D and Hargreaves, E (Eds.), *The SAGE Handbook of Learning*. London: Sage

Coe, R (2015) What makes great teaching? Paper presented at the IB World Regional Conference, International Baccalaureate, Den Haag NL, 31 October

Coe, R, Aloisi, C, Higgins, S, and Elliot Major, L (2014) *What Makes Great Teaching? Review of the Underpinning Research*. London: Centre for Evaluation and Monitoring, Durham University, The Sutton Trust

DfE (Department for Education) (2019) *ITT Core Content Framework*. London: HMSO

Loughran, J (2019) Pedagogical reasoning: The foundation of the professional knowledge of teaching. *Teachers and Teaching* 25(5), 523–535

Loughran, J, Berry, A, and Mulhall, A (2012) *Understanding and Developing Science Teachers' Pedagogical Content Knowledge*. Rotterdam: SENSE Publishers

Shulman, LS (1986) Those who understand teach: Knowledge growth in teaching. *Educational Researcher* 15(2), 4–14

Shulman, LS (1987) Knowledge and teaching: Foundations of the new reform. *Harvard Educational Review* 57(1), 1–23

Singh, P (2002) Pedagogising knowledge: Bernstein's theory of the pedagogic device. *British Journal of the Sociology of Education* 23(4), 571–582

Tyler, RW (1949) *Basic Principles of Curriculum and Instruction*. Chicago, IL: University of Chicago Press

Wiggins, G and McTighe, J (1998) *Understanding by Design*. Upper Saddle River, NJ: Merrill Prentice Hall

PART 2

ESSENTIAL PRACTICE: WHAT ARE YOU TEACHING?

Introduction

Teachers have to pay attention to their pupils' learning needs *and* the curriculum, and so thinking about what you are teaching is one half of the dual focus of teachers. The purpose of Part 2 is to help you turn the essential knowledge about learning, teaching, the curriculum and planning you considered in Part 1 into understanding of how to think about what you will teach. Part 2 has three chapters:

- Chapter 5 considers how to think with the curriculum, so you are able to plan for learning.
- Chapter 6 considers how to plan your teaching so that pupils learn the curriculum and are not kept busy in activities related to the curriculum.
- Chapter 7 considers how to develop your pupils' vocabulary and conceptual understanding of the curriculum content.

This section of the book therefore develops your disciplinary knowledge of teaching, i.e. how to think like a teacher by drawing on and using as tools the most significant and pertinent ideas about teaching that have developed over time.

5
HOW TO USE THE CURRICULUM WHEN YOU PLAN

Why is It Important to Think About How You Will Plan with Curriculum Coverage in Mind?

Teaching is a regulated profession, which means that aspects of what you do and why you do it are laid down in law. As a teacher, the minimum requirements of your practice and conduct are established in a set of professional standards, known as *Teachers' Standards* (DfE, 2011). In the preamble to the Overview of the standards (a helpful chart that summarises its key points), having strong subject knowledge is placed third, immediately after the standard that teachers are required to act with honesty and integrity. In other words, its position in the top three emphasises that subject knowledge is central to good teaching.

Standard 3 – A teacher must demonstrate good subject and curriculum knowledge – sets out that, alongside the role of every teacher to develop pupils' literacy (and, as a primary teacher, to understand systematic synthetic phonics and early maths teaching strategies), a teacher must:

- know subject and curriculum areas
- foster and maintain pupils' interest in the subject
- address pupils' misunderstandings
- understand how the subject and the curriculum have developed
- value scholarship (i.e. the subject as a form of disciplinary knowledge)

Similarly, the National Curriculum is 'essential knowledge' that all pupils are entitled to learn so that they can take up their future role as 'educated citizens' (DfE, 2014: 6). In other words, you have a responsibility to teach the curriculum well and your pupils have a right to develop the knowledge, skills and understanding set out in the curriculum. This means that you need to develop ways of thinking about the curriculum so that you can:

- plan to teach bearing in mind how pupils learn
- understand the content of the curriculum

so that:

- you are able to respond to your pupils and adapt your teaching
- answer the questions your pupils ask (including some you might not have anticipated)
- be able to offer your pupils multiple and different examples and explanations to ensure they gain understanding at a deeper level as they form mental representations and develop schemas (in other words, to know how to make the content meaningful to particular pupils so that they can assimilate and integrate new and prior knowledge)

As a new teacher, you are likely to be provided with a template for lesson planning. The intention behind such models for lesson planning is that they scaffold you towards being able to plan lessons by yourself. They also ensure that what some schools term as 'non-negotiables' are included. These are the compulsory elements of lessons, as decided by the headteacher. However, lesson plan forms and templates can lead to a misconception: that lesson planning is all about learning how to fill in the sections on the form as an end product in itself or are evidence of good teaching *per se*. By contrast, lesson planning is a process and a way of thinking – your hard thinking about your pupils and the curriculum and how to bring them into relation with each other so that your pupils think hard about the curriculum content.

What Should You Think Hard About When You Plan to Teach Curriculum Content?

Thinking about what you have to teach can be overwhelming at first (and indeed any time you teach a new topic or area you may feel anxious about your subject knowledge too). This is because it is so important to get things right. You will not want to teach something incorrectly, create confusion during a lesson or set up misconceptions for the lessons and years to come. This sense of responsibility can be compounded for primary teachers because of the breadth of subjects that need to be taught each year.

Strong subject and curriculum knowledge is not a fixed entity – all teachers are revising and refining what they know throughout their teaching careers. Your aim is to focus on becoming a curriculum thinker and developing your knowledge of the content of the curriculum over time. A four-stage approach has been developed to enable teachers to focus on their approach to thinking about the curriculum as they plan their lessons. The purpose of these four stages is that you develop deep knowledge of the subject content so that your understanding of it is fluent and flexible. Fluent and flexible understanding of the subject content is the platform on which you can base adaptive and responsive teaching of your pupils. The following four stages use the subject of geography as a worked example to show you how to use the process.

Stage 1: What Does the National Curriculum Require?

First, and even if you are working from a published scheme or school plans, check what the National Curriculum has to say about the area of study. It is a good idea to have a printed or electronic copy of the National Curriculum in your planning folders (see www.gov.uk/government/publications/national-curriculum-in-england-primary-curriculum).

For example, the section on Geography has three sections:

1 Purpose of Study.
2 Aims.
3 Attainment Targets:
   - Subject Content Key Stage 1
   - Subject Content Key Stage 2

The commentary column in Table 5.1 models how you should interpret the curriculum and infer the implications for what you need to understand in full so that you can teach the subject content correctly.

Analysing the National Curriculum requirements for each subject is an important starting point for being a curriculum thinker because it helps you to identify the key aspects of the curriculum:

1 What powerful knowledge will pupils secure that will help them learn as they continue to study geography?
2 What second-order concepts of geography are pupils learning that enable them to think like a geographer?

Stage 2: Identify Curriculum Topics

Subject content is broken down into topics for each Key Stage. The topics provide another level of detail about what pupils should know, understand and be able to do by the end of each Key Stage. For example, in geography, four types of knowledge, understanding and skill are specified:

1 Locational knowledge.
2 Place knowledge.
3 Human and physical geography.
4 Geography skills and fieldwork.

Table 5.2 sets out these topics by Key Stage.

It goes without saying that in order to teach these topics, you need to have the knowledge, understanding and skills yourself. It is helpful then to think about these topics by asking the following questions, which give you the perspective of a pupil in the class who does not yet have this knowledge. You can then begin to consider the connections and sequencing of the curriculum:

1 What needs to be learned by pupils in each of these four areas?
2 What is the core content in each of the four areas?

3 What complex concepts will they be building to develop their geographical understanding over time?
4 How will the content you will teach build on what pupils already know, understand and be able to do?
5 What complex concepts will they be building to develop their geographical understanding over time?
6 What 'thinking like a geographer' knowledge are they developing via the second-order concepts?
7 What confusions about these geographical topics will you need to clarify in order to unlock the new knowledge you are teaching them?
8 What vocabulary will need to be taught to the pupils?

Table 5.1 How to analyse the National Curriculum as a planning document

Area of study section	Important information for planning	Commentary
Purpose of study	Should inspire in pupils a curiosity and fascination about **the world and its people**	So, the golden thread running through each lesson is the idea of the world and its people
	Should equip pupils with **knowledge about** diverse places, people, resources, and natural and human environments	So, there are five broad knowledge topics: places, people, resources, natural and human environments
	Deepen understanding of the Earth's key physical and human processes	This indicates the foundational concept that links the topics
	Deepen their understanding of the interaction between physical and human processes, and of the formation and use of landscapes and environments	This indicates that interaction, formation and use will be the key concepts that develop understanding
	Geographical knowledge, understanding and skills provide the frameworks and approaches **that explain how** the Earth's features at different scales are shaped, interconnected and change over time	This explains how pupils will apply what they learn in geography lessons (pupils will be able to explain **how** the Earth's features are shaped, interconnected and change over time)
Aims	**Develop contextual knowledge** of the location of globally significant places – both terrestrial and marine – including their defining physical and human characteristics and how these provide a geographical context for understanding the actions of processes	This sets out what pupils **need to know**: 1 Where places on land and sea are 2 The key characteristics of these places 3 How these places help us understand processes
	Understand the processes that give rise to key physical and human geographical features of the world, how these are interdependent and how they bring about spatial variation and change over time	This sets out what pupils **need to understand from their knowledge**: 1 The key features in the world 2 How human and physical features of the world are linked 3 How the key features have changed over time

(Continued)

Table 5.1 How to analyse the National Curriculum as a planning document (*Continued*)

Area of study section	Important information for planning	Commentary
	Ensure pupils are competent in the **geographical skills** needed to:	
	• collect, analyse and communicate with a range of data gathered through experiences of fieldwork that deepen their understanding of geographical processes	This sets out what pupils **need to be able to do with their knowledge** (i.e. how to apply and how they are able to think like a geographer) When doing fieldwork, gather data that pupils can use **to make sense of** the processes of interdependence and change
	• interpret a range of sources of geographical information, including maps, diagrams, globes, aerial photographs and Geographical Information Systems (GIS)	Be able **to use the tools** of geography as a geographer to think like a geographer
	• communicate geographical information in a variety of ways, including through maps, numerical and quantitative skills, and encourage writing at length	Be able **to share their geographical knowledge** like a geographer (in maps, data analysis and in essays)
Attainment targets	By the end of each Key Stage, pupils are expected to know, apply and understand the matters, skills and processes specified in the relevant programme of study	This definition of the purpose of Attainment Targets is helpful because it will inform your backwards planning. By looking at where pupils need to be by the end of each Key Stage, you will be able to recognise what you need to cover in each subject, in terms of the curriculum, in order for pupils to make improvements
Subject content Key Stage 1	Pupils should develop knowledge about the world, the United Kingdom and their locality They should understand basic subject-specific vocabulary relating to human and physical geography and begin to use geographical skills, including first-hand observation, to enhance their locational awareness	By comparing the overviews of each Key Stage, you can see what content each Key Stage has in common and how the content progresses to the end of Year 6 This is helpful because you can identify how pupils will later use what you are teaching them now and are able to frame what you are doing at the moment with what they will know, understand and do in later lessons and years
Subject content Key Stage 2	Pupils should extend their knowledge and understanding beyond the local area to include the United Kingdom and Europe, and North and South America This will include the location and characteristics of a range of the world's most significant human and physical features They should develop their use of geographical knowledge, understanding and skills to enhance their locational and place knowledge	Knowledge of geographical areas includes Europe and North and South America (not just the UK and where they live, as in Key Stage 1) This is new content not covered in Key Stage 1 This shows the purpose underpinning how pupils will use what they have learned to enhance their knowledge of place and location

Table 5.2 The subject content of geography topics

	Key Stage 1	Key Stage 2
Locational knowledge	**Name and locate** the world's seven **continents** and five **oceans**	Locate the world's countries, using maps to focus on **Europe (including the location of Russia) and North and South America**, concentrating on their environmental **regions**, key **physical** and **human characteristics, countries** and major **cities**
	Name, locate and identify characteristics of the **four countries and capital cities of the United Kingdom** and its surrounding **seas**	Name and locate the **counties and cities of the United Kingdom**, geographical **regions** and their identifying **human and physical characteristics**, key **topographical features** (including hills, mountains, coasts and rivers) and **land-use patterns**, and understand how some of these aspects have **changed** over time
		Identify the **position and significance** of latitude, longitude, Equator, Northern Hemisphere, Southern Hemisphere, the Tropics of Cancer and Capricorn, Arctic and Antarctic Circle, the Prime/Greenwich Meridian and time zones (including day and night)
Place knowledge	Understand geographical similarities and differences through studying the human and physical geography of a **small area of the United Kingdom**, and of a small area in a **contrasting non-European country**	Understand **geographical similarities and differences** through the study of human and physical geography of **a region of the United Kingdom, a region in a European country and a region in North or South America**
Human and physical geography	Identify **seasonal and daily weather patterns** in the United Kingdom and the location of **hot and cold areas of the world** in relation to the Equator and the North and South Poles Use basic **geographical vocabulary** to refer to: key physical features, including: beach, cliff, coast, forest, hill, mountain, sea, ocean, river, soil, valley, vegetation, season and weather key **human features**, including: city, town, village, factory, farm, house, office, port, harbour and shop	Describe and understand key aspects of: **physical geography**, including: climate zones, biomes and vegetation belts, rivers, mountains, volcanoes and earthquakes, and the water cycle **human geography**, including: types of settlement and land use, economic activity including trade links, and the distribution of natural resources, including energy, food, minerals and water

(Continued)

Table 5.2 The subject content of geography topics (*Continued*)

	Key Stage 1	Key Stage 2
Geographical skills and fieldwork	**Use world maps, atlases and globes** to identify the United Kingdom and its countries, as well as the countries, continents and oceans studied at this Key Stage **Use simple compass** directions (North, South, East and West) and locational and directional language (e.g. near and far, left and right) to describe the location of features and routes on a map **Use aerial photographs and plan perspectives** to recognise landmarks and basic human and physical features Devise a simple map and use and construct basic symbols in a key Use simple fieldwork and observational skills to study the geography of their school and its grounds and the key human and physical features of its surrounding environment	**Use maps, atlases, globes and digital/computer mapping** to locate countries and describe the features studied **Use the eight points of a compass, four- and six-figure grid references, symbols and key** (including the use of Ordnance Survey maps) to build pupils' knowledge of the United Kingdom and the wider world **Use fieldwork to observe, measure, record and present** the human and physical features in the local area using a range of methods, including: **sketch maps, plans and graphs, and digital technologies**

Key Takeaways

- Thinking hard about the specific content of the subject will help you to learn how to secure your pupils' subject knowledge and to make good judgements about how your pupils will use it, now and in the future (i.e. how to make the subject content learnable over time).
- Identify the specific ideas, concepts, vocabulary and facts that pupils absolutely need to know.
- Consider what subject content will be most important and useful to your pupils.
- Be sure that you can clearly articulate what it means to make progress in the subject content (try saying it out loud to a colleague and to the class).
- Be sure you have a clear 'picture' of what pupils are expected to know, understand and be able to do by the end of Year 6.
- How will any lesson you teach encourage your pupils to be readers, writers and thinkers in the subject?

Suggested Activity

Because one of the challenges of a primary school teacher is the need to develop your knowledge and understanding of subject content over time, it is useful to be aware of the associations that exist to develop the subject knowledge of teachers. For example, if you wanted to build your knowledge of geography, you can join The Geographical Association (https://geography.org.uk) or the Royal Geographical Society (www.rgs.org/join-us/). The Council for Subject Associations (www.subjectassociations.org.uk/the-cfsa-directory/) lists all the subject associations for subjects on the National Curriculum, many of which have heavily reduced rates for trainee and early career (EC) teachers.

Stage 3: Thinking About the Curriculum in Relation to Memory and Understanding

As we have seen in stages 1 and 2, the substantive knowledge that makes up the curriculum in primary geography is focused on four forms of geographical knowledge: locational knowledge, place knowledge, knowledge of the process that make up physical and human geography, and geographical skills and fieldwork. This is the detail that pupils need to learn, and this detail is underpinned by the concepts listed below.

Concepts in geography draw out the links between processes and ideas and are ways in which pupils learn how geography is structured. Geographical concepts stay relevant to the subject content of geography learned at any age or stage. As a teacher, once you are aware of the foundational concepts in the subject you are teaching, you can then think of them as a frame by which to connect the components that make up the knowledge and skills of the subject content. Concepts, then, are central to teaching and learning in any subject, and in geography they are generally agreed to be:

- Place
- Space
- Scale
- Interdependence
- Physical and human processes
- Environmental impact
- Sustainable development
- Cultural awareness
- Cultural diversity

It is helpful to be aware that whatever chunks of knowledge make up your lesson that you can connect them to one of the concepts listed above. This is because these concepts help to make sense and link together what is being taught in any one lesson.

It is useful, then, to link your knowledge of the curriculum with your knowledge of how pupils learn. This can be thought about by asking:

1 What knowledge needs repeating and emphasising so that it can be remembered over time?
2 Which ideas link knowledge and skills together so that pupils develop understanding?
3 How will pupils use their knowledge and skills to make sense of the world in terms of the geographical concepts listed above?

In this way, you will be clear about which building blocks in a lesson or sequence of lessons will enable your pupils to be successful later at more complex geographical tasks. In other words, as a teacher, you are drawing on your knowledge of the most important ideas in each subject to work out the best order in which to teach them so as to help your pupils, learn, remember and understand the subject content. Be aware that you are also aiming for pupils to reach the point where they are able to make inferences with what they have learned. For example, Table 5.3 sets out how the components of locational knowledge and geographical skills and fieldwork might be sequenced over the time from Year 1 to Year 6.

Stage 4: Consider Your Role in Creating the Culture for Learning

However well you are able to think through the curriculum that you will teach, how you present this content is equally important. Often new teachers are so focused on remembering the lesson they have planned that they forget to show their enthusiasm about what is to be learned. Good teaching turns on the social understanding of the teacher. While you need to think about your pupils and where they are in terms of learning the subject content (i.e. by imagining what is difficult for them and what they do not yet know about the subject content), it is also vital to model attitudes about learning the subject to your pupils. You should aim to show that:

- you are interested in the content
- you are enthusiastic about the content
- you think learning this content is valuable
- you emphasise the language development associated with the subject content so that pupils develop the cognitive tools to think in the subject

Table 5.3 An example of how curriculum content in geography can be sequenced over time to help pupils learn, remember and use it in their time in primary school

Year	Locational knowledge	Geographical skills and fieldwork
1	Know the names of the four countries that make up the UK and name the three main seas that surround the UK Know the name of and locate the four capital cities of England, Wales, Scotland and Northern Ireland	Know which is North, East, South and West on a compass Know their address, including the post code
2	Know the names of and locate the seven continents of the world Know the names of and locate the five oceans of the world	Know and use the terminologies: left and right, below, next to
3	Know the names of and locate at least eight European countries Know the names of and locate at least eight counties and at least six cities in England Know the names of four countries from the southern hemisphere and four from the northern hemisphere	Use maps to locate European countries and capitals Know and name the eight points of a compass
4	Know the names of and locate at least eight major capital cities across the world Know where the main mountain regions are in the UK Know, name and locate the main rivers in the UK Know where the equator, Tropic of Cancer, Tropic of Capricorn and the Greenwich Meridian are on a world map Know what is meant by the term 'tropics'	Use maps and globes to locate the equator, the Tropics of Cancer and Capricorn and the Greenwich Meridian Know how to plan a journey within the UK, using a road map
5	Know the names of a number of European capitals Know the names of, and locate, a number of South or North American countries	Know how to use graphs to record features such as temperature or rainfall across the world
6	Know about time zones and work out differences	Use Google Earth to locate a country or place of interest and to follow the journeys of rivers, or roads Know what most of the Ordnance Survey symbols stand for Know how to use six-figure grid references

Key Takeaways

- It is important to develop your knowledge of the subject content of the curriculum that you will teach.
- It is useful to identify the foundational concepts that make up the subjects that you teach.
- It is useful to identify the substantive knowledge that makes up the topics of the subject content and understand how pupils will be using the skills that rely on this knowledge as they progress through the Key Stages.
- It is important that you can demonstrate excitement and enthusiasm about the subject content because this will encourage pupils to feel it is worthwhile, especially when they find some of the subject content difficult to learn or remember.
- Always look ahead to see how what you are teaching develops in the years to come so that you can lay the foundations between the different curriculum components and are clear about how conceptual understanding in the subject develops over time.

Conclusion

The time you invest in understanding subject content as you plan will be repaid many times over when you are actually teaching. This is because developing deep knowledge of subject content will enable you to be confident to respond to your pupils and adapt your teaching. It will mean that you are not afraid that you know the answer when pupils ask questions and that you will be able to generate multiple examples, explanations and stories to bring the subject content to life for your pupils and to make it meaningful.

References

DfE (Department for Education) (2011) *Teachers' Standards*. London: HMSO

DfE (2014) *The National Curriculum in England Key Stages 1 and 2: Framework Documents*. London: DfE. Available at: www.gov.uk/dfe/nationalcurriculum. Ref: DFE-00178-2013

6
HOW TO PLAN FOR WHAT YOUR PUPILS WILL LEARN, NOT WHAT THEY WILL DO

Why is It Important to Think Hard About What Your Pupils Will Learn Rather Than Prioritising Fun Things for Them to Do?

In Part 1, we looked at the key ideas you need to know about learning, teaching, the curriculum and planning. In Part 2, we are looking at how you turn those ideas into action. This chapter discusses a threshold concept of teaching – a core idea in a subject, where understanding that concept is key to transforming the way you understand a whole subject, allowing you to move on in your learning (Cousin, 2006) – which you will revisit and reuse every time you plan a lesson or a sequence of lessons. Concentrating on the threshold concepts – on what you want your pupils to learn – rather than on what they will do, and seeing it in action for the first time will be a 'lightbulb moment' and will transform your approach to lesson planning. However, thinking about what your pupils will learn by completing tasks and activities is a form of teacher thinking and something you will need to focus on for every lesson if you want your teaching to have an impact on your pupils' learning.

In this chapter, we consider the role of framing learning intentions and success criteria before you design tasks. When you observe an experienced teacher in action, they can make identifying learning look easy, but in fact they are drawing on the complex knowledge that we have addressed in Part 1 and lots of practice, developed through their previous planning, to be able to do this. Remember, it is a habit of mind that teachers draw on every time they plan.

When you were a pupil in school, you probably remember that you spent your time in lessons doing 'the work' that the teachers asked you to do. So, it is natural that when you first begin teaching, you operate on the basis of your experience of being a pupil in school, and consequently make the work that your pupils will do in your lessons the a starting point. However, as Mary Alice White, a professor of psychology and education at Teachers College, USA, famously observed:

> The analogy that might make the students' view more comprehensible to adults is to imagine oneself on a ship sailing across an unknown sea, to an unknown destination. An adult would be desperate to know where he [sic] is going. But a child only knows he is going to school ... the chart is neither available nor understandable to him ... very quickly, the daily life on board ship becomes all important ... the daily chores, the demands, the inspections, become the reality, not the voyage, nor the destination. (White, 1971: 340)

In other words, not all the pupils will share the same ideas as their teachers about what they are meant to be doing in the lesson and the crucial link between the activity and its purpose in terms of their learning (i.e. why it is useful as part of the greater scheme of things). It is also important to remember that learning involves change (think back to the theories we reviewed in Chapter 1), and thus necessarily involves risk and possible difficulties for the learner. So, understanding the teacher's pedagogical reasoning (why they want you to do an activity and how that will help you learn and make progress as a learner in a particular subject) provides much needed clarity and motivation. It is also respectful of your pupils as learners and their learning process. Imagine sitting in a seminar and being asked to complete all sorts of tasks while not knowing why you should do them. You are simply expected to 'do as you are told'. How might that make you feel? Anxious, rebellious, or bored perhaps? Clarifying learning intentions and specifying success criteria draw on your 'know-why' as a teacher, as you use your pedagogical reasoning to plan for learning. Equally important, however, learning intentions enable your pupils to know why they are learning, how they are getting better and how the sequence of the curriculum joins up. As humans, we seek meaning, and your clarity and specificity enables your pupils to consider the question 'What does it mean?' as they learn the subject.

It is important to note at this point that there can exist a tension in planning. We know that learning a subject in school is both a cognitive and social process, so pupils need the opportunity to learn and remember and apply what they are learning through cognitive and social processes, not just by listening. Thinking up fun and engaging things for your pupils to do can be an important aspect of the creativity and professional judgement of teachers. However, while it can be rewarding, it is also sometimes time-consuming, so make sure you invest your planning time wisely and don't lose your evenings to a laminator or cutting up bits of card! And remember to plan activities with learning in mind, to ensure that your pupils learn what you want them to.

There is a chance that neither you nor your pupils can judge if they learned what you hoped they would. Equally, at the early stages of learning to teach, or when teaching content with which you are less familiar, identifying the intended learning can make it difficult to think up engaging, interesting and varied activities that take learning beyond the teacher simply telling the pupils what it is they want their pupils to learn (an issue we address in Part 3). Thus, an important related skill is designing tasks and activities that cause pupils to think in terms of the intended learning.

What Should You Think Hard About So That You Plan to Teach for Learning?

Before the National Curriculum was revised in 2014 (DfE, 2013), the *National Inspection Framework* (Ofsted, 2005) judged the quality of teaching on the extent to which pupils made progress against certain assessment objectives. Teachers had to be able to demonstrate that their pupils had made progress against these criteria and that pupils knew what they had to do to reach the next assessment target. It had an impact on how teachers taught:

- Lessons were driven by assessment targets
- Progress towards targets needed to be regularly demonstrated by pupils in the lesson (every 20 minutes was typical)

Consequently, there was a focus on the immediate, visible and short-term surface features of the lesson, with plans for teaching prioritising pupils' ability to demonstrate progress in their learning by recalling facts from their working memory. However, the National Curriculum was revised to focus on what the curriculum should cover rather than the focus on the previous version which was emphasised how it should be assessed, which means that we now draw on different ideas to plan teaching.

The ideas about learning set out in Table 6.1, which you will use as knowledge-in-action when you plan lessons, also link to two important ideas about the curriculum: progression and

Table 6.1 Concepts from learning theory that teachers use to plan lessons

Key ideas about learning used to plan teaching			
Learning is relatively permanent CHANGE	The CHANGE relates to how an ACTION is performed	The CHANGE can be seen as an EXPANDED CAPACITY in the learner in terms of knowledge, skill or understanding	The learner is now able to 'do' something that they COULD NOT DO BEFORE
• Teachers plan to support the long-term memory • Teachers plan to support deeper schema development • Learning is recognised as happening OVER TIME			

Table 6.2 Concepts from curriculum theory that teachers use to plan lessons

Curriculum Concept	Using this key idea as you plan
Progression	What does it mean to GET BETTER in this subject?
Sequencing	What is the best ORDER to teach this subject-matter to support learning over time?

sequencing (see Table 6.2). Both are important because as a teacher you have a dual focus: your pupils' learning and the curriculum you teach that they have to learn.

Having considered the ideas that shape starting to plan, the next section will look at how you identify learning when you plan. It looks at the first two steps in the process:

1 Clarifying learning intentions.
2 Specifying success criteria.

Step 1: Clarifying Learning Intentions

This section draws on the work of some leading researchers in their specific fields of expertise, who have informed how teachers begin to plan their teaching.

Gage: Identify What Your Pupils Will Do With What They Will Learn

Nathaniel Gage (1917–2008) was an American psychologist at Stanford University in California. He pioneered the scientific understanding of teaching. Along with his co-author, David Berliner, Gage identified that teachers should begin their planning by asking themselves three questions:

1 What do you want your pupils to learn?
2 How should your pupils behave (think, feel, move) differently after you have taught a topic or scheme?
3 Have you ever wished a teacher had told you more clearly what you should have been learning and why (and how can you make sure your own pupils do not feel this way)?

They argued that in 'the background to every kind of teaching is the question "What do you want to accomplish?"' (Gage and Berliner, 1998: 31). For example, a history teacher may want their pupils to draw on historical sources to explain present-day events. But if the teacher does not explain this, then the pupils assume that they are simply required to memorise what they are taught. In clarifying your intention for their learning, you explain to pupils what they should learn to do with the content of the lesson. In this example, that would be that they should look at contemporary problems from a historical perspective.

Gage and Berliner (1998) identify that one key reason makes it difficult for new teachers to formulate clear learning intentions: word magic. Word magic is when a key term or definition is expressed in the most convoluted and esoteric terms possible. They explain that word magic can be found in many curriculum documents, wherever the documents express ideal and often global educational aims. For example, in the Statutory Guidance for the Languages Programmes of Study of the National Curriculum, the purpose of studying languages states: 'Learning a foreign language is a liberation from insularity and provides an opening to other cultures. A high-quality languages education should foster pupils' curiosity and deepen their understanding of the world' (DfE, 2013: 1). Because such ideas are so important, it can be hard to deconstruct them to levels of a topic or scheme. So, the first step to clarifying learning intentions is to think of them in terms of observable behaviours – what you want to see your pupils *do* with what they have learned. In other words, what action is now made possible because of the change brought about by learning. Activities are undertaken to cause learning so that pupils can then act in the world with what they have learned – activities and tasks are not undertaken as an end in themselves.

The Languages Programmes of Study states that an aim of learning languages is to 'understand and respond to spoken and written language from a variety of authentic sources' (DfE, 2013: 1). Gage asks teachers to think about the aim as a learning intention. Is this a clear, explicit learning intention? Is it stated in observable behaviours? What do we mean by 'understand' and 'respond'? He argues that unless you spell out what your pupils do when they 'understand' and 'respond', your intention for your pupils is ambiguous (Gage and Berliner, 1998). It is important to be clear in this way because of you and your pupils' relationship to knowing the subject: you 'know', and they are the 'unknowers'. Recognising your pupils' perspective from their tables in your classroom, and explaining the purpose of the lesson in terms of their future observable behaviours, helps you to clarify your learning intentions, which in turn helps your pupils to learn. Table 6.3 offers a support to help you identify what pupils do with what they have learned.

There are two further steps to help you clarify learning intentions when you plan your lessons:

1 Specify the conditions under which the behaviour is expected to occur (e.g. using a specific resource or tool, setting parameters such as a certain time-fame, or what it is you are looking for from the pupils when they undertake a task).
2 State the minimum levels of acceptable performance, i.e. the success criteria (see below for more details).

Key Takeaways

- Does the learning intention describe what the pupils will be doing when they have demonstrated that they have achieved the learning intention?
- Does the learning intention describe the important conditions under which the pupils will be expected to demonstrate competence?
- Does the learning intention indicate how the pupil will be evaluated? Does it describe the lower limit of acceptable performance?

Table 6.3 Identifying possible observable behaviours by pupils (what will they do with the content once they have learned it)

Intention	Examples of observable behaviours	Example of a learning intention
Knowledge	to recall to recognise to acquire to identify to define	Pupils will be able to recall the dates of the two World Wars
Comprehension	to translate to transform to put in words to rephrase to restate	Pupils will be able to give examples of protein when discussing a healthy meal plan
Application	to generalise to choose to develop to organise to use to transfer to restructure to classify	Pupils will be able to pronounce the words of Frère Jacques accurately when singing the song
Analysis	to distinguish to detect to classify to disseminate to categorise to deduce to compare to contrast	Pupils will be able to distinguish facts from opinions when reading a newspaper article
Synthesis	to write to produce to constitute to transmit to originate to design to formulate	Pupils will be able to propose a plan for a school assembly to the rest of the class
Evaluation	to judge to argue to validate to assess to appraise to decide	Pupils will be able to argue the case for and against a particular course of action

Gagné: Identify the Human Capability to be Established by Your Teaching

Robert Gagné (1916-2002) was an American psychologist at Florida State University. He pioneered instructional theory and design. It was Gagné who first identified that the clearer the objectives for learning are, the easier it is for pupils to learn (Gagné et al., 1992). Similar to other psychologists, he recognised that the school curriculum is organised on the basis of what society requires from its citizens and that certain 'human capabilities' need to be explicitly taught to children to ready them for adult life. Gagné named five major human capabilities: intellectual skill, cognitive strategy, verbal information, motor skill and attitude (Gagné et al., 1992). Thinking in terms of these five categories helps teachers to identify and clarify learning intentions. Gagné suggested that a pupil being able to achieve a changed action is made possible by the new mental representation they have developed though the activities teachers have designed to cause such learning (Gagné et al., 1992). Conceiving the intended learning in terms of its intended development of human capacity helps you to pinpoint the learning. Table 6.4 sets out Gagné's five kinds of learned capabilities, providing definitions, examples in practice and evidence of learning.

Table 6.4 Identifying learning intentions in terms of the development of human capabilities

Category of human capability	Definition	Example	Evidence of learning
Intellectual skills	Enables pupils to interact with their environment in terms of symbols or conceptualisations Learning an intellectual skill means learning how to do something of an intellectual type What is learned is procedural knowledge An intellectual skill can have the function of becoming a component of further learning or more complex intellectual skills	Learning how to identify a poem by its rhyme pattern is an intellectual skill	To know whether a student has learned an intellectual skill, the teacher observes a performance of that skill, e.g. showing what a metaphor is in one or more specific instances
Cognitive strategies	The pupil's own learning, remembering and thinking behaviour Such skills improve over a relatively long period of time as the pupil engages in more and more learning and thinking A cognitive strategy may be selected by the pupil as a mode of solving a new problem	For example, how a pupil manages their own behaviour when they are reading with the intent to learn something	Such strategies may be used in many different situations where the pupil thinks and learns

(Continued)

Table 6.4 Identifying learning intentions in terms of the development of human capabilities (*Continued*)

Category of human capability	Definition	Example	Evidence of learning
	Most cognitive strategies are domain-specific, although inference and induction are more general strategies (learned over a long period of time)		
Verbal information	This is the kind of knowledge we are able to state It is often called knowing that or declarative knowledge Over time, we learn a great deal of verbal information or verbal knowledge It is the kind of information we are expected to be able to recall readily Verbal information is important when transferring learning from one situation to another	Recounting events or applying rules to situations	Such information is usually seen by pupils communicating among themselves orally or in writing
Motor skills	Pupils are expected to learn a range of motor skills	This may include physical activities as well as learning to write	It is inferred when the pupil can perform the action in a variety of different contexts
Attitude	Often referred to as the affective domain, the effect of an attitude amplifies pupils' positive or negative reactions towards something Rules are often expected to establish socially approved attitudes towards other people, towards knowledge and learning, and towards self-efficacy An attitude is the persisting state that modifies pupils' choices of actions	Teachers tend to infer pupils' attitudes towards objects, people and events from the choices of action they take Often school learning is successful in modifying attitudes in a positive frame, e.g. in developing a learning environment of high expectations	In practice, teachers tend not to formally assess attitudes, but they can notice them in the choices pupils make about their personal courses of action/about the courses of action they take

Key Takeaways

- It can be difficult to pinpoint and express learning intentions.
- Curriculum documents are often expressed in general rather than in the specific terms that make for effective learning intentions.
- Gagne's five categories of human capabilities (intellectual skill, cognitive strategy, verbal information, motor skill and attitude) can act as a checklist to help you pinpoint the specifics of learning and identify how it will contribute to the intended change in your pupils' abilities.

Hattie: Match the Learning Intention to the Learning Phase

John Hattie is professor of education and director of the Melbourne Research Institute at the University of Melbourne in Australia. He produced two syntheses of meta-analyses in relation to achievement to identify the learning strategies that can be linked to achievement in learners (Hattie, 2009, 2023). From this work, he developed a model of learning that divides the learning process into phases of learning outcomes: surface learning, deep learning and the transfer of learning to new situations. Hattie argues that identifying the phase of learning helps the teacher to clarify the learning intention. Identifying the learning phase also supports the teacher to identify the most useful preceding and follow-up phases in the learning process.

The aim of the teacher is to enhance all three. Hattie's model includes seven phases of learning. Each phase is as important as the others (i.e. it is not a hierarchal model) and does not imply an order or a sequence. The skill of the teacher rests in being able to identify the relevant learning phase and when their pupils need to move on to another phase. Thinking about learning intentions in terms of what pupils can already do; how they approach their work especially when it might be difficult or challenging and designing elements of tasks so that pupils can complete some aspects of it by themselves can help you compose them. According to Hattie, learning outcomes can be divided into surface learning, deep learning and the ability to transfer learning to new situations. Each element also includes an acquisition phase and a consolidation phase (see Table 6.5). Thinking about your intention for learning in terms of the phase of learning is a useful tool for clarifying the learning itself because it helps you to identify the most meaningful content at that phase.

Table 6.5 sets out the distinguishing features of each phase of Hattie's model.

Hattie (2014) argues that what pupils bring and then take away from their learning in school can be thought of as:

- skill – the attributes of prior achievement the pupil brings, which links to Vygotsky's Zone of Proximal Development (Vygotsky, 1978)
- will – tendencies to respond to certain situations
- thrill – taking an achievement-focused approach to learning, in which teachers develop strategies to successfully complete tasks by themselves

Table 6.5 Phases of learning outcomes (Hattie, 2009)

Phase of learning outcome	Feature	Timing of learning: acquisition and consolidation
Surface learning	Studying without much reflecting on either purpose or strategy Learning many ideas without necessarily relating them Memorising facts and procedures routinely	Involves a retrieval process using short-term memory This process involves transferring the knowing and understanding from long-term memory back into short-term working memory **Acquisition** Pupils are able to reproduce learning in a performance by: record keeping, summarising, underlining and highlighting, reviewing records, rereading, note taking, mnemonics, attention focusing, planning, seeking information, selecting main idea, and memorising **Consolidation** Pupils begin to invest in their learning by encoding it: knowing it more, or is it well learned? (by repetition) and remembering it more, or can the memory be accessed when it is needed? (by retrieval). It involves a willingness to practise, be curious and explore, and a willingness to tolerate ambiguity and uncertainty in this investment phase It involves practice testing, spaced and mass practice, teaching test taking, interleaved practice, rehearsal, and knowing how to seek and receive feedback
Deep learning	Seeking meaning Relating and extending ideas Looking for patterns and underlying principles Checking evidence and coming to conclusions Examining arguments cautiously and critically Becoming actively interested in lesson and topic content	It involves a retrieval process of actively processing and rehearsing the materials as this increases the likelihood of moving knowledge to the long-term memory It involves transferring the knowing and understanding from long-term memory back into short-term working memory so that the automised learning becomes the ideas in the pupil's mind **Acquisition** Via self-regulation (knowing what to do when you do not know what to do), and as such becoming one's own teacher, making decisions about what to do, when and how. Such skills are: planning, evaluation and reflection, peer tutoring, asking questions, and questioning for clarification **Consolidation** Via self-talk strategies: self-verbalisation, self-questioning, self-monitoring, help seeking, elaborating self-consequences, self-explanation, collaborative and cooperative learning, elaborative interrogation, engaging in Socratic questioning

(*Continued*)

Table 6.5 Phases of learning outcomes (Hattie, 2009) (*Continued*)

Phase of learning outcome	Feature	Timing of learning: acquisition and consolidation
Transference	The skill to transfer learning to new situations By developing adaptive thinking, pupils can develop a meta-routine for deciding between learning strategies across a range of contexts and outcomes	It is a dynamic process (not fixed or static) that requires pupils to actively choose and evaluate strategies, consider resources and surface information, and receive and seek feedback to enhance their adaptive skills Transfer is often assisted by seeing the same idea in at least two different contexts, particularly when pupils differentiate the applicability conditions of solutions and have multiple opportunities to detect similarities and differences It is important to teach pupils to pause before attempting to address a new problem and detect the similarities and differences between previous tasks and the new one

Key Takeaways

- Rather than focus on achievement as the only outcome of learning, Hattie's learning process approach promotes the intertwining of skill (what pupils already know), thrill (the aspects of the task they can complete alone) and will (their resilience when tackling something new or difficult) during learning.
- Think of learning as moving from 'surface learning' (recall of facts) to 'deep learning', (conceptual understanding), not as simply learning at a surface or deep level but also in terms of developing pupils' dispositions, motivations and achievement.
- As a new teacher, you may consider the key intentions for learning in terms of Hattie's three learning outcomes. For example, the extent to which your learning intention addresses:
  - the will, i.e. the willingness of your pupils to invest in more and deeper learning.
  - the thrill, e.g. the emotions associated with successful learning, such as curiosity and a willingness to explore what we do not know.
  - skills, i.e. the content and deeper understanding of the content.

Wiliam: The Language of Learning Intentions

Dylan Wiliam is Emeritus Professor of Educational Assessment at UCL Institute of Education. He argues that curriculum documents of all types are often written in a register that is suitable for adults, and for adults in their professional roles as teachers (Wiliam, 2011). The documents use technical terms and subject-specific jargon that is familiar to educators but is not yet familiar to pupils (because that is what you are yet to teach them!). It is therefore necessary for teachers to adapt the phrasing into more age- and experience-appropriate language so that the language of learning is not a barrier to pupils' understanding of what they are about to learn.

However, there are some terms and phrases that are central to the subject discipline and learning them over time is also key to thinking about that subject. In these instances, you need to consider how and when to teach pupils the terms specifically, so that they adopt the ways of thinking (see 'will' in the section above) that help to define each subject and its 'official' language, thus enabling pupils to think like an artist, or a geographer or a computer scientist, etc.

Wiliam (2011) suggests that for primary school-aged children the following acronyms are useful for getting pupils started with learning intentions, success criteria (see the next section for further information) and helping pupils to see where and how this particular learning fits in with other things they have done:

- WALT – We are learning to...
- WILF – What I am looking for?
- TIB – This is because...

In summarising Wiliam's ideas, Jones (2021) suggests three golden rules for designing learning intentions:

- Be clear – learning intentions must be crystal clear in terms of content and language so every child in the class can understand
- Be specific – you and your pupils must know exactly what needs to be learned and how
- Be desirably difficult – the level of challenge should be desirable for all pupils in the class (although, as the next section on success criteria explains, this does not mean that the learning intention should be differentiated, because all children are entitled to the same learning)

Jones also suggests that adding the phrase 'so that' to your learning intention may help your pupils to understand not only what they are learning, but also why. This is similar to Wiliam's (2011) use of TIB. You are sharing the purpose of the learning with your pupils, which motivates them to take a risk to learn something new and helps them to connect the parts of the learning to the whole (an underlying concept or a big question).

Key Takeaways

A learning intention is a description of the change that you hope to bring about in terms of what your pupils will be able to do in the future, which may not necessarily be judged in the moment. It is useful to ask yourself the following questions so that you can be clear about your learning intention when planning a lesson:

1. What do my pupils need to know?
2. What do my pupils already know?
3. How can I help my pupils to learn what they need to learn? (This will support you in specifying the success criteria and designing pertinent activities and tasks.)

Step 2: Specifying Success Criteria

Success criteria are linked to learning intentions but perform a different job for both you and your pupils. Whereas learning intentions describe the change that the learning will bring about for the pupils, success criteria describe the steps to successful performance of that action. They are the means by which the teacher knows that the learning intention has been satisfied. Hattie (2014) helpfully describes learning as a hill to climb – from where the pupil is now to where they need to be – linking it to Vygotsky's Zone of Proximal Development – the difference between what a pupil can do with help and without help – but focusing on goals. The purpose of success criteria is to help pupils to understand what the teacher will use to judge their work (what I am looking for). As a teacher, this means that you need to be clear about the criteria by which you will judge if your learning intention has been successfully achieved. It also means that your pupils can learn how to judge for themselves if they have been successful. Success criteria are useful because they help both you and your pupils to monitor the progress in their learning by checking throughout the lessons that they understand the success criteria. Your aim is that pupils understand what success looks like and, as such, it is a means by which they can connect and organise what they are learning.

Success criteria, then, are descriptions of the desired performance in the learning tasks and activities that the pupils will undertake in the lesson. Whereas learning cannot be judged in the moment, performance in the task can, and success criteria help you and your pupils to do this. In other words, success criteria have the job of breaking down into manageable chunks the learning intentions to help pupils achieve the desired goals or outcomes in terms of the content, knowledge or skills to be learned. The success criteria are then linked to the learning intention and those links should be clear to you and your pupils. Success criteria can be used to show pupils what success looks like through modelling and the use of examples (you may think of this as WAGOLL – what a good one looks like). This is because models and examples help pupils to understand what the change that the learning is intended to bring about looks like, i.e. their future self, who has been changed by the knowledge, skill or understanding acquired through the process of learning.

Success criteria can be differentiated because the steps to success may be different in nature and quality for different groups of pupils. However, the learning intention is the same because all pupils are entitled to learn the same curriculum. And in reverse terms, success criteria provide a way for you to think about scaffolding and devising a plan to remove scaffolding to ensure the pupils' work supports learning and not only the performance of tasks.

Clarke (2005) identified that success criteria often indicate whether a pupil can transfer what they have learned into a different context. This is an important point because if a teacher confuses the learning intention from which the success criteria are developed with the context for learning, the result can be that the teacher only directly teaches what will be tested. It can result in a shallow and narrow experience for pupils, which does not enable pupils to transfer their learning to a new context. Understanding that a learning intention outlines what pupils will know, understand and be able to do by the end of the lesson that they could not do before and that success criteria are the individual steps in each task or activity that together take the pupil to that successful endpoint. As teachers, we are interested not only in our pupils' ability to do what we have taught them, but also their ability to apply their newly acquired knowledge to similar, but different contexts.

Key Takeaways

- Understanding the difference and relationship between learning intentions and success criteria helps you to distinguish between your learning intention and the tasks and activities that take place in your lesson. Ask yourself:
  - What are my learning intentions for this lesson?
  - What do I expect my pupils to learn as a result of this task or activity?

Conclusion

We have established that it is helpful for pupils to understand what they are expected to learn and do, and why it matters. This process relates directly to formative assessment and the role of checking for understanding as you teach, because it is a means by which you establish:

- where pupils are in their learning
- where they are going
- how they will get there

Similarly, in the process of lesson planning, this means the following three steps:

1 Clarify the learning intentions.
2 Specify the success criteria.
3 Design activities that will lead to the required learning.

It also means that pupils have a framework for formative dialogues with you and other pupils because it enables them to:

- ensure understanding
- identify success
- determine what is difficult
- discuss strategies for improvement
- reflect on their progress

However, it does not mean that there is only one way in which to share the learning intentions and success criteria with pupils. The two most common misconceptions are that this should always happen at the start of the lesson and that it should be written down. Thinking about how and when to share information about intended learning and the features of success with the class is important and integral to lesson planning. Not every lesson needs to follow an identical format. Sometimes the excitement and curiosity you want your pupils to feel in a lesson will be dissipated if they know the outcome at the start. There are other approaches you can take. For example:

- you may want to co-construct detailed success criteria with your pupils from an outline (as long as *you* define what good looks like, not the pupils!)
- you may want to spend time looking at examples of quality work with pupils so that they learn how to identify strengths and weaknesses in others' work and then see their own work in these same terms
- you may ask pupils to design their own questions, quizzes and tests as this enables you to gain a real insight into what pupils think they have been learning!

Finally, ensuring your pupils understand the learning intentions and success criteria builds a culture of respect and is motivating for pupils because it recognises that learning can feel risky. By its very nature, when you learn, you are doing something you were not able to do before. Enabling your pupils to understand your intent and the purpose of your activities addresses your pupils' emotions directly. Your actions can create an environment that supports and values not only learning, but also the learning process and the pupil in their role as learner.

References

Clarke, S (2005) *Formative Assessment in Action*. London: Hodder Murray

Cousin, G (2006) An introduction to threshold concepts. *Planet* 17(1), 4–5. DOI: 10.11120/plan.2006.00170004

DfE (Department for Education) (2013) *The National Curriculum in England Key Stages 1 and 2: Framework Documents*. London: DfE. Available at: www.gov.uk/dfe/nationalcurriculum. Ref: DFE-00178-2013

Gage, N and Berliner, D (1998) *Educational Psychology*. Boston, MA: Houghton Mifflin

Gagné, RM, Briggs, LJ, and Wager, WW (1992) *Principles of Instructional Design*. New York: Harcourt Brace Jovanovich

Hattie, J (2009) *Visible Learning: A Synthesis of over 800 Meta-analyses relating to Achievement*. Abingdon: Routledge

Hattie, J (2014) The role of learning strategies in today's classrooms. *The 34th Vernon-Wall Lecture*. Presented at the Education Section of the British Psychological Society, Milton Keynes, 8 November

Hattie, J (2023) *Visible Learning: The Sequel. A Synthesis of over 2,100 Meta-analyses relating to Achievement*. Abingdon: Routledge

Jones, K (2021) *Wiliam and Leahy's Five Formative Assessment Strategies in Action*. Woodbridge: John Catt Educational

Ofsted (2005) *National Inspection Framework*. London: Ofsted

Vygotsky LS (1978) *Mind in Society; The development of higher psychological processes*. London: Harvard University Press

White, MA (1971) The view from the student's desk. In Silberman, ML (Ed.), *The Experience of Schooling*. New York: Holt, Rhinehart and Wilson

Wiliam, D (2011) *Embedded Formative Assessment*. Bloomington, IN: Solution Tree Press

7
HOW TO PLAN SO TALK SUPPORTS LEARNING

Why is It Important to Plan for Classroom Talk?

Much staff time in school is spent on calculating the costs and benefits of different resources for teaching. However, classroom talk costs nothing and is one of the most effective resources for teaching and learning (Education Endowment Foundation, 2021), and it is often overlooked. How talk is used in classrooms is certainly not implemented as systematically as a new scheme of work or an IT system might be. Yet classroom talk – both teacher talk and pupil talk – is a powerful tool for learning, so it is important for you to be able to use the talk that takes place in your classroom to the fullest extent. Classroom talk works so powerfully to support learning because of the direct relationship between our use of language and our thinking. It is therefore important to distinguish between the different aspects of talk that take place in a classroom and their purposes:

- Teacher talk is when you question, explain or model, i.e. you use teaching techniques and strategies as a stimulus for pupil talk.
- Pupil talk is when pupils use their talk for learning.
- Dialogic teaching creates a learning environment for quality interactions.

In this chapter we concentrate on teacher talk and pupil talk. Dialogic teaching is taken up in Chapter 9 on planning for quality interactions, in the context of planning a learning environment that develops confident speakers. Other teaching techniques and strategies that also promote pupils' talking and listening skills are covered in Chapter 11 on planning for scaffolding and modelling.

Specifically, there are three important reasons why you should plan for the talking that is going to take place in your classroom:

1 It is a skill for life.
2 It is a vehicle for learning.
3 It is a means of pupil engagement.

Classroom Talk: Developing a Skill for Life

Being able to communicate well allows people to fully participate in the wide variety of situations and a range of social interactions that make up life in modern Britain. It is a lifelong skill that can be developed in the classroom by encouraging pupils to use spoken language well. Planning your lessons in terms of classroom talk will enhance the life opportunities for your pupils. Secondary school education, university education and employment opportunities become more available to pupils who are proficient speakers and listeners. Modelling and using ambitious vocabulary, different forms of social interaction and how to discuss and disagree politely and effectively supports your pupils in developing their oracy skills.

Classroom Talk: A Vehicle for Learning

Speaking and listening are important educational goals in themselves, but they are also a means for learning every subject on the school curriculum. Learning in school mostly happens as a result of social interactions. It is through talk that pupils secure their understanding (by articulating what they comprehend or using what they now know) and it is how you, as a teacher, check for understanding in lessons. In other words, talk helps pupils learn well. It does this in two ways:

1 By developing literacy skills and therefore making every subject accessible.
2 By helping pupils to think and understand.

Pupils who have lots of opportunities to verbalise what they are learning are better able to solve problems and to reason, and to transfer what they have learned to new contexts. Classroom talk for learning can be exploratory, as pupils look to make sense of new ideas, but also prepared and rehearsed by pupils for more formal contexts, such as in debates and presentations. You may therefore want to encourage your pupils to share different perspectives by building and challenging ideas.

Classroom Talk: A Means for Engagement

While it is important to teach your pupils to be skilful in articulating their ideas and to attain better because they are able to make sense of what and how they are learning, learning to listen to and speak with others who have different experiences from your own is the foundation for the equal, diverse and inclusive society that is modern Britain. Furthermore, pupils, as children, have a right to express their ideas and for their views to be taken seriously. Listening, without the opportunity to verbalise, neglects what we now know about how best to learn. It is important that you, as a teacher, are able to communicate clearly, but teaching is not the same as you simply telling and pupils listening. You need to give pupils the chance to rehearse what they want to say before they share it with the whole class (think, pair, share) and to monitor participation to ensure that all pupils speak during the course of each day, and that pupils listen to each other and use each other's ideas.

Classroom Talk: Past and Present

Talk is the way in which we share ideas and think with other people. In the classroom, teachers use talk to ask and answer questions, explain ideas, challenge pupils' previous knowledge, develop understanding and provide feedback. However, talk in schools has been a source of dispute for at least the last 40 years. One of the continuing and unresolved points of debate turns on the impact of insisting that all pupils speak in Standard English in order to raise educational standards and questioning the place of regional accents and dialects. Most significantly for planning lessons, pupil talk, especially talking with peers, is sometimes seen as being tantamount to time off task, that directly leads to low-level disruption. In addition, some teachers worry about losing control when they create time and space for pupils to talk to each other in their lessons. Indeed, the Oracy All-Party Parliamentary Group's (APPG) inquiry into the development of spoken language skills found that fewer than half of primary school teachers reported being confident in their understanding of the 'spoken language' requirements outlined in the National Curriculum (Oracy APPG, 2021).

However, meta-analytical research of 154 studies on oral language interventions undertaken by the Education Endowment Foundation (EEF) (2021) found that teaching approaches that emphasise the importance of spoken language and verbal interaction in the classroom have a very high impact (an additional six months' progress over the course of a year) for very low costs. The analysis suggests that developing pupils' spoken vocabulary works best when it is taught in relation to current content and when pupils are required to use their new vocabulary in active and meaningful ways. Specifically, the EEF suggests four effective approaches:

1 Encourage your pupils to read aloud and then to talk about what they have read with you and the rest of the class.
2 Model how to infer through the use of structured questioning.
3 Include group and paired work that allows pupils the opportunity to share their thought processes.
4 Design activities that implicitly and explicitly extend the spoken language of pupils.

Furthermore, the EEF's analysis of the evidence suggests that teachers should link spoken language activities to the curriculum so that both language development and their learning of the curriculum mutually benefit one another. They also recommend that teachers should explicitly teach the use of spoken language at least three times a week, every week of the school year.

Key Takeaways

- Plan your lessons with the aim that every pupil has an opportunity to talk in lessons during the day.
- Consider planning some lessons where the tasks and activities are not based on pupils being expected to write in their books. Rather, you can focus on pupils spending that particular lesson speaking.

What Should You Think Hard About So That You Plan for Classroom Talk?

It is important to think about the talk that you initiate as a teacher (teacher-initiated talk) as your first planning priority when you are a new teacher. This is because teacher-initiated talk is the form of talk that begins any interaction in your classroom. It is the classroom talk that you use to explain, teach and ask pupils to remember what they have learned. Teacher-initiated talk is the most common form of classroom talk, but it is also the classroom talk whose quality you directly control and for which you are directly responsible. Teacher-initiated talk typically takes the form of initiation–response–evaluation (IRE), and focuses on questions (often closed questions), recall answers and feedback. In particular, it is helpful to think of your teacher-initiated talk in three ways when you plan, so that you can share this explicitly with your pupils as a meta-commentary on the purpose of their talking and how it will help them to learn:

1 The role of talking and listening in relation to their learning.
2 The role of verbalisation.
3 The link to the structure of your lessons.

How Do Pupils Interpret the Role of Talk in Their Learning?

Gipps, McCallum and Hargreaves (2016) researched the practice of expert teachers and how it impacted their pupils. They observed and interviewed expert teachers of Year 2 and Year 6 for 18 months to develop a case study of the most effective primary teacher classroom practice. They found that pupils regarded talk as an important process for learning. In particular, Year 6 pupils were very conscious of the place of talking and asking questions in learning. Pupils thought that when they asked the teacher a question, it helped them to find out something new or to confirm their thoughts. They said that when teachers asked them questions, it helped them to clarify their ideas or gain feedback on how they were doing. Year 6 pupils believed that talk helped them in the following ways:

- Talking with a friend was a way of getting an easier explanation
- Talking one to one with the teacher was a way to seek clarification or get some feedback

- Talking with other pupils gave [them] ideas about different ways of tacking a problem
- Debating was a way to hear what other people thought and to learn new facts
- Brainstorming helped pupils to connect ideas together (Gipps et al., 2016)

The Year 2 children in the study described talking for learning in terms of one-to-ones with the teacher or another adult. They saw this talk as a way to clarify an idea they had been taught rather than as a means to explore ideas.

Both the Year 2 and Year 6 pupils thought that listening to the teacher was an important way to learn. It is why you should prepare what you will say to the whole class when you plan your lessons, so that what you say is crystal clear and not confusing). Year 6 pupils valued listening to the teacher when new and difficult ideas were being explained or when instructions for a task were detailed. Pupils also made sure to eavesdrop when the teacher was explaining something to other pupils, because it often clarified puzzling questions and yielded useful tips on how to proceed. Whereas Year 2 pupils reported that they listened carefully to the teacher so that they received information and instructions from the teacher, Year 6 pupils believed that listening to the teacher and then discussing ideas helped them to connect new and established learning.

Key Takeaways

- Your pupils expect that your talk will help them to learn. It is important to allocate some of your planning time to the key explanations that will take place in the lesson so that they are concise, focused and clear.
- It is useful to write down the important explanations, questions and instructions that will happen in the lesson you are planning as a sort of script. Remember that you are trying to connect what your pupils already know with the new information you are supplying in your explanation or instructions for a task. So when you are writing your script, think about what it might be like to not know what you are explaining.

What Will Your Pupils Say in Your Lessons?

You teach by what you say and the actions you undertake. Similarly, giving your pupils the opportunity to verbalise is an important part of the learning process because it enables them to process what they are learning as well as affording them the opportunity to understand what you have been teaching them. As such, you need to think about the types of talk that enable pupils to engage in high-quality talk for learning. As a teacher, you should plan for four types of talk that your pupils can use to support their learning: discussion, deliberation, argumentation and dialogue. How each benefits learning is set out in Table 7.1.

Table 7.1 How pupil talk supports learning

Talk type	How it benefits learning
Discussion	Your pupils learn to exchange ideas and information
Deliberation	Your pupils learn to weigh the merits of ideas, opinion or evidence
Argumentation	Your pupils learn to weigh the merits of ideas, opinion or evidence
Dialogue	Your pupils learn to work towards a collective understanding in an interactive way

Key Takeaway

- In each section of the lesson, think hard about when your pupils will have the opportunity to verbalise what they have been learning and what will be the best form of talk to aid learning. This is important because it gives your pupils the chance to process and check their understanding of what you have been asking them to think about and do.

What is the Link Between What Pupils Talk About and How the Lesson is Planned?

There are three important planning questions that help to frame classroom tasks and activities in terms of pupil talk. These questions can be categorised as the purpose (why), form (how) and participation (who) of classroom talk. Table 7.2 sets out the questions to ask yourself about the role of pupil talk in your classroom and what you need to think about when you plan pupil talk to support learning.

Table 7.2 Thinking about the purpose, form and participation of pupil talk

Category of planning question	Question to ask yourself about classroom talk	Next level of planning detail
Purpose	Why will pupils talk?	Will pupils discuss? Will pupils deliberate? Will pupils argue? Will pupils work with each other to achieve a collective understanding?
Form	How will pupils talk?	What concrete, visual or spoken tools will help pupils in their talk? How will interactions be explicitly modelled, valued and explained to the class as learning in its own right and linked to improved comprehension? How are the tools and the interactions referred to as part of the routines and expectations of the class over time?
Participation	Who will talk and to whom?	Who has a voice in this lesson? Who is the audience for the talk in the lesson? How will participation be valued?

Table 7.3 A summary of the teacher talk to practise and perfect at key stages in a lesson

Stage of lesson	Strategy for you to practise in terms of teacher talk	Type of classroom talk	Aim
Introduction	Informing Scaffolding	Interactive	To motivate pupils
Class engaged in activities	Teacher tours the room	1:1 between the teacher and individual pupils	To check and observe so teacher can gauge pupil understanding of and progress on activity for learning To identify and demonstrate reteaching To model 'better ways of doing aspects of the task' so that pupils can immediately act on feedback
Plenary	Summarise what has been achieved or not	Repeat teaching Remind pupils of key knowledge Share examples of pupils' work Describe what was correct or demonstrated learning and understanding	To draw the whole class together so pupils have a sense of the progress they have made and to motivate them

Typically, lessons follow a similar format: teachers tend to use the same strategies at the same stage of the lesson. In the early stages of teaching, this is particularly beneficial because it gives you the opportunity to really hone your teaching skills. So, think hard and get very good at using classroom talk by planning the purpose, form and participation for pupil talk at the different stages of the lesson, and maximise the potential of the different teaching strategies. However, you also need to consider your own talk as a teacher, and Table 7.3 provides a template for the different types of teacher talk that you need to plan for and practise using at different stages of the lesson.

Alongside planning for and becoming skilled at using particular forms of teacher talk as the first stage of thinking about planning what you are teaching, you also need to think about the general learning environment in your classroom in terms of talk. There are three action points to consider:

1 Make sure that every day your classroom is rich in high-quality talk. You can achieve this by being clear to yourself when you plan and also with your pupils when you teach about the purpose of their talk.
2 Create a range of opportunities for talk that covers all modes of speech: formal and presentational, imaginative, creative or talk as a tool for thinking.

3 Think of each mode of talk in terms of its potential for teachable moments and tell your pupils they are getting better at communicating in a range of registers over time.

Activities to Help You Maximise Talk When You Plan Your Lessons

- Practise reading aloud all texts that you will share with the class before the lesson to ensure that you model good reading and so aid comprehension
- Explicitly extend the spoken vocabulary that your pupils use
- Prepare structured questions that aim to develop reading comprehension
- Plan to spend time in every lesson discussing the content of the curriculum, making sure you include a wide range of pupils' voices and contributions so that the class can come to a collective understanding

Self-Reflection

After you have taught a lesson, think it over not in terms of what you asked, or your instructions or explanations, but focus on what the pupils said in the lesson and what you did with what they said.

Key Takeaways

- The learning that you plan for should be focused on what pupils already know, enabling you to identify misconceptions and encouraging your pupils to reflect on and engage with their own learning.
- Pupils should be encouraged to think about the learning process and how to improve their knowledge and skills.
- Focus on your pupils' speaking skills so that you can support their language development.
- Make sure that your pupils' writing is underpinned by speaking.
- Encourage your pupils to use a wide and relevant range of vocabulary when speaking and writing.
- Model an ambitious use of language.
- Ask questions that develop pupils' thinking skills and encourages them to begin problem-solving.
- Encourage your pupils to ask why things happen and to explain their thinking.

Planning for Talking Together as a Whole Class

In the very early days of learning to teach, you will rightly focus time and energy on the occasions when you are speaking to the whole class. It is important to think about and plan carefully for what you will say at these times in your lessons because you will want to ensure your knowledge of the curriculum is accurate and that the class is paying attention to what you tell them. However, very swiftly, you will appreciate that the focus of your planning when you will talk to the whole class is not best placed *solely* on what you say, but on how you *involve the pupils* in what you are saying.

As first introduced in the section 'What should you think hard about so that you plan for classroom talk?', much classroom talk follows the pattern of initiation–response–evaluation (IRE). Sometimes 'evaluation' is replaced by ' 'feedback' (IRF) or 'initiation–response–response' (IRR). As a new teacher, IRE in your lessons often takes the form of rapid, content-based questioning and follow up, which aims to guide pupils to a particular point in the lesson or a shared 'correct' answer. It is helpful to note that in some cases the retrieval practice part of lessons follows this structure, although retrieval practice sessions tend to focus much more on the questioning part of interactions because their purpose is to support pupils to remember content. However, there are ways in which you can plan more effectively to get the whole class to talk together with you as you implement this foundational structure of teacher talk. It is very helpful to think about your teacher talk as having a structure such as IRE because it enables you to consider what you say in terms of creating the conditions for learning. The section below outlines how to plan IRE for whole class talk that will involve your pupils in what you are saying to the class.

Initiating the Whole Class Talking With You

The first step is to realise that when you begin to talk to the whole class, you are initiating a conversation whose purpose is to further learning in some way. So, the purpose of your discussion opener is to promote thinking. You can promote thinking through the use of open-ended questions or prompts to promote curiosity (Knight, 2022):

- What can you say about?
- What have you noticed?
- What do you think will happen?

Questioning is a particular and widely researched teaching tool. However, when initiating a whole-class discussion, it is useful to think about using open-ended questions whose higher-order nature asks pupils to draw on their skills of analysis, evaluation and synthesis. The main aim is that you are asking pupils to think, not just remember, what they have been told someone has thought. Whole-class discussion in your classroom will be more productive if you:

- are clear about the learning objective to which the discussion relates
- ensure the pupils have enough prior knowledge to have something to draw on when they talk about it
- give opportunities for pupils to rehearse what they want to say to the whole class in smaller groups or pairs first

Key Takeaway

- Effective whole-class discussion that supports learning does not typically take place spontaneously and in an unstructured way, but is initiated by the teacher after careful planning and preparation.

Ensuring Pupils Respond in Whole-Class Discussion

Your aim for whole-class discussion is that it should be inclusive of all your pupils. You want to avoid the same few pupils dominating the discussion and the same few pupils never contributing to it. There are two approaches you can use to achieve this aim. First, give pupils specific roles and methods of joining in so that it is clear how everyone will participate from the outset. It will become an ongoing classroom routine over time. Second, ask accessible questions and prompts (as mentioned above). It is important not to assume or presume whom you think is capable of participating in what way in the discussion, because this will negate the culture of high expectations and learning you are working to create with the class. In fact, high-quality discussion is a means of creating an inclusive culture and of enabling pupils to access the learning because it is a powerful tool to prepare pupils for writing and reading. So, spend time building in lots of opportunities for small group and pair talk before moving onto a whole-class discussion. You want your whole-class discussion to create a culture for learning that includes three elements:

1 Your pupils are validated because small group and pair discussion assures all pupils that their ideas are worth paying attention to.
2 It gives you the chance to walk around the room and eavesdrop so that you can reinforce learning and decide whom you will target a question to later.
3 It builds the notion that whole-class discussion is a collective activity, not an opportunity for individuals to talk to the whole class (Knight, 2022).

Key Takeaway

- As you develop your skill at talking with the whole class for the purpose of thinking, and as you get to know each class you teach more deeply, you may start to recognise the part that active listening can play in whole-class discussion. The first step is to create a culture where every child knows it is safe to speak.

Evaluating (or, Better Still, Responding or Feedback): An Important Third Step

Often in class your interactions will involve just two stages: a question and an answer. Sometimes, the question-and-answer interaction involves a third step, where the teacher offers a brief comment on the pupil's answer, which essentially finishes the exchange. It can be powerful to use this third step not to evaluate, but to respond or to offer wider feedback. For example, rather than evaluate pupils' contributions and answers in whole-class discussion, you might instead:

- ask a follow-up question or series of questions
- challenge the pupils' answers by querying or elaborating on what they have said through asking for clarification or justification
- encourage collective thinking by marking important points in the discussion, redirecting questions, offering opposite examples, modelling thinking aloud and recapping the discussion so far

Key Takeaway

- Whole-class talk is a way of learning in its own terms and can be a key part of your lesson.

Pupils Talking With Each Other in Your Lessons

The section above on the whole class talking with you emphasised the importance of pupils talking together in small groups or pairs as a rehearsal or as preparation for whole-class discussion. Sometimes, pupils talking in small groups gets a rather 'bad press' and can be seen as time wasted or as a way for low-level disruptive behaviour to appear. In other words, sometimes pupils talking to each other is seen as unproductive. However, the opportunity to verbalise what is being learned is an important step in the learning process. Using small groups or pairs for talking in your lessons is a valuable teaching strategy, but it needs to be done well to maximise its support of learning, and that requires preparation by you, the teacher.

Small group talk needs to be properly structured by you in your planning so that pupils can scaffold each other's learning and support each other's metacognitive thinking. The key benefits for learning are that small group talk provides an opportunity for your pupils to say out loud what they are thinking in order to promote their thinking and develop deeper understanding. Such talk is a chance for pupils to both rehearse and practise their contributions in larger groups, but also to externalise their previous knowledge before applying it later in tasks (as we discussed in Chapter 1).

Small group talk is best built into lessons when you:

- teach your pupils the necessary skills
- provide lots of opportunities for pupils to practise the skills
- set out specific ground rules
- provide scaffolds and structures within each talking task
- design activities that actually need to be thought about through talk

In other words, it is important to be explicit with your pupils that talk has an *exploratory purpose*. Otherwise, pupils might be assuming that the purpose of small group talk is to argue with one another or for one person to persuade the others that they are correct. By naming talk and its purpose as exploratory, you are also being clear with your pupils about *how* they should talk together. In exploratory talk, ideas emerge through:

- speculation
- questions
- checking
- clarification

Planning for Exploratory Talk

Small group and pair talk is best planned for as a frequent, low-stakes activity interspersed throughout each lesson. As such, it is part of how you sequence learning when you plan. There are several factors to bear in mind as you sequence small group talk in your structuring of sequences of learning:

1 Is the topic in question worth talking about?
2 Do your pupils have enough previous knowledge to draw on?
3 Is the talking task pitched at the right level to get started, but is it also sufficiently challenging?
4 Is the talking task open-ended? (i.e. pupils are not pursuing one correct answer – this is best served using a different strategy, such as teacher questioning or retrieval practice)
5 Is it a task best done with other people? (i.e. pupils need to collaborate, not compete)
6 Is the outcome of the task a shared perspective rather than talk itself?

What Should You Do When Pupils are Talking Together?

When your class is engaged in small group or pair talk, you have an important role to play to promote thinking and learning. Your role is not to sit and watch. In fact, small group talk provides an opportunity for important teaching interactions so that your pupils end the talking task better able to explain, question and respond. Gillies (2016) argues that teachers have three important teaching functions during small group and pair talk:

1 Prompting for reasons to support ideas.
2 Modelling how to present and use ideas.
3 Challenging pupils with counter-arguments.

So as your pupils talk to each other, you should circulate the room and interrupt their talk (after eavesdropping) by:

- challenging understanding
- encouraging metacognitive thinking
- raising inconsistencies
- focusing on pertinent ideas
- asking thoughtful questions
- making connections

Key Takeaways

- Small group and pair talk are best used frequently, in short bursts and built up over time.
- Select small group talk as an activity when your pupils have knowledge to draw on. An ambiguous, challenging task benefits from talking with the aim of developing a shared perspective.
- Your pupils need to be pre-taught how to engage in small group and pair talk, and its exploratory purpose should be made explicit so that pupils understand how to participate.

Being a Teacher Who Uses Talk Well

Voice 21 is an organisation that promotes classroom talk and researches how teachers can cultivate effective classroom talk. Voice 21 is an organisation that emerged from the work of the Oracy All-Party Parliamentary Group's inquiry into the provision and impact of Tracy education in the UK (2019-2021) (Oracy APPG, 2021). It promotes classroom talk and researches how teachers can cultivate effective classroom talk. It has published as set of benchmarks to guide teachers in their planning of classroom talk (Voice, 2021). Table 7.4 sets out the types of actions teachers can incorporate into their lesson planning to ensure that when pupils talk in the classroom, they are thinking and learning.

Table 7.4 Actions you can take to ensure your pupils benefit from talk in your lesson

Teacher benchmark	Teacher actions			
Sets high expectations	Establishes and models ambitious and challenging norms for talk	Ensures that pupils understand the expectations for talk in the classroom	Opportunities for talk are regular, purposeful, appropriately pitched and thoughtfully planned to ensure that pupils are well prepared to meet expectations	
Values every voice	Supports all pupils to participate in and benefit from talk in the classroom	Listens meaningfully to pupils	Encourages pupils to develop their ideas forever	Creates a culture in which pupils encourage each other to develop their ideas further
Teaches talk explicitly	Understands what good talk looks like in whole class and small group contexts	Intentionally teaches the skills of talking	Plans for talk to support learning	Looks for opportunities for pupils to develop their talking skills over time
Uses talk to help learning	Pupils have the opportunity to interact with the teacher and their peers	Pupils are encouraged to articulate, justify and expand their ideas	Pupils have the opportunity to share, develop and consolidate their understanding through talk	
Helps pupils get better at talking	The teacher sets out to notice progress in talk and uses this to inform their design of activities	Pupils have the opportunity to reflect on and get meaningful feedback on that book from their teacher and the other pupils		

Next Steps

This chapter has considered how and why you should plan for your teacher-initiated talk, your small group talk and whole-class talk. It has suggested some foundational ways in which you should think about talk when planning your lessons. However, it is also important to think about the next steps in talk that your pupils will take as they move onto secondary school, and your own next steps as you become a more experienced teacher.

Pupil Progression

As your pupils move onto subjects at Key Stage 3, be aware that they will learn more subject-specific vocabulary and key terms.

Teacher Progression

Over time, you and your class will become more skilful at the types of talk outlined in this chapter. However, there is another form of talk pedagogy – dialogic teaching – which will advance your skills even more. We discuss this topic specifically in Chapter 9. Alexander has been a significant figure in primary education in England. From 2006-17 he initiated and directed the Cambridge Primary Review. The focus of his research has been talk in teaching and learning. Alexander (2020) defines dialogic teaching is when high quality talk is used to enhance pupil engagement, learning and understanding.

The chapters in Part 3 will detail the practical skills to progress your teaching, from structuring lessons to embedding opportunities for talk in your classroom, from scaffolding and modelling, to planning so your pupils remember and so that you can check if they are learning.

Conclusion

When you provide opportunities for talk in your classroom, you are supporting your pupils' learning in three ways:

1 By talking about what they know and sharing their perspectives, your pupils have the opportunity to remember information and retrieve it by thinking deeply about it.
2 Well-designed talking tasks encourage your pupils to work hard at thinking about what they are learning, and such effort helps to bring about deep learning.
3 Well-designed classroom talk lowers cognitive load because such talking tasks operate from the class's collective working memory.

It is important to remember that talk in classrooms needs to be explicitly taught, which means you need to plan well to make it happen. In other words, successful classroom talk does not arise if pupils are just left to get on with it by themselves. Good teaching is pupil-centred and planning for classroom talk enables you to focus on your pupils' use of language to develop their thinking and learning.

References

Alexander, R (2020) *A Dialogic Teaching Companion*. Routledge
Education Endowment Foundation (EEF) (2021) *Oral Language Interventions*. London: EEF

Gillies, R (2016) *Enhancing Classroom-based Talk: Blending Practice, Research, and Theory*. Abingdon: Routledge

Gipps, C, McCallum, B, and Hargreaves, E (2016) *What Makes a Good Primary School Teacher? Expert Classroom Strategies*. Abingdon: Routledge

Knight, R (2022) *Classroom Talk in Practice Teachers' Experiences of Oracy in Action*. Maidenhead: Open University Press

Oracy All-Party Parliamentary Group (APPG) (2021) *Speak for Change Inquiry*. Inquiry Report. London: Oracy APPG

Voice 21 (2021) *The Oracy Benchmarks*. Secretariat for the Oracy All-Party Parliamentary Group. London: Voice 21. Available at: www.voice21.org

PART 3

ESSENTIAL PRACTICE: HOW WILL YOU TEACH?

Introduction

A plan is what you intend to do in an imagined future time. A lesson plan, then, is a set of pre-decisions made about your intended actions or the strategies you will deploy in order to reach a pre-determined endpoint. In the case of you as a teacher, this endpoint relates to your pupils' knowledge, skills and understanding of the curriculum. Your lesson plan is based on the teaching and learning principles that make up the foundation of your teacher knowledge (your know-that or declarative knowledge). Lesson planning is about the use of your knowing why you will act (your professional judgement), which you then practise and refine as teaching techniques (your know-how or procedural knowledge) over time. As you develop your knowledge-in action (i.e. how you respond in the moment when you are teaching your plan) to your class, you will become more expert.

Part 1 described the key declarative knowledge you need as a new teacher about learning, teaching, the curriculum and planning. Part 2 described how to think about what you are teaching as you apply this knowledge to understanding planning for teaching. Part 3 addresses how to plan how you will teach. It covers the procedural knowledge that is the basis for your know-how or the teaching techniques and strategies that will shape what you say and do in the actual lesson you are planning. Chapter 8 looks at how to structure a lesson plan in terms of the order of who will do what and when to maximise both learning and teaching. Chapter 9 considers how to ensure that what you and your pupils say and dominate every lesson maximised opportunities for learning. Chapter 10 outlines how to plan tasks and activities in lessons. Chapter 11 sets out how you can offer guidance (modelling) and assistance (scaffolding) to your pupils when you teach. Chapter 12 shows how you can use your understanding of memory, how it can be built into your planning and how you can check for understanding as you teach and how to assess for learning.

8 HOW TO STRUCTURE A LESSON

Why is It Important to Understand the Structure of a Lesson?

A primary school lesson is not a natural social event that unfolds under its own momentum; its purpose is to maximise the opportunities for teachers to teach and for pupils to learn. A lesson therefore needs to be explicitly structured to achieve its specific purpose. Most schools and all training providers require teachers to plan lessons using templates for lesson planning, which are reviewed in lesson observations and through professional development.

A lesson plan template is a model of a structure of a lesson. There are different templates in use at any one time, but they all provide examples of structures of lessons and aim to develop your understanding because they require you to pay attention to different elements and phases in a lesson structure. Templates are helpful to leaders of schools and training providers because they are a way to develop consistency of practice and are a means to reinforce a desired approach to teaching. For example, a lesson plan template may have a box that asks the teacher to include a starter activity or Do Now Activity (DNA) for the first few minutes of the lesson as pupils are entering the classroom and settling down. Using lesson plan templates as examples of how to teach helps you to move from seeing what good teaching looks like to understanding how good teaching works.

However, for new teachers in particular, the use of lesson planning templates can give rise to certain misconceptions about lesson planning. A lesson plan is not a product, but a process. The template acts as a scaffold to support your thinking about what you and your pupils will say, do and think during the lesson so that the curriculum content becomes part of what pupils know, understand and can do at the end of the lesson that they could not do at the beginning of the lesson.

Lesson planning is not an administrative task or just 'paperwork' – it is your prime task and the foundation from which you will get better at teaching over time. By structuring your lesson into a plan, you are practising thinking like a teacher. It can be useful, therefore, to differentiate between lesson planning, where you decide the activities of the lesson, and lesson preparation, where you consider the decisions you will make in order to teach the lesson to your particular class.

What makes lesson planning a difficult skill to acquire in the early years of teaching is the tension between the big picture of the curriculum and the small steps of the activities that make up a lesson. This is compounded in the early days of learning to teach, when you might be asked to plan and teach small sections of a lesson, and consequently tend to think of a lesson as a series of things to be done. The danger is that you can successfully complete a lesson plan template and teach a series of activities, but can fail to connect each of those steps to the curriculum learning that is the purpose of the lesson. This is because what happens when you plan a lesson is enacted thinking (the link between thinking about action to come): when you think about what you will say and do that will give pupils things to say and do so that they think hard about the lesson content. Lesson preparation also impacts your ability to be perceptive when you are teaching the lesson, and subsequently enables you to teach better. It does this in two important ways:

1 'A key part of teaching responsively is reading the reactions and needs of your pupils as we teach' (Lemov, 2021: 39).
2 'To perceive well, you will need to prepare for what you'll be looking for and, ideally, free up as much working memory as possible to be available, unencumbered, for observation' (Lemov, 2021: 39).

Furthermore, lesson plan templates are a useful for avoiding three common difficulties when learning to teach:

1 A lesson takes place in a fixed amount of time. Maximising the time available for learning is important because it is your most precious resource. It can be common to find that you 'run out of time' in a lesson, so by allocating time to the various elements of your lesson, you can make your plan realistic and ensure the curriculum is covered. It also allows you to review what needs to be readdressed in subsequent lessons in the sequence.
2 This leads to the second common difficulty, which is that new teachers are often over-ambitious in terms of how much material they think they can cover and do not appreciate how much time aspects of the lesson can take.
3 Finally, it is important to realise that not all boxes on your lesson plan template are always of equal importance. It is important to plan in more specific detail the instructions, explanations and questions you will give to the class. By scripting out the important things that you say to the class, you can ensure that you are clear and can avoid confusing your pupils. This practice also increases your confidence when you speak to the whole class.

In sum, lesson planning enables you to both structure and order how learning will happen and helps you to think through what you will do as a teacher to cause learning to happen.

What Should You Think Hard About When You Structure Your Lesson?

Double Planning

The Great Teaching Toolkit (Coe, 2020) defines structuring a lesson in terms of breaking down a whole lesson into its separate elements and processes:

- Sequence and match learning tasks to your pupils' needs and readiness.
- Share by signalling key elements of the structure of the lesson (learning objectives, rationale, overview, key ideas and stages of progress).
- Scaffold to make tasks accessible and then remove scaffolding so that all pupils succeed at the required level.

To be able to do this, experienced teachers use a process called 'double planning' (Lemov, 2021: 58). Whereas a lesson plan describes the series of activities that the teacher will lead during the lesson (detailing your key instructions, explanations and questions when you are teaching something for the first time and especially when you are a new teacher), double planning pays close attention to what *the pupils will be doing* at each stage of the lesson. Lemov (2021) provides an example: a lesson plan states that the teacher will read a passage, but a double-planned lesson considers what the pupils will be doing as the teacher reads the passage – listening for key points, making notes.

Double planning is when the teacher thinks about and plans for what the pupils will do. As a planning process it has two major advantages:

1 It enables you to see the lesson from the perspective of the pupils, and thus gives you an insight into whether the lesson is engaging.
2 It enables you to see the lesson in terms of its pace, and thus requires you to manage the variety of ways in which pupils will participate in the lesson.

Without double planning, many new teachers inadvertently plan lessons where pupils are essentially listening all day, rather than being actively and cognitively engaging with the curriculum. Double planning only requires that you make a simple adjustment to the lesson plan format with which you are working: just add two columns – one headed '*What I will say and do*' and the other headed '*What my pupils will say and do*'.

All in One Place

Double planning is beneficial because it enables you to look at your lesson from the perspective of your pupils and ensures that you are actively engaging them throughout the lesson. You can also use the lesson plan preparation to enable you to be more present to your pupils in the lesson itself. This can be achieved by structuring your lesson plan so that it works as a tool to help you teach. Table 8.1 details four techniques you can use to benefit your teaching, helping you to free up time so that you can be more present to your pupils.

Table 8.1 Four techniques for structuring your lesson plan

	Structuring your lesson	The benefit to your teaching
1	Have a **copy** of the resources the pupils will use in the lesson alongside you as you double plan the lesson; read them and consider how they will be used by pupils in the lesson	You will be better able to evaluate if the resources actually help pupils achieve the lesson objective or if they are likely to confuse You will also be able to see how you will want pupils to engage with them as part of the flow of their activities and so be better prepared to give instruction and explanation about what your pupils need to do You may choose to annotate your copy of the resources to remind yourself about your observations as to how they are to be introduced and used
2	Allocate **time** slots to each activity that you and your pupils undertake	This will help you to ensure that you allocate time in accordance to the key learning that needs to happen Otherwise, the beginnings of lessons can take too long; the middle part overruns and you are not left with sufficient time to consolidate learning It also ensures that you are mindful of the depth and breadth of content you can attend to during the lesson Over time, you will be accurate about how long an activity takes and can also be aware of what can be achieved in 5,10, 20 minutes, etc.
3	Prepare a **mini-checklist** or a few sentences about what you are looking for when your pupils 'say or do' in the lesson First, this acts as a double-check to make sure that you are really clear about what you are looking for from your pupils in the lesson It also frees up your working memory in the lesson because you understand what an ideal answer looks like and so this helps you organise and reinforce in your own mind what you want to see and hear when your pupils respond in the lesson So rather than thinking 'What's the answer?' as your pupils take part in the activity, instead you will be free to think 'Where and how are they confused?' and this is you thinking like a teacher	Doug Lemov (2021: 46) calls this technique 'exemplar planning'. He argues that 'a prepared teacher is a happy and poised teacher – who can express herself more fully and makes better decisions in the moment. She knows where she's going and isn't anxious or worried about what's next, how to do it, and how long it will take; her working memory is freed to listen carefully to pupils' answers or to improvise explanations where needed during the lesson because she knows where she wants it to go and can steer it there as gently or decisively as needed. She is a teacher who finds it easy to laugh alongside her pupils and celebrate their work.'
4	**Scribble** and annotate or stick sticky notes onto your lesson plan before, during and after you teach the lesson Such scribbles can often take the form of 'stage directions' and reminders to yourself about the content, the pupils and the insights you had about the lesson	This habit of putting all your thoughts about the lesson in one place and not on separate sheets of paper (because you will find yourself thinking about the lesson at other times alongside when you sat down and planned it the first time) frees you up from having multiple documents and allows you to act on your thoughts while your memories and ideas of the lesson are still fresh

Key Takeaways

- Lesson planning is not a paperwork exercise where the completed lesson plan is the goal. Rather, lesson planning is a way of helping you to think like a teacher. Writing a plan is an important cognitive process.
- Lesson planning will help you to get better at teaching by freeing up your working memory so you are better able to respond to your pupils.
- Lesson planning reflects what you know about the process of learning and the skilful techniques of teaching.
- Double planning helps you to understand your lesson from the perspective of your pupils, so you can plan a lesson that will keep them actively engaged with their learning throughout.

Structuring for Good Behaviour: Habits and Routines

How to 'Do' High Expectations

When a new teacher watches an expert teacher and then takes over the lesson, often the behaviour of the class deteriorates. Whereas the expert teacher made teaching look easy, slowly the lesson can unravel when a new teacher takes over, even when they are teaching the same lesson plan to the same class. The reason for this rests in the often-unnoticed way that the expert teacher has structured the lesson for good behaviour.

Similarly, and directly related to this experience, one of the most common phrases about teaching refers to the need for 'high expectations', yet it can be difficult for a new teacher to know how to 'do' high expectations. The phrase can sound like a platitude, but it is something that expert teachers do and is something that you can learn to do by structuring your lesson.

When an expert teacher double plans for what both they and their pupils will say and do, they are also developing a running commentary as to *how* they want the pupils to say and do the planned activities. This is how the teacher conveys the high expectations they have for their pupils. For example, rather than offering the instruction 'Please get your books out', an expert teacher will add how they want the instruction to be followed: 'Please get your books out *in silence*'. In other words, high expectations for both good behaviour and good attitudes to learning are part of a golden thread to the teacher's speech to the class. Everything a teacher says to the class is a comment on how the class is to behave or gives feedback on how well the class followed the expectations for behaviour in the instruction.

As a new teacher, you will learn to talk to the class in a way that determines what high expectations mean. Over time, your classroom talk and actions will develop and become automatic. In the early days of teaching any new class, it is worthwhile annotating your lesson plan to remind you to tell the class how you want them to undertake every aspect of the lesson and the school day. You need to be explicit about classroom routines as part of how you structure your lesson.

Key Takeaway

- High expectations are conveyed to the class *continuously* and are constantly reinforced for all pupils by the teacher's positive framing of behaviour for learning alongside the questions, instructions and explanations the teacher says to the class.

Classroom Routines for Transitions and Inclusion

Routines are part of setting high expectations and are a key way of building a positive learning environment. Routines are the pre-emptive strategies that create the space for supportive relationships between teachers and pupils. They enable pupils to meet the social and academic expectations the teacher has for the class. By teaching classroom routines explicitly, the teacher enables their pupils to learn good habits for learning.

It is useful to structure your plan around the changes that take place in the lesson and through out the school day – these are often termed as *transitions*. The key transitions to structure into your lesson plan are notes to yourself about what you will say to the pupils at the following points of change in the lesson:

1 Meeting and greeting pupils as they enter the classroom.
2 Getting pupils to sit down quickly and quietly.
3 Ensuring a calm and purposeful start to the lesson.
4 Ensuring pupils are looking and listening when you speak to the class.
5 Ensuring pupils leave the classroom in a quiet and orderly manner.

Structuring your lesson will also support you in your responsibility to include all pupils. Inclusive teaching brings about positive outcomes for all pupils, not just vulnerable pupils. Inclusive teaching is not a bolt-on to your teaching, but is best achieved by a series of small actions throughout the lesson. In other words, inclusion is how you make the learning work for everyone and is part of the structure of your lesson in the form of:

- the tweaks you make to your plan as you respond to pupils (facilitated by your double planning)
- how pupils are welcomed into the classroom
- how pupils are involved in the lesson
- connecting the lesson content to the experiences and needs of the pupils (facilitated by your double planning)

Key Takeaways

- Certain moments are especially significant for learning in a lesson.
- Paying attention to what you will say about these points of change to your pupils as part of the structure of the lesson will enable you to create a positive and inclusive environment for learning.

Structuring Your Lesson for Good Behaviour and Learning: The Theory

How your pupils perceive you as a teacher and consequently the culture for learning you develop in your classroom is shaped by everything you say and do over time. Theo Wubbels and Mieke Brekelmans are professors of education at Utrecht University. They undertook a 25-year study to examine teacher behaviours in order to understand their effect on teacher–pupil relationships, and the impact they have on pupil outcomes (Wubbels and Brekelmans, 2005). They mapped the modes of communication used by teachers and concluded that what teachers say and how they say it are highly influential on pupil outcomes. They recommended that new teachers should focus on communicating the persona of an experienced teacher when addressing the whole class. They can do this by considering what they say and do (their gestures and behaviours) and how pupils are likely to perceive their words, actions, and behaviours. Wubbels and Brekelmans (2005) defined two aspects and two levels of teacher communication (see Table 8.2).

Table 8.2 Ways in which teachers communicate in their classrooms

Aspect 1 of communication	Content	What the teacher says and does
Aspect 2 of communication	Relation	How the teacher says and does it
Level 1 of communication	Message	Individual instances of communication
Level 2 of communication	Pattern	The habits of communication that forge the relation between the teacher and the pupils over time

Their study showed that pupils' perceptions of their teacher and the relationship between teachers and pupils are important and developed through how the teacher presents themselves to their pupils. Teachers who are directive, authoritative and tolerant develop pupils who achieve well and have positive attitudes to learning the subject, but their key finding was that:

> to give pupils appropriate freedom and responsibility during group and independent work, it appeared to be important for a teacher to be a strong leader in central lesson segments. (Wubbels and Brekelmans, 2005: 15)

Pupils respond better to opportunities for independent learning when the teacher has first established their influence as the principal leader of learning in the classroom. Wubbels and Brekelmans argued that such influence is established by structuring the lesson so that the teacher is dominant (the teacher determines the pupils' activities) and co-operative (the teacher shows approval of the pupils and their behaviour). They suggested that experienced teachers demonstrate dominant and co-operative characteristics by structuring certain behaviours into their lessons (see Table 8.3). New teachers should aim to emulate these behaviours, and in so doing will acquire the persona of an experienced teacher.

Table 8.3 The behaviours that experienced teachers structure into their lesson to achieve good pupil outcomes and attitudes (Wubbels and Brekelmans, 2005)

Dominant behaviours by the teacher	Co-operative behaviours by the teacher
Noticing what is happening in the classroom	Showing an interest
Organising	Being considerate
Setting tasks	Being able to make a joke
Giving orders	Inspiring trust and confidence
Explaining	
Holding attention	

One tool that teachers can use to develop these behaviours is to incorporate meta-communication into their lesson planning. Meta-communication is communication about communication. Wubbels and Brekelmans (2005: 20) define meta-communication in the classroom as 'communication about how teachers and pupils communicate with each other'. An example of meta communication is when teachers specify the audience and purpose of any communication during the course of a lesson. By explicitly demonstrating how they want pupils to communicate in class through their own practice, teachers use meta-communication to create and maintain a positive learning environment. You can structure meta-communication into your double planned lessons by using scribbles, annotations and scripted notes before, during and after the lesson.

Key Takeaways

- Structure your lesson to give you opportunities to display the dominant and co-operative behaviours of experienced teachers.
- Before you structure independent learning opportunities for pupils in the lesson, first establish yourself in the role of principal leader of learning when you teach.

Structuring Your Lesson for Good Behaviour and Learning: What to Practise

Structuring your lesson plan on the basis of techniques you can use to create a healthy atmosphere and to establish positive working relationships between you and your pupils, which you can then perfect over time, will help you get better at teaching more quickly. Robert Marzano is an educational researcher in the United States who has focused his work on establishing research-based strategies for classroom management. He states that while much of the teacher's time in class is taken up with the activities of teaching, effective teachers also spend time on creating conditions that are conducive for learning (Marzano, 2003a). This is why it is important to plan not only for what you and your pupils will say and do relating to learning and teaching, but also for the good behaviour that leads to learning. Marzano argues that the development of what he calls 'withitness' is the key difference between more expert teachers and less skilled others. 'Withitness' is being keenly aware of and alert to what inhibits learning so that teachers can counteract it before it occurs (Marzano, 2003a: 5). Teachers can plan for it by being fully present in class.

While it can seem to new teachers that expert teachers' excellent classroom management arises from the charisma, confidence or some hidden magic, in fact it is mostly due to their behaviour in the classroom. In a meta-analysis of more than 100 studies, Marzano and Marzano (2003b) found that the most effective teacher–pupil relationships rest on teachers creating a positive working atmosphere and demonstrating the assertive persona of an expert teacher. They describe assertiveness as 'the teacher's ability to provide clear purpose and strong guidance regarding academic and pupil behavior' (Marzano and Marzano, 2003b: 8).

Table 8.4 lists the techniques they suggested that new teachers use to create a positive working atmosphere (co-operation) and the assertive persona of an expert teacher (dominance). These approaches can be structured into your lesson plans as scripts, scribbles and annotations.

Key Takeaways

- There are routines, techniques and processes that you can structure into your lesson plan that will bring about better teaching and learning.
- These routines, techniques and processes enable you to be an authority in your classroom, but also empower pupils and actively involve them in the classroom.
- Pupils do not like teachers who cannot control the class.
- Communicate clearly and often with your pupils; they need to know you and you need to know them.

Table 8.4 Techniques to structure into your lesson plan to develop a positive classroom atmosphere and your own assertiveness (Marzano and Marzano, 2003b)

Positive working atmosphere (co-operation)	Assertive persona of an expert teacher (dominance)
Using a wide repertoire of verbal and physical cues to react to pupils' off-task behaviour, such as raising your hand or putting fingers to your lips	Using assertive body language: standing up straight, managing the physical space between you and pupils and matching your facial expression with what you are saying (e.g. looking disappointed when pupils don't follow a routine and you are reminding them of what you want them to do)
Giving clear recognition of appropriate behaviour and sometimes rewarding such behaviour with tokens, etc.	Using an appropriate tone of voice, speaking clearly and deliberately in a pitch that is slightly elevated from your normal classroom speech, not showing emotion in your voice (particularly not demonstrating extreme emotion, such as anger or frustration)
Holding the whole class accountable for good behaviour by referring to your expectations of the whole class and commenting on when they are being met	Persisting with instructions until pupils respond appropriately, not ignoring any inappropriate behaviour, not being side-tracked by pupils blaming or arguing but listening to legitimate explanations by pupils
Keeping in contact with pupils' homes and informing parents of the rewards and sanctions you use but also when pupils are behaving well for learning	
Providing clear goals at the start of a lesson in terms of what will be learned in the lesson	
Beginning the lesson by explaining to pupils what they will achieve by the end of the lesson so that they understand how they will learn	
Taking a personal interest in your pupils' lives and concerns	
Finding ways for pupils to use their own agency and autonomy to learn, and not expecting pupils to merely passively follow orders	
Being equitable and positive to all pupils by maintaining eye contact with all pupils, moving freely around the room, acknowledging and commending the contributions through physical gestures and linking one pupil's ideas to another's, providing wait time for pupils to think before they answer questions, and asking all pupils to answer questions, not just the ones who put their hands up	

Rosenshine's Influence in England and Wales

Since the Literacy and Numeracy National Strategies were introduced in England in the 1990s, the structure of a lesson that is most commonly used has been a 'three-part lesson'. A three-part lesson consists of a starter – a planned activity that involves everyone at the start of the lesson – the main body of the lesson, and finally ending with a plenary, which functions to bring the learning to a conclusion. However, a different approach, which was first developed in the USA in the 1980s (Rosenshine, 1980) became popular here in 2020. Instead of the three-part structure, it draws on Rosenshine's (2005) emphasis on what teachers 'do' pedagogically *within* the structure of a lesson. Rosenshine (2005) found that teachers structure their lessons around three functions of teaching and that, as a result, effective teaching is based on ten principles (Rosenshine 2010, 2012). The three teaching functions are:

1. To teach in small steps – presenting only small parts of new material at single time.
2. To guide pupils' practice – having presented a small amount of material, the teacher models the activity, asks pupils to try the activity, pupils then work in small groups on the activity, and the teacher asks questions and helps pupils with their work.
3. To use cognitive processing strategies – the guiding procedures that help pupils to complete less-structured activities, such as procedural prompts, models and scaffolds, to help pupils build the learning to do more complex tasks.

Rosenshine's ten principles of effective teaching (he used the US term 'instruction') (2010, 2012) are:

1. Begin a lesson with a short review of previous learning.
2. Present new material in small steps with pupil practice after each step.
3. Ask a large number of questions and check the responses of all pupils.
4. Provide models.
5. Guide pupil practice.
6. Check for pupil understanding.
7. Obtain a high success rate.
8. Provide scaffolds for difficult tasks.
9. Require and monitor independent practice.
10. Engage pupils in weekly and monthly review.

Although sometimes used by schools as a checklist for how to teach, Rosenshine intended these principles to set out the steps that an effective teacher takes within the structure of a particular lesson. The structure of a lesson is a tool, not an end in itself. Following the steps will not turn you into an expert teacher. It is how you use the structure that counts. You should use the structure to help you decide how you want to use the time available to teach the content of the lesson to the particular pupils in your class. In other words, use the lesson structure to help you decide how you will help your pupils to learn.

Key takeaways

- Introduce pupils to new content.
- You should structure your lesson to include activities that allow pupils to practice using what they are learning and allocate significant amounts of time for question-and-answer sessions.

Conclusion

It is helpful to think about your lesson in terms of the order of what will happen and when. This chapter has set out several ways in which a lesson can be structured and how these elements of a lesson can be thought of in terms of what you and your pupils will say and do in whole-class, small-group and individual activities. However, as well as thinking about the organisation of the children in the class at certain phases of the lesson, it is also important to think about how the nature of the activity will reinforce the learning of the curriculum.

References

Coe, R, Rauch, CJ, Kime, S, and Singleton, D (2020) *Great Teaching Toolkit: Evidence Review*. Cambridge: Evidence Based Education and Cambridge Assessment International Education. Available at: https://www.cambridgeinternational.org/Images/584543-great-teaching-toolkit-evidence-review.pdf

Lemov, D (2021) *Teach Like a Champion 3.0: Techniques that Put Students on the Path to College*. San Francisco, CA: Jossey: Bass

Marzano, RJ (2003a) *Classroom Management that Works: Research Based Strategies for Every Teacher*. Alexandria, VA: Association for Supervision and Curriculum Development

Marzano, RJ and Marzano, JS (2003b) The key to classroom management. *Educational Leadership* 61(1), 6–13

Rosenshine, B (1980) How time is spent in elementary classroom. In D.Denham and A. Lieberman (Eds) *Time to Learn: A review of the beginning teacher evaluation study* (pp. 107–126). Washington DC: Institute of Education.

Rosenshine, B (2005) Advances in research on instruction. *The Journal of Educational Research* 88(5) May–June), 262–268

Rosenshine, B (2010) *Principles of Instruction: Educational Practices Series – 21*. Geneva: UNESCO International Bureau of Education

Rosenshine, B (2012) Principles of instruction: Research-based strategies that all teachers should know. *American Educator* Spring 12–18

Wubbels, T and Brekelmans, M (2005) Two decades of research on teacher–student relationships in class. *International Journal of Educational Research* 43, 6–24

9
HOW TO PLAN FOR QUALITY INTERACTIONS

Why is It Important to Plan for Quality Interactions?

As a practising teacher, for much of your teaching day you will be concerned with what you and your pupils say and do. In Chapter 10, we consider the role of task design in planning lessons, as this addresses planning for activities and what you and your pupils will do, but in this chapter, we look at what is said in the classroom.

'Quality interactions', which is a term more commonly used in the teaching of 3–7-year-olds, applies to all ages and phases of teaching. In the 3–7-year-old classroom, 'quality interaction' refers to the adult being attuned and responsive to the child. It also focuses on the back and forth of conversation, such as eye contact, turn taking, following the child's lead, and sharing attention on what interests the child, alongside modelling and scaffolding to expand and extend what the child says. Many expert primary teachers continue to think in this way when they teach their key stage 2 class because it reminds them of the purpose of classroom talk: to enable their pupils to learn better because they are engaged in quality interactions with their teacher and the other children in the class. From birth, children are hard-wired to seek out interaction, and nurturing, responsive interactions are vital for the development of children. As Professor Robin Alexander set out in the introduction to his seminal work, *Towards Dialogic Teaching: Rethinking Classroom Talk* (2004: 9):

> Talk has always been one of the essential tools of teaching, and the best teachers use it with precision and flair. But talk is much more than an aid to effective teaching. Children, we now know, need to talk, and to experience a rich diet of spoken language, in order to think and to learn. Reading, writing and number maybe the acknowledged curriculum basics, but talk is arguably the true foundation of learning.

For several decades there has been a trend to focus on what new technologies can offer to the classroom, but it is important 'to remember that teaching is fundamentally about human relations … what happens between you and your class, with or without a computer in the room' (Scott, 2015: 150). Language is your primary teaching tool. It is therefore very important to understand how language can be used to support your classroom management and to help your pupils learn the curriculum content and develop their social and cognitive skills. This chapter addresses how you should best talk in your classroom and how you can best encourage your pupils to speak.

First, the chapter looks at how you can plan talk for teaching and talk for learning, and draws on the work of Alexander, who developed the concept of dialogic teaching. Then it develops the idea of how to structure lessons for quality interactions. It outlines how you can best use the five phases of your lessons, and your teaching approach at each phase, to include all the children in your class and to create an effective learning environment. It explains the teaching approach of SEN specialist Sara Alston (2021), and shows how her understanding of how to plan for the five different phases of a lesson links with the pedagogic principles of Barak Rosenshine (2010, 2012).

What is Talk for Teaching and Talk for Learning?

The three most common forms of teacher talk are:

1. *Rote:* the drilling of facts, ideas, and routines through constant repetition.
2. *Recitation:* the accumulation of knowledge and understanding through questions designed to test or stimulate recall of what has been previously taught or to cue pupils to work out and answer from the clues provided in the question.
3. *Instruction:* telling the pupil what to do, and/or imparting information, and/or explaining facts, principles, or procedures. (Alexander, 2004: 30)

Much whole-class teaching is a particular form of teacher talk – you talk and the pupils listen, interspersed with question and answer or call and response. In such whole-class teaching, teachers tend to use one of five common oral techniques to build pupils' new understanding on their past activity:

1. *Recapitulation:* summarise and review what has gone before.
2. *Elicitation:* asking a question designed to stimulate recall.
3. *Repetition:* repeating a pupil's answer, either to give it general prominence or to encourage an alternative.
4. *Reformulation:* paraphrasing a pupil's response, to make it more accessible to the rest of the class or to improve the way it has been expressed.
5. *Exhortation:* encouraging pupils to 'think' or 'remember' what has been said or done earlier. (Mercer, 2000: 131–146)

Two further forms of teacher talk tend to occur less frequently:

1. *Discussion:* the exchange of ideas with a view to sharing information and solving problems.
2. *Dialogue:* achieving common understanding through structured, cumulative questioning and discussion which guide and prompt, reduce choices, minimise risk and error, and expedite 'handover' of concepts and principles. (Alexander, 2004: 30)

Thus, dialogic teaching is more concerned with the back and forth of conversation between you and your pupils. Mercer (2000) described this process as 'interthinking' – a reciprocal process in which ideas are bounced back and forth and, on that basis, children's thinking is taken forward. For example, rather than just respond to *what* you think about your pupils' answers, in dialogic teaching you would also comment on *why* you have those thoughts, i.e. you substantiate or explain your response, but you also encourage pupils to respond *further* to your what and why response.

While acknowledging that all forms of talk have a place in the classroom, dialogue has a particularly vital part to play to ensure that pupils are 'empowered in their learning now, and later as adult members of society' (Alexander, 2004: 39). Alexander (2004) noted that the culture of the classroom needs to allow for shifts from transmission-only teaching to joint work between teachers and their pupils. He described the essential features of the dialogic classroom in terms of five principles (Alexander, 2004: 28):

1 *Collective:* teachers and pupils address learning tasks together, whether as a group or as a class, rather than in isolation.
2 *Reciprocal:* teachers and pupils listen to each other and share ideas and alternative viewpoints.
3 *Supportive:* pupils articulate their ideas freely, without fear of embarrassment of 'wrong' answers, and help each other to reach common understandings.
4 *Cumulative:* teachers and pupils build on their own and each other's ideas and chain them into coherent lines of thinking and enquiry.
5 *Purposeful:* teachers plan and facilitate dialogic teaching with particular educational goals in view.

Siraj et al. (2019), in their 17-year longitudinal study of effective primary teaching, were disappointed by how few examples of such dialogic teaching and learning they observed, but they noted that it occurred in the teaching of the most effective teachers in the most effective schools. They concluded that any dialogic teaching and learning was better than none. Siraj et al. (2019) set out the foundations that these most effective teachers had put in place. Dialogic teachers:

- had a desire to engage with their pupils at every level
- arranged their classrooms, routines and resources so that their pupils could be self-reliant
- were extremely sensitive to their pupils' needs
- modelled, encouraged and insisted on good relationships
- provided a collaborative environment

These foundations were critical because the teachers created an 'arena for dialogic learning. Because pupils knew their opinions and contributions were respected and valued, they could engage confidently in dialogue with each other and the teacher. Because they learnt in a particularly positive and supportive environment, they were able to attempt new learning challenges more easily' (Siraj et al., 2019: 166).

Alexander (2004) argued that teachers should plan their teaching so that pupils develop their learning through the following types of pupil talk:

- narrate
- explain

- instruct
- ask different kinds of questions
- receive, act and build on answers
- speculate and imagine
- explore and evaluate ideas
- discuss
- argue, reason and justify
- negotiate

These types of talk are based on the following four skills:

1 Listen.
2 Be receptive to alternative viewpoints.
3 Think about what they hear.
4 Give others time to think. (Alexander, 2004: 39)

It is clear that fostering dialogic teaching is a mark of your ability to teach skilfully and effectively. However, it is also apparent that a dialogic classroom prepares pupils to take up their place in the world with more confidence, with an interest in words and language and understanding the importance of listening as well as speaking.

How to Plan for Talk for Teaching and Talk for Learning

The aim of teaching dialogically is so that your pupils, over time, develop a rich vocabulary, are able to speak confidently, clearly, informatively, expressively and succinctly, have the capacity to engage with, and communicate in, different registers and genres, and have the ability and motivation to listen to others. Table 9.1 summarises the factors and conditions you should plan for in order to introduce dialogic teaching into your classroom.

As a teacher, your talk for teaching will happen within three types of teaching interaction: whole-class teaching, teacher-led group work, and in one–one interactions with your pupils. Table 9.2 sets out what dialogic teaching looks like in these teaching interactions.

When pupils are engaged in talking with each other for learning, i.e. in pupil-led group work, five learning behaviours can be seen:

1 Pupils listen carefully to each other.
2 Pupils encourage each other to participate and share ideas.
3 Pupils build on their own and each other's contributions.
4 Pupils strive to reach common understanding and agreed conclusions.
5 Pupils respect minority viewpoints.

Table 9.1 What to bear in mind when you plan talk for teaching and talk for learning (adapted from Alexander, 2004)

What to plan	How to plan
Classroom setting	• Use different settings and tasks: whole class, teacher-led group work, pupil-led group work, and individual pupil-work • Change the classroom layout to meet the needs of tasks and for different types of learning talk • Plan the classroom layout to support concentration and to ensure distractions and interruptions are kept to a minimum
Lesson starters and stages	• Ensure lesson starters, transitions and plenaries are no longer than they need to be and do not last longer than your pupils' concentration span • Do not let writing episodes of the lesson extend beyond the time they require • In-lesson starters, transitions and conclusions are concerned with ideas rather than procedures
Tasks	• Plan tasks that benefit from talk-based activities as well as reading and writing activities • Make the phrase, 'Let's talk about it' as familiar as 'Let's write about it' • Allocate the time on task as a precious resource
Teaching and assessing	• Teaching should be pacey in terms of cognitive ground covered rather than for the speed of activity or interaction • Shift from interactions which are brief and random to those which are both longer and more sustained • Monitor the balance of written to oral tasks and consider giving more prominence to oral tasks than you might have done previously • Practise assessing your pupils on the basis of their understanding of what they say as well as by checking what they have written
Modelling	• Make notes on your plan to remind yourself to be sensitive to your expression, gesture, body language, physical stance and location in the classroom and its impact on classroom talk • Make notes on your plan to remind yourself to model a rich vocabulary, to be confident, clear, informative and succinct in speech, to use a range of registers and genres, and to promote good listening

Table 9.2 Observable behaviours in a classroom where talk is used to support teaching

Whole-class teaching Teacher-led group work	One–one interactions with your pupils…
• Questions are structured to provoke thoughtful answers • Answers provoke further questions • Answers are seen as the building blocks of dialogue rather than the end point • Talk is balanced between encouraging participation and extending understanding • Pupils are encouraged to ask questions and provide explanations • Pupil talk is managed by shared routines rather than through hands-up activities • Those who are not speaking are recognised as listening, looking, reflecting and evaluating • Pupils learn that different school subjects and different social circumstances demand different registers and are taught how to use them • Pupils are confident enough to make mistakes and learn that mistakes are to be viewed as something to learn from rather than to be ashamed of	• last long enough to be of use to the pupil • are teaching-focused rather than used to manage behaviour • provide diagnostic feedback, on which pupils can build

A particular teaching strategy that is a good way to start improving talk for teaching and learning in your classroom is your use of questioning and how you manage your pupils' answers. Table 9.3 sets out what you should plan for so that your use of questions and answers begins to move your classroom to becoming a dialogic space for teaching and learning.

Table 9.3 Using questions, answers and feedback to support talk for learning

Talk for teaching **Questioning in whole class, group or individual interactions**	**Talk for learning** **Develop your pupils so that they respond to your questions by...**	**Talk for teaching** **How to feedback to your pupils' responses to your questions**
• Anchored in the content of the lesson • Builds on previous knowledge • Elicits evidence of pupil understanding • Creates the opportunity for a range of responses, i.e. closed/narrow, open/discursive and speculative ('what is?' and 'what might be?' questions) • Balances open-endedness with guidance and structure • Gives children time to think	• answering the question in depth rather than worrying about spotting the correct answer • moving beyond yes/no or simple recall to offering extended answers involving reasoning, hypothesising and thinking aloud • being considered and discursive rather than brief and quick to finish	• Instead of offering simple positive, negative or non-committal judgement, or merely repeating the pupil's answer, offer informative diagnostic feedback on which pupils can build • Reformulate pupils' responses in a way that does not signal approval or disapproval • Use praise discriminatingly and appropriately and avoid habitual praise, such as 'good boy', 'very good', 'excellent', 'brilliant', etc. • Keep lines of enquiry open rather than close them down • Encourage pupils to articulate their ideas openly and confidently, without fear of embarrassment or retribution if they are wrong

Plan your lessons so that you have a balance between pupils answering questions by putting their hands up and you deciding who should answer. Ensure you mix up your classroom talk between asking questions and telling, informing and explaining the curriculum. Reduce habitual praise and replace it with feedback that informs, extends and encourages. Finally, develop your skill in synthesising the understanding you want to achieve when leading whole-class discussions.

Key Takeaways

- Expert primary school teachers utilise dialogic classroom practice to support learning.
- Take an active role as a speaker and listener in your classroom by guiding your pupils' use of language and modelling the ways language can be used for hard thinking.
- Establish an appropriate set of ground rules for talk in your classroom.
- Ensure that group activities are well designed to elicit debate and joint reasoning.
- Plan lessons to have a balance between pupils answering questions by putting their hands up and you deciding who should answer, and ensure you balance asking questions against you telling, informing and explaining the curriculum.

Why is It Important to Plan for Inclusion?

So far, we have discussed how you might plan a lesson using different teaching interactions by explicitly thinking about the roles of your talk for teaching and the talk for learning of your pupils. However, we can also consider these forms of interaction in terms of the different phases of the lesson. The key phases of a lesson that you can plan for are:

- Phase 1: transition, entering the room and getting ready to learn
- Phase 2: engaging the whole class in the delivery and receiving of instructions
- Phase 3: individual pupils working as a class
- Phase 4: group work that includes pupils
- Phase 5: the last five minutes of the lesson (Alston, 2021)

This section outlines how you can plan your lessons in these five phases to achieve two long-term teaching aims:

1 To create an effective learning environment for all.
2 To create an environment that is inclusive to the needs of individual pupils.

Planning for Inclusion in Terms of Language

As Alston (2021: 1) states: 'Inclusion is hard if you think of the lesson as one long marathon with lots of differentiated points along the way for lots of different children. Instead, it's easier to think of the lesson as a series of routines and priorities that can become enmeshed in good practice and that can be useful for all children, not just those identified as SEN.'

Planning a lesson that is inclusive comes down to:

- understanding and catering for the needs of all pupils by considering each pupil's learning strengths and difficulties
- determining how to support each individual child

It is important to think about the language you use to describe the children you teach, and those with SEN in particular. For example, focusing on a pupil's needs and how those needs are demonstrated by behaviours helps you to see the child in optimistic and understanding ways rather than being resentful of the stress and disturbance they might cause to a lesson. Even a subtle shift from labelling a child in terms of their needs (i.e. Jane is an autistic child) to recognising that the pupil is a child first who has strengths and needs (i.e. Jane is a child *with* autism) prevents obscuring the child from your view as their teacher. In this way, you are better able to see each pupil as an individual and not as a set of assumptions based on their SEN labels.

Planning for Inclusion as Good Teaching

The most inclusive teachers are focused on good teaching, but they emphasise particular aspects of what they do. Table 9.4 sets out some aspects of good teaching practice and the inclusive actions teachers take to ensure all their pupils are able to learn as effectively as possible.

Table 9.4 Inclusive actions for quality interactions

Aspect of good teaching	Inclusive actions for quality interactions
Relationships with pupils	1. Think carefully about your use of language to build trust 2. Consider the impact of your language on how a child might feel about themselves 3. Model being able to admit when you make a mistake and apologising when you get something wrong 4. Use specific praise so that your pupils know what they are being praised for and why
Relationships with parents	1. Build trust with parents by sharing good as well as bad news 2. Use everyday language and avoid educational jargon 3. Think carefully how to communicate about attainment and progress, particularly for pupils who are not making age expectations year on year or whose development is atypical
Relationships with other staff in your classroom	1. Communicate regularly about the pupils in your class and their learning 2. Explain what you are teaching and why ahead of each lesson so that they can offer effective support and be a good explainer of the planned learning to the targeted pupils 3. Ask for and listen to their feedback on what the pupils have learned
Importance of the use of visuals	1. Visuals reinforce and help deliver key messages and instructions 2. Plan your use of visuals for instructions that you often repeat, to pre-warn of regular transitions and for new or technical vocabulary 3. Use visuals as *aides-mémoire* to help pupils embed and take ownership of their learning
Support reading	1. Focus on language development in every lesson and in every subject 2. Think of support strategies that do not always require reading skills to access them 3. Focus on reading aloud so that dysfluency does not become inaudible and thereby drops as the number one learning priority
Time	1. Balance quieter and noisier learning times 2. Avoid possible high-stress lessons one after another so that your pupils can stay calm and self-regulated 3. Plan for quiet times to support focus and concentration 4. Rethink what fun might be – unpredictable events and changes to routine (such as at Christmas and the end of term) can provoke anxiety and make life more difficult to cope with, so share the plan so that children know ahead of time, include quiet time and routine among the change and allow for opt-outs and quiet spaces 5. Work preventatively at the start of the year, week, day and new unit to avoid things becoming an issue and to build effective differentiation into each phase of the lesson to support the next stage of learning (this will save you time, effort and physical and emotional energy in the long run) 6. Teach the skills for learning (listening, note-taking, etc.) as explicitly as you might teach other classroom routines

The next section goes into the next level of detail and sets out what quality interactions look like at each of the five phases of the lesson. It links quality interactions with Rosenshine's ten principles (2010, 2012) so that you can see how they link to the key processes of effective teaching.

Inclusion as Quality Interactions at Each Phase of the Lesson

Planning your lessons based on simple and consistent routines and then applying tweaks and adaptions is the process which is at the heart of successful and inclusive teaching. Because you are thinking of small tweaks and adaptions, rather than complex processes, quality interactions for inclusive teaching are more likely to be better implemented by you and easier for your pupils to understand. Table 9.5 lists the phases and suggests lesson activities, what the activities aim to achieve and how they do so.

Table 9.5 Planning for quality interactions in each lesson phase (adapted from Alston, 2021)

Phase	Lesson activity	Aim	How
1	Transition, entering the classroom and preparing to learn	To start the lesson calmly	• Be warm and welcoming • Establish clear routines • Build confidence • Build self-belief
2	Delivering and receiving instructions and whole class engagement	To communicate in order to be understood by all	Use simple, reiterated instructions and check to see if children understand
3	Individuals working as a class	To enable pupils to participate independently	• Differentiate • Prompt • Praise • Vary approaches
4	Individuals fitting into a group of learners	To ensure groups are places of belonging for all and that they promote and extend learning while developing pupils' social skills	• Plan routines • Use routines to assign roles • Promote self-esteem • Reward participation • Reward inclusivity
5	The last five minutes	To end the lesson in a way that will fully prepare and enable all pupils to engage in the next activity	• Be warm • Be encouraging • Establish clear routines • Build confidence • build self-belief

Rosenshine's Principles of Instruction and Quality Interactions

Barak Rosenshine (1930–2017) was a professor in educational psychology at the University of Illinois. His research career focused on effective ways of teaching and developing models of teaching that describe the steps teachers should take to better support pupil learning. Two of his articles (Rosenshine, 2010, 2012), which are freely available on the internet, became very popular in England when they were summarised by ex-headteacher Tom Sherrington into handy mini-guides in 2019. Rosenshine summarised some teaching principles taken from the research fields of cognitive science and classroom practice. They were intended to be particularly useful when the teacher's objective is to enable their pupils to master a body of knowledge or learn a skill which can be taught in a step-by-step manner (the principles are less relevant to analysis, problem-solving or creative activities).

Rosenshine's article in *American Educator* (2012) was a version of an article written for the UNESCO International Bureau of Education (IAE) the International Bureau of Education (IBE) (Rosenshine, 2010). The latter was the 21st in a series of pamphlets produced by (IBE), each of which was designed to be easily accessible in many different countries and to take the form of a simple, practical list of ten principles. Each principle linked to a suggested research reading (although of the 25 references, only three were more recent than 2000, even when the article was written in 2010). In recent years, some schools have used the principles as a checklist to judge teaching, but this was never the original intention. Rather, the aim was to use his principles to inform your judgement about how you wish to teach and as an *aide-mémoire* when planning your teaching. As such, some of his principles are a useful prompt and reminder about how you might best plan for talk for teaching and talk for learning. They are set out in Table 9.6, with the principles that refer to inclusive quality interactions highlighted in italic. It is worth noting that in his first pamphlet (2010) he lists 17 principles as well as the ten that he eventually focuses on in both (Rosenshine, 2010, 2012).

Table 9.6 A summary of Rosenshine's principles of instructions with those most relevant to inclusive quality interactions italicised

17 principles of instruction	10 principles of instruction
Begin a lesson with a short review of previous learning	Undertake a daily review
Present new material in small steps with pupil practice after each step	Present new material using small steps
Limit the amount of material that pupils receive at one time	*Ask questions*
Give clear and detailed instructions and explanations	Provide models
Ask a large number of questions and check for understanding	*Guide pupil practice*
Provide a high level of active practice for all pupils	*Check for pupil understanding*
Guide pupils as they begin to practise	Provide scaffolds for difficult tasks
Think aloud and model steps	*Obtain a high success rate*
Provide models of worked-out problems	Facilitate independent practice
Ask pupils to explain what they have learned	Carry out a weekly and monthly review
Check the responses of all pupils	
Provide systematic feedback and corrections	
Use more time to provide explanations	
Provide many examples	
Reteach material when necessary	
Prepare pupils for independent practice	
Monitor pupils when they begin independent practice	

Key Takeaways

- Plan routines, adaptions and tweaks in your classroom and share them with your teaching assistant (TA) or other adults so they are aware of them and why they are being implemented. This way you create shared expectations.
- Be consistent in how you adapt lessons to meet the needs of the children you teach so that pupils do not become anxious about the changes.
- Listen carefully to your pupils and involve them in your plans to support them and meet their needs.
- Remember that your pupils may have ideas about how best to support their needs.
- Connect the beginnings and endings of your lessons to the other parts of the school day and plan your routines and adaptions to fit in with the wider approach of the school.

Conclusion

Talk is at the heart of teaching. Teachers plan to achieve pupil understanding rather than pupil recall. Really good teachers plan their talk and plan how their pupils will learn from learning to listen and to speak. However, when you plan your lessons to allow time for you to listen carefully to your pupils, you also do two important things: you signal that your pupils matter to you (which is a powerful tool in creating good, productive relationships with your pupils) and you discover what they have learned and have yet to master.

References

Alexander, R (2004) *Towards Dialogic Teaching Rethinking Classroom Talk*. Thirsk: Dialogos UK

Alston, S (2021) *The Inclusive Classroom: A New Approach to Differentiation*. London: Bloomsbury

Mercer, N (2000) *Words and Minds: How We Use Language to Think Together*. London: Routledge

Rosenshine, B (2010) *Principles of Instruction: Education Practices Series – 21*. Geneva: UNESCO International Bureau of Education

Rosenshine, B (2012) Principles of instruction: Research-based strategies that all teachers should know. *American Educator* Spring, 12–18

Scott, C (2015) *Learn to Teach, Teach to Learn*. Cambridge: Cambridge University Press

Sherrington, T (2019) *Rosenshine's Principles in Action*. John Catt

Siraj, I, Taggart, B, Sammons, P, Melhuish, E, Sylva, K, and Shepherd, D (2019) *Teaching in Effective Primary Schools: Research into Pedagogy and Children' Learning*. London: UCL Institute of Education Press

10
HOW TO PLAN FOR WHAT YOUR PUPILS WILL DO IN YOUR LESSONS

Why is it Important to Plan for What Your Pupils Will Do?

This is an important question that goes to the heart of what it means to think like a teacher and to be able to plan lessons. For many experienced teachers, planning what your pupils will do in a lesson is one of the most creative, satisfying and engaging aspects of teaching: being a curriculum designer who is able to respond to the needs of the children in the class. However, it is also the aspect of learning to teach and to plan that can cause uncertainty for new teachers if they cannot think of suitable things for pupils to do.

First, imagine you have a Year 3 class and you have been asked to teach them a science lesson on the topic of light. When you look at the National Curriculum guidance, you notice that they need to learn that light is reflected from surfaces. And then your mind goes a blank. How can you help 30 seven-year-olds understand this? You could just tell them, but if you want them to integrate this knowledge about light with their everyday knowledge, you realise that you need to design something for them to *actually* do in the lesson. How might you interpret and plan from this curriculum information and enact it as you teach the lesson?

As a second example, Year 4 maths has the following topics: number and place value and rounding; addition and subtraction; multiplication and division; fractions, decimals and percentages; measurement; geometry (the property of shapes and position, direction and motion); and statistics. You have been asked to plan a sequence of maths lessons for Year 4. What activity would you select for the topic of addition and subtraction? Specifically, what can you organise so that pupils estimate and use inverse operations to check answers to a calculation? You may think about what you did when you were at school, or you 'google' the question to find other teachers' resources, or you put the question into ChatGPT and, in doing so, find another layer of detail about what your pupils need to understand by the end of the sequence of lessons.

The danger in planning what your pupils should do in a lesson is that you are likely to have only a limited number of ideas and that, over time, you will teach every lesson in the same way. However, as a teacher, the purpose of your teacher knowledge is not just to deliver the content and then assess pupils afterwards. As a pedagogical designer, you need to draw on your knowledge of pupil development in the curriculum and how the curriculum progresses, and then be able to turn this knowledge into things that pupils can do. In other words, you will ask yourself the question 'To advance their learning, what will my pupils do?'

Important Theoretical Concepts to Shape Your Planning

There are three concepts derived from teaching theory that can shape your understanding of lesson planning. These three terms are most typically used to describe what pupils will do in a lesson and each one arises from a different school of thought. What pupils will do in a lesson can be described as:

- active learning
- tasks and activities
- guided and independent practice

The sections below explain these three concepts and summarise their theoretical background to inform how to think about what your pupils might usefully do.

Active Learning: Learning as a Generative Activity

Often new teachers talk about pupils being active in the lesson and think that this means that pupils need to be physically active. We know that, in fact, pupils are required to be cognitively active. What can seem like a passive experience, for example reading a book, can be planned by the teacher to produce meaningful learning. Nevertheless, planning what pupils will say and do so that they think hard is challenging for a new teacher.

Logan Fiorella and Richard E Meyer, professors of psychology at the University of California, researched effective learning strategies – the activities pupils engage in during a lesson that are intended to improve learning. In their book *Learning as a Generative Activity: Eight Learning Strategies that Promote Understanding* (2015), they outline eight activities that pupils can do in a lesson that will promote understanding of the content to be learnt. They developed the term 'generative learning', which they define as 'helping learners to actively make sense of the material so they can build meaningful learning outcomes that allow them to transfer what they have learned to solving new problems' (Fiorella and Meyer, 2015: vii).

Fiorella and Meyer identify three kinds of learning: rote learning, where pupils memorise information so they can remember it later; associative learning, where pupils build associations so that they can give a response to a stimulus; and generative learning, where pupils learn as a process of making sense of information in order to solve new problems. They define generative learning in terms of its cognitive processes. There are three cognitive processes that make up hard thinking:

1 Selecting – paying attention to relevant information and relating it to what is already known.
2 Organising – reorganising the new content into a coherent structure.
3 Integrating – integrating the cognitive structures with each other and with relevant prior knowledge activated from long-term memory by distinguishing what is important from what is not.

In generative learning, the pupil generates 'their own learning outcomes by interpreting what is presented to them rather than by simply receiving it as presented' (Fiorella and Meyer, 2015: viii). To teach well, you do not simply present the material to the pupils (as in the science and maths dilemmas presented earlier), but guide your pupils' cognitive processing in terms of selecting, organising and integrating the curriculum content through activities you plan for them to do. In other words, you would plan your lessons and what pupils will do in the lesson to help them get better at selecting, organising and integrating what you are teaching them.

Eight Generative Learning Strategies

Table 10.1 sets out, as an example, the eight generative learning strategies and maps them against the learning objectives identified earlier in the chapter. You will see that each suggested strategy across both subjects is identical. This is because the suggested activity is a springboard so that you can further specify aspects of the task in the particular subject. As you become familiar with thinking about lesson planning in terms of the eight learning strategies, you will

Table 10.1 Eight generative learning strategies (Fiorella and Meyer, 2015)

Strategy	**Year 3 Science: To learn that light is reflected from surfaces**	**Year 4 Maths: To learn how to estimate and use inverse operations to check answers to a calculation**
Summarise	Create a written or oral summary	Create a written or oral summary
Map	Create a spatial representation	Create a spatial representation
Draw	Create a drawing	Create a drawing
Imagine	Imagine a situation from life	Imagine a situation from life
Self-test	Design a personal test	Design a personal test
Self-explain	Identify the sections of the content that are confusing and create a written or oral explanation	Identify the sections of the content that are confusing and create a written or oral explanation
Teach	Explain the content to another pupil	Explain the content to another pupil
Enact	Act out the content	Act out the content

be able to think of a range of summarising, mapping drawing, imagining, self-testing, self-explaining, teaching and enacting activities for your pupils to do.

Your pupils need to learn in ways that produce transferable knowledge and skills. When you create tasks that generate learning, you are enabling your pupils to become people who can adapt to new situations, synthesise multiple sources of information and come up with creative solutions (Fiorella and Meyer, 2015: 16). Table 10.2 provides an overview of each generative learning strategy and what you need to be aware of as you use the approach to think of things for your pupils to do when you plan lessons.

Table 10.2 A summary of the eight learning strategies that promote understanding

Learning by	What it involves	Some things to be aware of
Summarising	Restating the main ideas of a lesson in the pupil's own words	Pre-teach how to summarise – how to select main ideas, make connections between them, and restate them in their own words
Mapping	Converting the lesson content into a concept map (words representing key ideas with connecting lines), knowledge map (concepts are linked by relationship, e.g. type of or evidence for) or graphic organiser (compare and contrast)	Can be time-consuming, so partly completed maps can be useful for pupils
Drawing	Deciding what should be included and how they should be arranged to represent the main ideas of the content	Make sure the effort of producing a drawing does not detract from the content to be learned
Imagining	Asking pupils to form mental images to illustrate the lesson content	Motivate pupils to persist in a task that requires no overt activity
Self-testing	Answering practice questions about previously learned content	Ensure pupils take repeat tests with feedback and that the practice test is very similar to the final tests Works best when it supports the retention of facts and concepts rather than applying knowledge
Self-explaining	Asking pupils to explain the content of a lesson to themselves during learning	Self-explanation can be applied to texts, diagrams or worked examples It supports pupils in generating inferences from content and metacognitive awareness
Teaching	Improving one's own understanding of previous content though teaching it to others	Works best if pupils are aware that they will go on to teach the content to others, and pupils are required to represent the content rather than restate it Teaching activities are the basis for many classroom tasks
Enacting	Engaging in task-relevant movements during learning	Concrete manipulatives can help promote the transfer of knowledge Make sure that pupils can connect how movements relate to abstract principles in the subject

Key Takeaways

- Think about what your pupils will do in terms of how the planned activity will ask them to select, organise and integrate the main ideas of the curriculum content.
- Think of active learning in terms of cognitive processes.
- Consider which of the eight learning strategies can be used to shape a lesson activity.

Tasks and Activities: Task Design

The theory of task design arises from the work of Vygotsky and has been developed by Walter Doyle, Professor Emeritus at the University of Arizona. He states: 'The tasks a teacher defines for a lesson or unit shape how pupils engage intellectually with the content of the curriculum, what tools and strategies they learn to use with this content, and what learning capacities they take away from these curriculum encounters' (Doyle, 2015: xiii). The aim of the task design is that pupils develop a higher-level understanding of the content. For the teacher, this involves:

- identifying the purpose of the task
- the resources or materials available
- which types of teaching and intervention allow pupils to process the information as they work their way through the task activities

Task design links with generative learning in that the emphasis of task design is active participation. It concerns the processes of pupils' learning. As a new teacher, when you design a task, you might ask yourself four questions:

1 What matters in the subject I am teaching?
2 How will tasks and activities help pupils to engage with the concepts of the subject?
3 How can I make the task demanding?
4 What are the processes of internalisation (when new knowledge becomes part of a schema) and externalisation (when knowledge is used to solve problems or applied in new situations) of the subjects' concepts that the tasks and activities require?

In this way, your task design links with your subject knowledge, and through the tasks you set, you introduce your pupils to the concepts of the subject and demonstrate how they connect to pupils' everyday experience of those concepts. The process of the intertwining of these two sorts of concepts, Scientific (i.e. to be taught in school) and everyday (pupils' everyday understanding of the world), is key to gaining understanding of the subject: pupils gain understanding of the abstract aspects of the subject, and the abstract aspects of the subject merge into how your pupils now see the world because their previous everyday experience has been enhanced by the new understanding (i.e. they have been 'changed' by learning).

However, although it can be difficult for new teachers to identify the abstract concepts that make up the content of the subject, they must also pay attention to the nature of the pupils' everyday knowledge, because without this awareness they will not be able to design tasks that enable pupils to merge the new and old experiences into understanding. As a new teacher, there are several questions you can ask yourself as you design tasks to help you do this:

1 How will the pupils' everyday understandings *be used* in the task?
2 What talk and language will pupils' *draw on* as their action in the activity?

Alexander (2000) explained the way in which teachers should distinguish between task and activity. The task is concerned with the cognitive demand that will bring about learning, whereas the activity can be thought of as the way these cognitive demands are presented for the purpose of teaching. By working with their peers and with you, your pupils will, by completing an activity, grasp and use the subject concepts. In other words, the activity demands that they think hard for themselves, but that this occurs by working with others in the classroom. Accomplishing a task, then, is not just about the subject content; it is also about the types of thinking and the situation that the activity creates. Doyle (1983) argues that there are two consequences of such task accomplishment:

1 The pupil acquires new information (in the form of facts, concepts, principles or solutions).
2 The pupil practises certain cognitive operations (in the form of memorising, classifying, inferring or analysing).

This new information or practice of cognitive operations is developed because the pupil has to obtain or produce the new information demanded by the activities in the task. In other words, your design of tasks and their related activities has the long-term aim of ensuring that pupils have to work things out for themselves while working with others in a classroom. In this way, pupils develop greater awareness of their own learning process *and* how their knowledge of the world is expanding.

Quadrant Model of Task Design

Anne Edwards, Professor Emerita at the University of Oxford, developed a quadrant model to help new teachers understand how to sequence tasks so that pupils not only internalise what they have been taught but, through their engagement with activities as part of the learning task, are also able to externalise (use and apply) their more mature understanding of the subject content (Edwards, 2015). In her quadrant model quadrants 1 and 4 are where knowledge is on display. In quadrant 1, the teacher displays knowledge by modelling and instructing. In quadrant 4, the pupils display knowledge in some form of summative assessment. Poor teaching is frequently characterised as the direct move from quadrant 1 to 4 because pupils have not had the chance to acquire or apply the knowledge for themselves.

Quadrant 2 is where pupils begin to work in highly structured ways with subject content. They take some control over it and explore what they can do with it. In quadrant 3, that same knowledge becomes a resource that pupils can deploy and test in problem-solving activities. By doing so, pupils begin to grasp the potential and limitations of what they know and are more firmly connected to a readjusted knowledge schema and the system of inferences that go with it.

Edwards' quadrant model points out the advantages of taking time in tasks and activities in lessons to enable pupils to both acquire and use – internalise and externalise – the substantive knowledge (the key concepts) and the syntactic knowledge (thinking like a subject expert who is able to infer, evaluate evidence and consider cause and effect) of the subject content.

The model is useful because it:

- points to the need for teachers to see learning as the pupils increasing their control of the subject content while also developing as learners themselves
- helps teachers to identify the different types of tasks required in each quadrant
- helps teachers to identify how their role as teacher changes in each quadrant
- helps teachers to identify where formative assessment can help to guide pupils' engagement

It is important to recognise the significance of quadrant 3. Quadrant 3 is a challenging stage in the sequence of learning for both pupils and teachers. This is because it is the point when pupils move into open-ended problem-solving activities, where they are trying to take control of the knowledge they have only just begun to grasp and use it to solve problems or to tackle rather more complex tasks. Consequently, the role of the teacher changes in quadrant 3. In this stage, most of the teacher's effort goes into planning the task, identifying at least some of the resources that can be used to engage pupils, and ensuring that pupils are able to use the strategies that will help them pursue, rather than be afraid of, the demands of the tasks. As a teacher, you are then positioned as a resource who is able to respond to pupils' questions and intervene if pupils are overwhelmed by the task.

However, it is important to note that both quadrants 2 and 3 need to be safe places for learning, where mistakes can be made, misunderstandings revealed and risks taken. It is therefore important to recognise and prepare for the social aspects of task and activity design because they can support the more emotional aspects of learning, such as dealing with mistakes and misunderstandings and what feels risky.

Using the quadrant model when thinking about task design will support you in two ways:

- being aware of the demands you make of pupils in the tasks you set
- being better able to position yourself as a resource to support learning

Key Takeaways

- Understanding the nature of the tasks and activities you design allows you to better support your pupils' metacognitive processes as learners. Good design of tasks and activities create active, aware and agentic learners.
- Careful task design moves pupils from partial understanding to the confident use of subject concepts. It also supports pupils' engagement, self-regulation and metacognitive awareness.
- Designing tasks is an opportunity for you to be both creative and to use your professional judgement as a teacher.
- Thinking about how what your pupils will do in a lesson helps them to learn the curriculum content.

Guided and Independent Practice

Rather than think about what pupils will do in lessons as activities and tasks, some teachers plan in terms of what pupils will practise. Perhaps, at one time, this way of thinking may only have been applied to practical subjects such as PE, music, art or technology, where pupils are practising particular skills, but it is now applied more widely to teaching and learning. The concept of practice, as applied to lesson planning, has arisen from four different theoretical sources, each of which sheds slightly different light on how you can think about what your pupils will do in the lesson. Each of the four approaches converges on two common points: how to use practice to support the learning of your pupils and, linked to this, what your role is when your pupils are practising?

Guided and Independent Practice: Rosenshine

In his principles of effective teaching, Rosenshine (2010, 2012) mentions 'practice' five times:

1 Present new material in small steps with pupil practice after each step.
2 Provide a high level of active practice for all pupils.
3 Guide pupils as they begin to practise.
4 Prepare pupils for independent practice.
5 Monitor pupils when they begin independent practice.

Rosenshine (2010) focuses on guiding pupil practice (Principle 5) and independent practice (Principle 9). Indeed, the term 'Requiring and monitoring independent practice' was coined by Rosenshine, and has since become part of teachers' professional language. The term 'guided practice' has been widely used since the 1980s. Rosenshine argues that the research suggests that:

> although most teachers provided some guided practice, the most successful teachers spent more time in guided practice, more time asking questions, more time checking for understanding, more time correcting errors and more time having pupils work out problems with teacher guidance. (Rosenshine, 2010: 17)

He states that the most successful teachers follow such guided practice with independent practice 'because a good deal of practice (overlearning) is needed in order to become fluent and automatic in a skill' (2010: 24). He mentions the need to become fluent in knowing facts and concepts for subsequent learning as well as the operations used to problem solve in subjects such as maths, science and language. It is important to appreciate that a link should exist between the content of guided and independent practice:

> The more-successful teachers provided for extensive and successful practice, both in the classroom and after class. *Independent practice should involve the same material as the guided practice.* If guided practice dealt with identifying types of sentences, then independent practice should deal with the same topic or, perhaps, with creating individual compound in complex sentences. It would be inappropriate if this guided practice contained an independent practice assignment that asked pupils do activities such as 'Write a paragraph using two compound and two complex practice sentences' because the pupils have not been adequately prepared for such an activity. *Pupils need to be prepared for their independent practice.* (Rosenshine, 2010: 24, emphasis added)

I Do, We Do, You Do: Gradual Release of Responsibility Model

The teaching strategy of *I do, we do, you do* was created by Doug Fisher and Nancy Frey, Professors of Language and Literacy at San Diego State University, in 2006. It was developed to support teachers to teach all aspects of reading and writing effectively. This teaching approach was developed from the Gradual Release of Responsibility (GRR) model, which was introduced by P David Pearson (Professor of Curriculum and Instruction at the University of Illinois) and fellow researcher Margaret C Gallagher (1983). The GRR model was originally applied to teaching reading comprehension, but is now used in all aspects of teaching and learning.

The GRR model arose from research to identify an effective way of teaching reading comprehension, following earlier research by Durkin (1978–1979) that showed that rather than teaching pupils how to understand, teachers simply required their pupils to answer questions. In other words, the teaching of comprehension was just asking and answering questions. The problem Pearson and Gallagher (1983) identified with this approach was that it perpetuated the gap between those who can and those who cannot answer the question.

As a form of practice, it did not help those who could not answer the question to refine what they were doing, nor did it help those who could not answer the question improve what they could not do. GRR was developed to support effective teaching by seeking to meet the needs of individual and small groups of pupils (rather than as a whole-class strategy) through targeted and individualised teaching. It requires the teacher to shift from assuming all the responsibility of the task to a situation in which the pupils assume all of the responsibility. As such, Pearson and Gallagher's GRR grew out of Vygotsky's work (1978) and his Zone of Proximal Proximity. Three concepts from the Gradual Release of Responsibility model have become key ideas for teachers:

1 Modelling – where the teacher or another pupil demonstrates how to do the task.
2 Guided practice – where the teacher and the pupil are sometimes jointly and sometimes separately responsible for enacting different steps in completing the task.
3 Independent practice – where the teacher has, at least for the moment, completely released responsibility to the pupil(s). (Pearson et al., 2019)

Fisher and Frey (2006) first identified that, as a teaching strategy, the GRR model could be understood in terms of four interactive and interrelated components in the teaching of reading. In the first two, the teacher has responsibility:

1 Focus lessons – in which teachers model their own metacognitive process as active readers. They model strategies that focus on increasing understanding of content of the text. Usually brief in nature, in focus lessons, the teacher establishes the purposes for reading and points pupils towards important learning objectives.
2 Guided instruction – in which teachers prompt, question, facilitate or lead pupils through tasks that increase understanding of a particular text.

Pupils assume responsibility in the remaining two components:

3 Collaborative learning – pupils consolidate their understanding of the content and explore opportunities to problem solve, discuss, negotiate and think with their peers.
4 Independent learning – this component is seen as the most important goal of good teaching. It allows pupils to practise applying skills and information in new ways. As pupils transfer their learning to subsequent tasks, they synthesise information, transform ideas and solidify their understanding. They become active readers and capable learners (Fisher and Frey, 2006).

Fisher and Frey (2008) developed their notion of the four components, representing them as:

- Focus lesson – I do it
- Guided Instruction – We do it
- Collaborative learning – You do it together
- Independent learning – You do it alone

Fisher and Frey (2006, 2008) argue that the most important point for the teacher to remember about both three elements of the Gradual Release of Responsibility model (I do, we do, you do) and their development of it into a the four-pronged teaching strategy is that neither the model nor the 'I do, we do, you do' is a linear approach to whole-class teaching. Rather, the pupils move back and forth between the components as they master skills, strategies and the curriculum content in small groups or in individual work. The GRR model differs from current permutations of modelling and practising 'I do, we do, you do' in that there are four components to the strategy (instead of three) and the 'we do' phase in Fisher and Frey (2008) has two distinct aspects: 'we do it' and 'you do it together'. In the 'we do it' phase practice is guided by the teacher, but in the 'you do it together' phase the pupils work together on a practice activity collaboratively. It is also important to remember that 'I do, we do and you do' is not simply endless repetition of the same learning point but centres around the responsibility for applying their understanding shifting to the pupils.

I Do, You Help: Natural Learning Theory

Don Holdaway (1930-2004) had global influence on how we teach children to read. He introduced both the practice of shared reading and the use of Big Books (Holdaway, 1979). Based in Auckland, New Zealand, his work began when he was asked to develop teaching techniques to support Maori children who were learning to read in traditional school settings. He noticed that while these children appeared to struggle to learn to read in school, they had mastered a complex language and clearly had many linguistic abilities. He realised that the developmental and natural processes of learning could be usefully applied to how children learn to read at school, and this was the starting point from which he developed his model. His model recognised the significance of children's natural aspirations to want to learn. He built on it by replicating the profound impact of the social experience of the bedtime story on children's reading ability and motivation (Holdaway, 1979).

Holdaway's model was linked to the way children learn naturally and socially with their parents and carers in that it identified and replicated the four phases of such learning sequences:

1 Demonstration – the child watches what the adult is doing.
2 Participation – the child joins in alongside the adult as they perform an activity.
3 Role play/practice – the child practises, and the adult enables and supports the child's efforts.
4 Performance – the child performs to the adult, who is an audience ('Watch me!') enjoying and validating the child's accomplishment.

Holdaway's learning model aligns with other forms of scaffolding (see Chapter 11), and his work on shared reading has expanded beyond helping children to read. It is also used in understanding how to teach all areas of knowledge and the skills that children need to learn in school. The processes of natural learning theory, in terms of the role of the teacher and the

4 You do, I watch	**1** I do, you watch
3 You do, I help	**2** I do, you help

Figure 10.1 The role of the teacher and pupil in natural learning theory

pupil, is summarised in Figure 10.1. Quadrant 1 describes the teacher explaining or modelling to the class (in the case of reading the teacher reads the book and the pupils watch and listen). In Quadrant 2 the children join in with aspects of the reading or tasks, but the reading is led by the teacher. In Quadrant 3, the children are reading and this time the teacher is providing assistance and support especially in terms of comprehension. Finally, in Quadrant 4, the pupils are able to read fluently, and the teacher is now listening.

The driving question that this model addresses is the key question parents and teachers ask themselves about their role in learning: 'What can my child (pupil) accomplish with assistance?'. In terms of pupils practising in the classroom, this model differs from 'I do, we do, you do' because, as with the work of Fisher and Frey (2008), the approach as four, not three phases. It is also important to note that the learning process is not sequential and linear; just as between parents and children, it is likely that much time will be spent moving between 'I do, you help' and 'you do, I help' as the child learns. The word 'help' is also significant because Holdaway's model acknowledges that when children are learning something complex (like reading), it will take time and the goal may not be complete mastery of every small step. Rather, the goal is reached by building up experience and expertise over quite long periods of time, through practice and familiarity.

Retrieval, Spaced and Interleaving Practice: Cognitive Science

Theories from cognitive science provide principles that may be applied to teaching and learning. Applied cognitive science is more limited and complex and the 'applications of cognitive science, while fully plausible given the basic science, are yet to be fully tested and found effective in the classroom' (Education Endowment Foundation (EEF), 2021: 7). Among the approaches teachers apply in their classroom, three relate to what you might plan for your pupils to do in your lesson in terms of practice, and what content they might practice. The three concepts are:

1 Retrieval practice – using a variety of strategies to recall information from memory (e.g. flash cards, practice tests or quizzing, or mind-mapping).
2 Spaced practice – spacing out retrieval practices over a longer period of time, rather than only doing them in one concentrated period of time.
3 Interleaving practice – switching between different types of problems or ideas within the same lesson or session.

In *retrieval practice*, you will remind pupils of previous learning rather than ask your pupils to recall it themselves. The strategy requires pupils to think hard about what they have retained and can recall. In other words, it tests for learning rather than recapping the information. Thus, it can be a better teaching strategy because retrieval practice will encourage your pupils to strengthen their memory on key concepts and information. It also helps both you and them to identify gaps in knowledge that can be retaught. Retrieval practice usually takes the form of:

- Multiple choice questions
- Short-answer fact questions
- Short problem-solving
- True/false questions
- Labelling diagrams
- Image recognition
- Recitation of quotes
- List creation (EEF, 2012: 21)

Spaced practice is a form of retrieval practice where content is revisited not at one time, but spaced over a lesson or a number of days, weeks and months, with unrelated content learning and activities taking place in-between. Spaced practice needs to be organised and planned by the teacher because there can seem to be little opportunity to revisit previous content and school timetables are often organised in blocks or units that can appear to work against revisiting content.

Interleaving is when the teacher teaches several topics at the same time so that pupils have to switch between the two topics leading to better retention. Spaced practice is when the teacher breaks down the topic but teachers it over time and in between time teaches totally different topics. The idea here is that it increases the likelihood of information being embedded in their long-term memory. In this way it is thought to support pupils in making comparisons and solving problems where pupils select strategies to generate solutions. It is important to note that much of the evidence of the effectiveness of interleaving practice has been focused on the teaching and learning of maths.

Retrieval, spaced and interleaving practice can help you to think about what content, when and which form of practice you may wish to use when you plan what your pupils will do in your lesson.

Key Takeaways

- You may want to think about how to plan what your pupils will do in your lesson in terms of what your pupils will be practising.
- Ensure that your pupils have lots of opportunities to apply what they have learned because, typically, teachers neither plan for enough practice nor devote sufficient time for pupils to practise deeply enough.
- It is also important to ensure that:
  - pupils get time in your lessons to practise independently (in some classes this never actually happens)

- ○ you stand back and resist the urge to step in and interfere.
- ○ some of the opportunities to practice occur in small groups as well as with individual pupils.
- Plan the way that time is used in your lesson so that you do not move from your input to them 'doing' the task, but to allow time for pupils to practise with your help. This is because pupils need time to grapple with the lesson content for themselves.

Conclusion

Many of the concepts and theories summarised in this chapter link with the notion that in teaching you are assisting so that pupils learn. It is useful to think about designing activities that require pupils to make something with the knowledge you have previously taught them, since, as a consequence, learning is generated. It is important to plan lessons that do not move from your input straight to pupils doing something for assessment purposes. Rather, when you plan a lesson, you should plan for guided practice, led by you, to take place as much as possible. Edwards' (2015) quadrant and the work of Fisher and Frey (2006, 2008) and Holdaway (1979), indicate that you should plan your lessons so as to spend as much time as possible letting pupils engage in practice, guided by you. As a teacher, you have an important role to play, and whichever approach you adopt, they all emphasise the significance of lesson planning that enables pupils to think hard, integrate and apply what they are learning.

References

Alexander, R (2000) *Culture and Pedagogy: International Comparisons in Primary Education.* Oxford: Blackwell

Banting, N (2022) The mathematical power of building to specifications. Paper presented at the British Columbia Association of Mathematics Teachers (BCAMT) Fall Conference, Whistler, BC, October

Doyle, W (1983) Academic work. *Review of Educational Research* 53, 159–199

Doyle, W (2015) *Designing Tasks in Secondary Education: Enhancing subject understanding and student engagement*, Thompson I (Ed). Thompson Routledge

Durkin, D (1978-1979) What classroom observations reveal about reading comprehension instruction. *Reading Research Quarterly* 14, 481–533

Edwards, A (2015) Engaging learners with knowledge. In Thompson, I. (Ed.), *Designing Tasks in Secondary Education: Enhancing Subject Understanding and Student Engagement.* London: Routledge

Education Endowment Foundation (EEF) (2021) *Cognitive Science Approaches in the Classroom: A Review of the Evidence.* London: EEF

Fiorella, L and Meyer, RE (2015) *Learning as a Generative Activity: Eight Learning Strategies that Promote Understanding*. Cambridge: Cambridge University Press

Fisher, D and Frey, N (2006) *Language Arts Workshop: Purpose for Reading and Writing Instruction.* Upper Saddle River, NJ: Merrill Prentice Hall

Fisher, D and Frey, N (2008) *Better Learning through Structured Teaching: A Framework for the Gradual Release of Responsibility*. Alexandria, VA: Association for Supervision and Curriculum Development

Holdaway, D (1979) *The Foundations of Literacy*. Portsmouth, NH: Heinemann Educational Books

Pearson, PD and Gallagher, MC (1983) The instruction of reading comprehension. *Contemporary Educational Psychology* 8, 317–344

Pearson, D, McVee, M, and Shanahan, L (2019) In the beginning: The historical and conceptual genesis of the gradual release of responsibility. In McVee, M, Ortleib, J, Reichenberg, J, and Pearson, D (Eds.), *The Gradual Release of Responsibility in Literacy and Practice* (pp. 1–21). Bingley: Emerald

Rosenshine, B (2010) *Principles of Instruction: Education Practices Series – 21*. Geneva: UNESCO International Bureau of Education

Rosenshine, B (2012) Principles of instruction: Research-based strategies that all teachers should know. *American Educator* Spring, 12–18

Vygotsky, L S (1978) *Mind in Society:The Development of Higher Psychological processes* Cambridge, MA: Harvard University Press

11
HOW TO PLAN FOR SCAFFOLDING AND MODELLING

Why is It Important to Plan for Scaffolding and Modelling?

Scaffolding and modelling are the basis of teaching because they are the main ways in which teachers provided guidance (modelling) and assistance (scaffolding) to their pupils. These words are also the first two professional words that become part of a new teacher's vocabulary. However, while these words are widely used by all types of teachers with different amounts of experience, fewer teachers have a solid understanding of what they mean in precise and specific terms and where they have come from in educational theory, evidence and research. By understanding exactly what these words signify, your use of them as teaching strategies is more likely to accurately reflect these important ideas about teaching, and consequently your teaching will be more effective and have a bigger impact on how your pupils learn.

What is Scaffolding?

Although many books and articles written for teachers talk about modelling, and emphasise in particular the use of worked examples, it is important to understand that *modelling is a form of scaffolding*. Scaffolding is a metaphor to describe the teacher's use of a verbal or written *temporary adaptive support* that enables the pupil to make progress towards becoming able to complete a task independently. The term and process were first identified by David Wood, Jerome Bruner and Gail Ross in 1976. They wanted to understand more about how an adult or expert helps someone. Specifically, they wanted to understand the process of tutoring between an adult and a child as they acquire skills and solve problems. Rather than approach this research with a hypothesis about how it might or should happen, they set up a problem-solving task (stacking 21 bricks into a pyramid) for 30 3-, 4- and 5-year-olds, which they closely observed. They noticed that children at different ages responded differently to the task (as you might expect given the developmental differences of 3-, 4- and 5-year-olds), but they also noticed that the teachers responded to three types of behaviour:

1 If the child ignored the task and just started to play, they would present pairs of bricks as mini-constructions to get them started.
2 If the child started the task, but overlooked a feature, the teacher would use a verbal cue to get them back on task.
3 If the child constructed the pyramid as had been demonstrated to them, the teacher would allow them to self-correct any errors.

Consequently, Wood et al. (1976) defined scaffolding as when a teacher helps a child to do actions that have a recognisable-to-the-pupil solution – the teacher helps the child to recognise where their learning is leading. They recognised that for a child to learn, they must be able to recognise the solution to the problem before they are able to solve the problem for themselves without assistance. The child must understand the end of the task as well as the process for completing the task: 'comprehension precedes production' (Wood et al., 1976: 94).

They also identified that to be an effective teacher, the teacher needs to focus on two things at the same time: first, the structure and solution of the problem to be solved, and second, the child's current conception of the structure and solution of the problem to be solved. Without bearing both ideas in mind, the teacher will not be able to generate feedback or devise situations to help the child get better at the task at that precise moment. In other words, teaching is dependent on both the task and the child, and the process of teaching is generated by the teacher thinking about both.

Wood, Bruner and Ross (1976) were able to provide a close definition of scaffolding, which they described in terms of six functions and their relation to teaching:

1 *Recruitment* – the teacher must elicit their pupils' interest in the task and the skills needed to complete it.
2 *Reduction in degrees of freedom* – the teacher must break the task down into very small steps. The steps must be small enough so that the pupil is able to see the right next step and an obviously wrong one.
3 *Direction maintenance* – the teacher must keep the pupils interested in and focused on the task, especially when a pupil might want to stay at the easy stage of the task that they can already do with confidence.
4 *Marking critical features* – the teacher should mark out or emphasise the key milestones in the task to make it clear to the pupil what is different between what they are doing now and will do next.

5 *Frustration control* – the teacher should be empathetic to the frustration of the pupil doing something they cannot yet do, but critically, this must not take the form of making the task easier because the pupils will develop too much dependency on the adults.
6 *Demonstrating* – the good teacher must not only model possible solutions to any task, but also perform an 'idealised' version of the task so that the pupil can copy those steps. The teacher imitates an idealised form of the solution to be attempted by the pupils with the aim that the pupil will be more able to closely imitate it.

As a teacher, to scaffold properly you need to:

- show patience and empathy
- hold two mental models: your own mental model of the problem to be solved and the pupils' mental model of the problem to be solved
- show the pupil the differences between where they are now in solving the problem and the solved problem
- know when to change the support you are offering the pupil so that they progress in solving the problem or completing the task

Scaffolding: The Link to Vygotsky

Although Vygotsky researched and wrote in Russia in the early 1930s, his work was not translated into English and widely known in the West until the early 1970s. Since then, many people have taken up his ideas and used them to explain aspects of teaching and learning. It is a common misconception to assume that it was Vygotsky who first devised and used the term scaffolding. He did not. Bruner adopted the metaphor from some of Vygotsky's colleagues, who were still working in Russia 30 years after Vygotsky's death, and, with Woods and Ross, applied it to their work (Woods et al., 1976) (Schvarts and Bakker, 2019).

The myth that the term scaffolding has come from Vygotsky is probably because of the way it is often merged with Vygotsky's Zone of Proximal Development (ZPD), which is the specific range of tasks that can be accomplished by a pupil with the help of the adult but lies beyond the capabilities of the pupil alone. The metaphor of the ZPD is concerned with the pupil's development: 'the distance between the actual development level as determined by independent problem solving and the level of potential development as determined through problem solving under adult guidance or in collaboration with more capable peers' (Vygotsky, 1978: 86). However, scaffolding is a part of the practice of the teacher. Researchers have used both metaphors to help explain the other (Schvarts and Bakker, 2019). There are five important points to consider from this research into scaffolding and the ZPD that will help you plan your scaffolding better:

1 Scaffolding tends to be used to address a brief episode of teaching, which comes to an end with the gradual withdrawal of scaffolding (Smagorinsky, 2018), although long-term scaffolding can continue until independence is achieved (Smit and Van Eerde, 2013).

2 Scaffolding is a process of teaching within the ZPD and, as a result, the pace of learning is far quicker (Woods et al., 1976).
3 A period of self-scaffolding follows the gradual withdrawal of external support by the teacher as the pupil practises the skill many times until the skill becomes automatic and the self-scaffolding is no longer needed (Schvarts and Bakker, 2019).
4 Scaffolding links to metacognition because the pupil mimics the teacher's 'think-alouds' until they become internalised by the pupil and part of how they self-regulate their own behaviour (Bickhard, 2005).
5 The gradual withdrawal of scaffolding should not be thought of as the removal of support by the teacher, but as the pupils appropriating the function for themselves (Zavershneva and Van der Veer, 2018).

Scaffolding: The Link to Rosenshine

In the 1990s, Barak Rosenshine was a professor of educational psychology at the University of Illiniois and Carla Meister was a local teacher and one of his PhD students. In the 1990s, they wrote three articles together, two of which (1992, 1994) shaped his highly influential *Principles of Instruction* (Rosenshine, 2010, 2012).

Rosenshine drew on constructivism to explain how learning happens: that learners actively construct knowledge rather than just passively taking in information and, as such, are active participants in the creation of their own knowledge. Rosenshine and Meister developed the theoretical framework for their research from Vygotsky's ZPD and Wood, Bruner and Ross's (1976) work on scaffolds. Subsequently, from their empirical research into the effective teaching, they developed the concepts of reciprocal teaching (also called guided practice) and cognitive strategies (the specific strategies pupils can use to solve problems, write or develop their reading comprehension) (Rosenshine and Meister, 1992, 1994).

Although Rosenshine does not explicitly mention scaffolding in his 17 teaching processes, it does feature in his eighth principle of instruction: 'Provide scaffolds for difficult tasks – the teacher provides pupils with temporary supports and scaffolds to assist them when they learn difficult tasks' (Rosenshine, 2010:8, 22). In this principle, scaffolding includes modelling (the steps taken by the teacher or their think-alouds as they solve the problem) or the use of tools (e.g. cue cards or checklists that finish the task for the pupil or model the completed task so that pupils can check their own finished work). Specifically, he lists six strategies that teachers should include in their lesson plans:

1 Provide prompts for the steps that may be used. For reading, these may be 'who', 'why' and 'how.
2 Write the title of what is being read. Skim read for the 4–6 main ideas and then find and add two or more important details.
3 Think aloud to show your thought processes so that pupils can observe the expert thinking that they can't usually access. Teachers can also ask pupils to think aloud as they problem-solve.

4 Show and discuss the mistakes and errors commonly made by pupils.
5 Devise and model how to use a checklist by which pupils can evaluate their completed work.
6 Show pupils very good models of the work that pupils are completing so that they can compare their own work with it.

Sherrington (2019), in his booklet *Rosenshine's Principles in Action*, suggests five ways in which a teacher can provide scaffolds for difficult tasks. As a teacher, you can plan to use the following:

1 Writing frames as sentence openers and answering questions.
2 Paragraph structures – PEE (Point–Evidence–Explain), PETAL (Point–Evidence–Technique–Analyse–Link) and SQuID (Statement–Quotation–Inference–Development).
3 An example produced by previous pupils or by the teacher, from which pupils identify strengths and areas for improvement.
4 Strategic thinking – labelling a task or problem so that pupils can identify the next steps in a process.
5 Anticipated common errors and misconceptions – highlighting these as potential pitfalls for pupils and using them as a checklist for self-checking and self-correcting by pupils.

Scaffolding: The Link to Lemov

Doug Lemov is Managing Director of Uncommon Schools, a charity that leads 44 schools in the USA. He has written three books under the heading *Teach Like a Champion* (2010, 2015, 2021), which describe 49, 62 and 63 teaching techniques that he observed effective teachers using. *Teach Like a Champion* (TLAC) is not a system of teaching, but a collection of concrete, specific and actionable techniques that teachers can select and try out in the classroom.

Three of his techniques address how a teacher may scaffold:

- Name the steps – break down complex tasks into steps that form a path to mastery (Lemov, 2010)
- Board to paper – model and shape how pupils should take notes in order to capture the information teachers present (Lemov, 2021)
- Group discussion – sometimes allow the pupils to discuss a topic without teacher mediation. Lemov calls this a 'batch process' [as the technique centres on selected groups of pupils forming a 'batch' of their own ideas before the teacher gives feedback] (Lemov, 2021)

'Name (take) the steps', which corresponds to Rosenshine's second principle: (Rosenshine, 2010, 2012) involves breaking complex tasks into simple steps so that pupils are encouraged to explore the question out loud: what is the process? Lemov advises not only deciding the steps yourself before teaching, but also giving each step a memorable name. When teaching, you should switch between solving the immediate problem or completing the task and reflecting on the process being used (which he calls the 'two stairways') so that pupils pay attention to both product and process.

'Board to paper' concerns modelling how pupils should make notes. Young children should learn to copy the teacher's notes, first by filling in blank spaces in a graphic organiser, and then by copying them on to a blank page. Needless to say, the teacher's version should show exactly how the notes should be presented. Your scaffolding should focus on how to make headings, subheadings, lists and mnemonics. A 'board to paper' sheet is not a worksheet, he argues, because its purpose is to scaffold pupils into the critical skill of making their own notes for learning.

Lemov's 'batch process' is a technique teachers can use as they scaffold pupils towards working autonomously in class and group discussion (Lemov, 2021). Rather than comment every time a pupil speaks, your action is to allow batches of pupil exchanges before you comment. The aim is not that pupils talk more, but that the exchanges between pupils are more useful and productive. Lemov suggests that this type of talk is scaffolded by you in two ways: you decide who will be involved in the exchanges and you use this technique as part of a short, daily activity (some schools begin by using the 'batch process' technique for one minute in every lesson and then build up).

Key Takeaways

- Scaffolding is a temporary adaptive support that the teacher provides until the pupils are able to complete the task for themselves. The task is shared until that point, which links to the model of Gradual Release of Responsibility (Fisher and Frey, 2008).
- Scaffolding in teaching can be understood as the transfer of the scaffolding function from external help (by the teacher) into internal help as the pupil refers to the voice in their head rather than just copying the teacher (metacognition and self-regulation by the pupil).
- Different pupils need different guidance when solving a problem or learning a task, and paying attention to each pupil's difference in competence (the relative breadth of each pupil's ZPD) will signpost you to what teaching is required next.
- Pupils must master a low-level skill before moving on to a skill at the next level.
- Your scaffolding will help pupils learn faster and achieve more.

What is Modelling?

Modelling was first identified by Wood, Bruner and Ross (1976) as something the teacher does as a way to scaffold learning, although they used the term 'demonstration' instead of 'modelling'. Demonstration was their sixth scaffolding function, and they defined it as being more than the teacher performing the task in front of their pupils. It involves the teacher not only showing how to undertake or complete a task, but also highlighting the key ideas involved. Importantly, the goal of demonstrating/modelling is not that the pupil then immediately tries to imitate what the teacher has just shown them. Rather, modelling works by helping the pupils to understand the solution of a problem or the completion of a task. Indeed, Wood et al.

argued that pupils cannot adequately imitate a task when they have no understanding of the end of the process.

Modelling is key to offering clear explanations and can take three forms:

1. Live modelling (often called think-aloud) – where the teacher narrates undertaking the task or solving the problem by talking through their decisions and choices so that internal debate and implicit processes are made explicit. In this way, the pupils gain insight into how an historian, scientist, artist or writer might think. The teacher can also use live modelling to reveal the way an effective learner might reflect as they work by asking 'why' and 'how' questions at each step and then explaining the answer out loud. An interactive whiteboard or a visualiser are good tools to use when you undertake live modelling.
2. A worked example – a step-by-step demonstration of how to perform a task or solve a problem. Worked examples can be used in displays around the classroom not only to convey your high expectations, but also as exemplars for what your pupils are learning. The goal is to provide pupils with many worked examples so that general patterns become clear. Over time, less fully worked examples can be used, leaving the pupils with more to complete. Showing pupils examples of good work also helps pupils to gain understanding of both the product and the process. Sherrington (2019) suggests that effective teachers use examples more frequently and use more examples than new teachers when they teach.
3. A conceptual model – a concrete explanation or graphical representation of something that happens in the real world.

'Provide models' is the fourth of Rosenshine's ten *Principles of Instruction* (2010, 2012). He suggests that teachers use worked examples (or, as he terms them, worked-out examples) as models because they provide pupils with cognitive support. They are effective because they allow pupils to concentrate on one step at a time. He also advocates two uses of prompts by the teacher during guided practice:

1. The teacher can provide prompts for pupils to use to question themselves as they work.
2. The teacher can ask many questions from which the pupil selects a prompt to use for themselves.

Key Takeaways

- While modelling can take up teaching time, it is a very good use of time.
- Showing pupils what it is they are trying to achieve and how to achieve it means that pupils get to spend more time synthesising and applying what they are learning.
- Modelling is also a huge motivator for your pupils because they can clearly see what it is they are being asked to do.

Conclusion

Research into the most effective primary school teachers shows that they adapt every aspect of their classroom practice to the specific needs of the individual pupil in their classroom. They recognise their pupils' particular needs by developing a good understanding of all the pupils in their class. They then design, select, develop and deliver learning materials that are suitable for the pupils' range of identified needs. They scaffold the work set for them and the outcomes that they expect from them (Siraj et al., 2019).

Scaffolding is part of the cycle of teaching and learning in the classroom. It draws on your observation of your pupils for signs of confusion or uncertainty and your deep subject knowledge of how the curriculum gets progressively more complex through the key stages. It enables your pupils to integrate the key concepts of the specific subject with their everyday knowledge through tasks designed and supported by the teacher. The nature of the temporary adaptive support is to simplify the role of the learner in the task, not to simplify the task. Scaffolding reduces the extraneous load on your pupils' working memories and strengthens their schema, and it makes learning more efficient and manageable.

References

Bickhard, MH (2005) Functional scaffolding and self-scaffolding. *New Ideas in Psychology* 23(3), 166–173

Fisher, D and Frey, N (2008) *Better Learning through Structured Teaching: A Framework for the Gradual Release of Responsibility*. Alexandria, VA: Association for Supervision and Curriculum Development

Lemov, D (2010) *Teach Like a Champion: 49 Techniques that Put Students on the Path to College*. San Francisco, CA: Jossey-Bass

Lemov, D (2015) *Teach Like a Champion 2.0: 62 Techniques that Put Students on the Path to College*. San Francisco, CA: Jossey-Bass

Lemov, D (2021) *Teach Like a Champion 3.0: 63 techniques that Put Students on the Path to College*. San Francisco, CA: Jossey-Bass

Rosenshine, B (2010) *Principles of Instruction: Education Practices Series – 21*. Geneva: UNESCO International Bureau of Education

Rosenshine, B (2012) Principles of instruction: Research-based strategies that all teachers should know. *American Educator* Spring, 12–18

Rosenshine, B and Meister, C (1992) The use of scaffolds for teaching higher-level cognitive strategies. *Educational Leadership* 49(7), 26–33

Rosenshine, B and Meister, C (1994) Reciprocal teaching: A review of the research. *Review of Educational Research* 64(4), 479–530

Schvarts, A and Bakker, A (2019) The early history of the scaffolding metaphor: Bernstein, Luria, Vygtosky, and before. *Mind, Culture, and Activity* 26(1), 4–23

Sherrington, T (2019) *Rosenshine's Principles in Action*. Woodbridge: John Catt

Siraj, I, Taggart, B, Sammons, P, Melhuish, E, Sylva, K, and Shepherd, D (2019) *Teaching in Effective Primary Schools: Research into Pedagogy and Children's Learning*. London: UCL Institute of Education Press

Smagorinsky, P (2018) Deconflating the ZPD and instructional scaffolding: Retranslating and reconceiving the zone of proximal development as a zone of next development. *Learning, Culture, and Social Interaction* 16, 70–75

Smit, J and Van Eerde, D (2013) A conceptualisation of whole-class scaffolding. *British Educational Research Journal* 2(1), 22–31

Vygotsky, LS (1978) Interaction between learning and development. *Readings on the Development of Children* 30(3), 565–581

Wood, D, Bruner, J, and Ross, G (1976) The role of tutoring in problem solving. *The Journal of Child Psychology and Child Psychiatry* 17, 89–100

Zavershneva, E and Van der Veer, R (Eds.) (2018) *Vygotsky's Notebooks: Perspectives in Cultural-Historical Research* (Vol. 2). Singapore: Springer Nature

12 HOW TO PLAN SO THAT YOUR PUPILS REMEMBER WHAT YOU HAVE TAUGHT

Why is It Important That Your Pupils Remember Your Lessons?

One of the challenges of being a teacher is that there is just so much material to get through. The curriculum is full of content and is knowledge-rich, and there are continual cries in the media, and from various policy groups, that more and more issues should be addressed and taught in school. The consequence is that teachers feel under pressure to 'power on through' the curriculum and to just keep going forward – each day and each lesson tackling something new. This is known as 'massed or clustered practice where material is covered in a single lesson or a linear and sequential succession of learning' (Education Endowment Foundation (EEF), 2021: 15). However, the outcome to that approach is also frustrating because what you had taught, and thought you could count on your pupils knowing, is not remembered by them. This presents you with a dilemma – how should you ensure your pupils remember crucial content in the long term?

The best approach to the challenge of ensuring your pupils remember core knowledge in the long term is to build 'remembering' into your lesson planning. This is achieved by drawing on what we know about memory and learning to decide how and what you plan to revisit over time. The key message is to think about teaching the curriculum not in terms of moving forward in a straight line, but rather by spiralling upwards, while circling back and forth making links and connections. Indeed, it works better not to think about planning as making your lessons 'fun and engaging', but about making them 'memorable'.

Your long-term aims should be that:

- you plan lessons that incorporate repetition and build in emphasis so that pupils' understanding is deepened, and they are increasingly able to think in terms of the subject you are teaching

- you plan lessons that enable pupils to recall and retain what you have taught, and they have lots of opportunities to apply and use what they have learned in activities

Reflections

Reflecting on Recall

You may have taught a really good lesson, but what have the pupils retained? How do you know what they have retained? Do you support children with working memory issues?

Reflecting on Retention

Do you know what your pupils recall a couple of weeks after the lesson? What are your pupils retaining that can be applied in later lessons?

How Can Theories About Learning Help You Plan Memorable Lessons?

As a teacher, you can draw insights from several theories about learning to address the challenge of planning lessons so that your pupils will later remember what you have taught them. Table 12.1 summarises these insights, which were covered in detail in Part 1 of this book.

Table 12.1 Summary of educational theory that informs how to plan lessons that support pupils' memory

Theory	Key issue	Why it is important	Implications for your lesson planning
Cognitive Load Theory	Working memory (WM) capacity	WM has a limited capacity – you should be mindful not to overload pupils with too much information at once	Present new information in manageable chunks, allowing pupils the chance to process and transfer it to long-term memory effectively (by practising after each new step)
Cognitive Load Theory	Intrinsic and Extraneous Cognitive Load	Intrinsic Load is the inherent complexity of the material Extraneous Load is the unnecessary cognitive load imposed on your pupils by the approach you take to teaching the material	Minimise Extraneous Load to give learning the best chance Use clear and concise teaching materials, activities, explanations and questions to avoid pupils becoming confused or distracted

(Continued)

Table 12.1 Summary of educational theory that informs how to plan lessons that support pupils' memory (*Continued*)

Theory	Key issue	Why it is important	Implications for your lesson planning
Cognitive science	Spaced practice (also known as spaced learning, distributed practice and the spacing effect)	Spaced practice (revisiting key concepts, ideas or skills over longer periods of time) increases the likelihood of knowledge being embedded in pupils' long-term memory	Revisit a specific concept or idea several times during the course of one week or once or twice a week over many weeks You may wish to experiment with spacing within a lesson by breaking the lesson up into short intervals of time (say 10-minute slots) to revisit a key concept or idea over and again (but fill the space between the slots with unrelated material)
Schema Theory	Pupils organise information into mental frameworks or schemas (also known as scripts or mental models)	Build on pupils' existing schemas and connect new information to prior knowledge to help pupils remember	Introduce concepts in a structured manner and be very explicit in pointing out the connections to related ideas and previous learning Use comparisons and analogies to add depth or address misconceptions Require pupils to elaborate on and question concepts and ideas to strengthen, develop and transfer learning
Cognitive science	Retrieval practice involves the process of pupils recalling information from memory with little or no prompting	Testing learning (low-stake tests such as individual questions and quizzes) works better than restudying or recapping material	Design • Quizzes • Flashcards • Discussion prompts • Multiple choice questions • Short-answer fact questions • Short problem-solving • True/false questions • Labelling diagrams • Image recognition • Recitation of quotes and definitions • List creations
Constructivism	The constructivist approach emphasises active cognitive engagement (thinking hard) and pupil-led learning	Activities that encourage exploration, problem-solving and critical thinking (after knowledge has been taught) support remembering because they generate learning	Plan hands-on activities for your pupils to do that require them to connect their everyday knowledge with the curriculum material
Self-regulated learning	Teach metacognitive strategies	Guide pupils in setting goals, monitoring their understanding and reflecting on their progress	Provide opportunities for pupils to assess their understanding and to replan their next steps accordingly

(*Continued*)

Table 12.1 Summary of educational theory that informs how to plan lessons that support pupils' memory (*Continued*)

Theory	Key issue	Why it is important	Implications for your lesson planning
Motivation and affective factors	Consider the emotions of your pupils	Consider the affective factors of boredom, anxiety, enjoyment, anger, shame, pride and happiness, and which ones are experienced by pupils in your classroom Consider intrinsic (from within the pupil in terms of their interests, curiosity, feelings of interest, personal satisfaction and achievement) and extrinsic (from rewards, incentives and punishments) motivation and how to be aware of and use both side by side in your classroom	Connect the curriculum content to your pupils' personal interests, hobbies and achievements, and to real-world experience and events
Cultural-historical theory	Zone of Proximal Development	Challenge your pupils to work within their optimal learning range and design tasks so that they achieve an optimal success rate of about 80% (i.e. they were learning the material, but were also challenged at the same time)	Present material that is neither too easy nor too difficult Build in regular checks for understanding in both guided and independent practice so that you can evaluate the level of challenge (stopping the work if you realise your pupils are having difficulty and then making the next steps smaller and introducing more practice)

Which Sections of the Lesson Plan Help Pupils Remember What You Have Taught?

There are six components of a lesson plan that you can use to help your pupils remember. They occur at the beginning of the lesson, in its structure and through the climate for learning you create.

You establish your intentions for the lesson right at the beginning. This is why it is important to focus on lesson content and not to make general administrative tasks an unintentional focus of your lesson.

There are two aspects of your lesson plan that can ensure your lesson begins effectively:

1 Engage your pupils' prior knowledge because this helps them to make connections in their minds and is also a foundation for the new information to come. This is often achieved

by questioning or quizzing but, depending on the age of your class, it can involve them creating (or co-creating with you and the rest of the class/group) knowledge or graphic organisers to represent their current level of knowledge, skill and understanding.

2 Provide learning objectives that clearly and concisely communicate what they will learn today, why a particular activity is taking place, and how the current learning fits into the overall structure. You can also provide examples of the types of tasks, problems and questions pupils will be able to do.

There are two aspects of your lesson plan that structure the lesson to support remembering by your pupils:

1 Break the lesson down into more memorable chunks (e.g. of 10, 15 or 20 minutes) so that your hand is 'forced' into presenting information in small steps, followed by mini-activities that encourage pupils to practise what they have learned. This will also prompt you into organising the order in which you present the small steps into one that is most helpful for securing learning.
2 The small chunks or steps of your lesson provide you with an opportunity to repeat and review key concepts and how understanding of the concept is progressing and deepening during the lesson. It can be helpful to think of your lesson as containing lots of beginnings and endings (some teachers call these mini-plenaries).

There are two aspects of your lesson plan that support a climate for learning (sometimes called the learning environment) and they address the affective and motivation factors of learning:

1 Establish a consistent routine in your lessons by ensuring that pupils can predict the order of events throughout the day and the week. Share, teach and reinforce the routine so that pupils feel secure and develop a positive mindset that frees them up for learning (which can be stressful as well as exciting!).
2 Be aware of how long you expect children under the age of 11 to sit still in one place. Recognise their need for breaks, movement, change and variety. This is important because it supports pupils to improve their attention and to retain what they have learned.

Key Takeaways

- Spend time at the start of each lesson (say 3–8 minutes) discussing with the class: What will be new? What will be remembered? How will they use what they already know?
- Try starting each lesson with a daily review: 'What do we (now) know about x?'
- Use questioning and a variety of prompts to support pupils recalling and applying what they have learned.
- Do not always require pupils to share what they recall by writing it down. Think of other methods you can use.

- Support pupils to understand which bits of the lesson and tasks need to be remembered.
- Provide regular opportunities for pupils to revisit what they have learned to support their long-term understanding.
- Support pupils to see how different parts of the lesson relate to each other and fit together.
- Provide pupils with the opportunity to practise and develop a range of skills across the topic or curriculum.

Which Teaching Strategies Help Pupils Remember What You Have Taught?

Teachers select a range of different teaching strategies when they plan a lesson. Some of these are more useful than others when it comes to helping pupils remember the lesson content. Table 12.2 sets out 11 teaching strategies that align how your pupils remember the lesson content with cognitive development. You should look to include some of these in your lessons over a week but not in every lesson of every day!

How to Plan a Lesson So That Pupils Learn Through Internalising and Externalising Lesson Content

The process of learning involves both internalisation (the process of making the knowledge, skills and understanding taught one's own) and externalisation (demonstrating or using what has been learned in a new or different context). We examined both in Chapter 1. 'What is learning?' A lesson plan should therefore recognise both elements of the learning process and provide opportunities for both. Ensuring that your lessons focus on both aspects of the process of learning will enable your pupils to move beyond the recall of facts or, at its worst, using memory in a tokenistic way to just remember facts. Planning for internalisation and externalisation ensures your lesson planning considers the disciplinary traditions and concepts of the subject being taught, and supports the development of fluency in disciplinary processes as the concepts become more complex. For example, what do pupils in Year 6 know and can do that pupils in Year 3 do not? What do pupils in Year 3 know and can do what pupils in Year 1 do not?

Table 12.3 sets out teaching strategies for both:

- making the lesson content part of how the pupil sees the world (internalisation)
- making the lesson content part of how they are now able to operate in the world as a consequence of their learning (externalisation)

Table 12.2 Summary of different teaching strategies that support pupils' remembering curriculum content

Teaching strategy	Why it helps your pupils remember	Implications for your lesson planning
Visual aids	Supports understanding and retention	Use charts, diagrams, images and videos to help explain
Interactive activities	Allows active participation in the learning process	Try experiments, projects and role-play
Stories	Stories are both memorable and provide a context for curriculum content	Include stories that illustrate key concepts or real-world experience
Games and play	Games are enjoyable, motivating and memorable	Look to turn learning into some form of game whenever you can
Mnemonics and acronyms	They help pupils remember lists, sequences or specific information	Encourage pupils to come up with mnemonics and acronyms and 'perform' them as call and response or in a singsong voice
Music and rhymes	Rhythm and melody aid memory retention	Use chants, music, songs and rhyming to reinforce key information (almost everything can be sung as a song!)
Peer teaching	Fosters a climate for learning of trust and respect	Reinforces knowledge, skill and understanding because it is a real-life application of learning, and helps the peer tutee because the explanations can be pitched differently
Reflection and questioning	Reflection and questioning deepen understanding because they generate learning	Provide opportunities for pupils to talk about what they have been learning in meta terms and to ask questions of themselves, each other and you
Real-life examples	Relates the curriculum content to real-life experience and situations that pupils are likely to have already encountered	Help pupils to integrate new information with their everyday knowledge, and are also very motivating because pupils can see the relevance of what they are being asked to learn
Positive reinforcement	Use of praise and encouragement	Connects positive and optimistic association with the content, which is both motivating and more likely to be remembered
Variety	Not every child experiences learning in the same way. Different pupils have individual needs so if over time you vary your lesson structure and activities, you are more likely to meet those needs	While predictable routines contribute to make pupils feel safe while they are learning, it is also important not to repeat the same way of teaching all day, every day. Bored, uninterested pupils, for whom the day presents no surprises, will struggle to pay attention (which is the foundation of memory)

Table 12.3 Teaching strategies that can support pupils to learn through internalisation and externalisation

Internalisation strategy	Implications for your lesson planning	Externalisation strategy	Implications for your lesson planning
Facilitate discussion	Encourage pupils to share their thoughts, ask questions and express their opinions	**Create artefacts**	Models, posters, objects allow pupils to apply their knowledge in a different context
Use open-ended questions	Such questions prompt critical thinking about the content and require pupils to articulate their understanding so they then internalise concepts more deeply	**Use role play and simulations**	Enacting knowledge in the form of a play or recreating a real-life situation provides pupils with the opportunity to present their understanding of concepts outside their own minds
Include metacognition	Allow time for pupils to self-monitor and self-reflect so that they start to think about their own thinking processes and learning strategies	**Use presentations and demonstrations**	When pupils present what they have learned to an audience (e.g. the class, in an assembly), they consolidate what they have learned and identify gaps and misconceptions that can be clarified
Allow choice	Allow pupils to make decisions about some aspects of tasks, such as the format or writing. Having some control over one's work both motivates pupils and personalises the internalisation process	**Incorporate public recognition**	When effort and achievement are recognised (whether verbally, face to face, through reward systems or by communicating with and involving parents), pupils' motivation increases and the value of what is being learned is reinforced
Use graphic organisers, diagrams and concept maps	Visualising abstract ideas in the concrete form of a diagram helps pupils make connections between the elements of what they are learning	**Use journalling**	Writing *about* what they have learned helps pupils to turn 'the silent speech in their head' (internalisation) into the way they use what they have learned as they operate in the world (externalisation)

When you plan for both processes, you enable pupils to remember the lesson content. This is because you are promoting deep understanding and also the practical application of knowledge. Consequently, pupils are better able to communicate effectively and apply what they have learned in various new and different contexts.

Beginnings and Endings of Lessons: How to Use Your Learning Objectives to Make Your lessons 'Memorable'

It is important to plan the beginnings and endings of your lesson, especially carefully because these are the phases of the lesson when pupils are most likely to be paying close attention. Part 1, and in particular Chapter 8, have described in detail how to develop learning objectives. However, looking at the verbs in your learning objectives can also help you to identify how pupils may apply their learning, show understanding, and therefore what should form the focus of the recall and retrieval activities.

For example, if your learning objective contains the verb 'select' – 'By the end of the lesson, pupils will be able to select…' – it signals to you that your plan should reflect what is involved in selecting, in terms of phases and activities that support memory. This might be that:

- the steps of selection can be broken down into smaller sub-steps
- the think-alouds of a selection process can be used as prompts and questions
- other activities that have involved selection are recalled and the crucial content from them is revisited

By thinking carefully about the verb in your learning objective, you will be able to identify, emphasise and repeat the crucial knowledge and content associated with the verb. Christine Counsell (2003) compiled a useful list of words and phrases for thinking about learning objectives. Carefully identifying the verb will support you in identifying what needs to be remembered in the long term, and consequently what needs to be revisited in any particular lesson:

- extract
- give examples of
- relate
- choose
- connect
- link
- explain
- illustrate
- show the relationship between
- explain the relationship between
- comment upon
- remember
- recall
- ask questions about
- choose questions about
- prioritise
- create headings
- refine headings
- justify
- justify thinking concerning
- explain thinking concerning
- compare
- contrast
- define
- analyse
- join up
- shape
- organise
- reconsider
- reflect
- support a view that
- evaluate
- weigh up
- create
- construct

Using the 'I Do, We Do, You Do' and the Three-Part Lesson Planning Approaches More Effectively So They Support Memory Retention

As a new teacher, you are likely to be taught or required to plan lessons using the following two structures: the 'I do, we do, and you do' modelling sequence or the three-part lesson (starter, main body, plenary). There is no doubt that both methods of planning will support you to meet your professional requirement in the *Early Careers Framework* (ECF) (DfE, 2019a) and *Core Content Framework* (CCF) of Classroom Practice (Standard 4 – Plan and teach well-structured lessons) (DfE, 2019b: 17–19). However, there are some occasions where such planning structures may not fully support your pupils' memory retention. Therefore, it is helpful to be aware of possible limitations when using these planning formats and to consider how to maximise what your pupils remember of your lesson.

Table 12.4 sets out the three potential limitations of the 'I do, we do, and you do' modelling sequence (which is addressed in detail in Chapter 10) and how you can mitigate their impacts in the structure of your planning.

Table 12.4 How to ensure 'I do, we do, and you do' supports pupil memory retention

Issues with 'I do, we do, and you do' and memory retention	How to mitigate potential limitations with the planning structure
Limited cognitive engagement	It is important to consider how much time is spent on the 'I do' and 'we do' aspects of modelling If these phases dominate the lesson, there is limited time for pupils to actively process and internalise the information Without sufficient 'you do' time, pupils may struggle to remember the lesson content
Insufficient opportunities for retrieval practice	The 'you do' phase is very important for memory consolidation, but within it there needs to be lots of opportunities for retrieval practice (actively recalling information from memory) to gain the benefits of long-term retention
Over-emphasis on the 'I do'	If the 'I do' phase is dominated by teacher talk without pupil question and answer, pupils may switch off and disengage from the process

The three-part lesson was first introduced in England in 1997–1998 as a key component of the literacy and numeracy strategies. It encouraged teachers to follow a standard lesson plan for each 45- or 60-minute lesson. For example, in a numeracy lesson, the format was a starter session of up to 10 minutes of oral work, followed by 40 minutes on a main teaching activity, and up to 15 minutes of plenary time to sum up. The three-part lesson is still widely used in many schools. Earlier debates about the merits of exact timings of each part have dissipated, and the structure is now implemented with more flexibility rather than strict timings by the minute. However, there are still important issues to be aware of if you wish to use, or are required to use, this structure for planning your lessons. Table 12.5 summarises what you need to know to ensure your three-part lesson helps pupils to remember the lesson content.

Table 12.5 How to ensure the three-part lesson structure supports pupil memory retention

Issues with the three-part lesson and memory retention	How to mitigate potential limitations with the planning structure
Lack of variation in learning activities	Ensure that just because your lesson plans have a three-part structure that you do not always use the same sorts of activities in the same order. Try to vary the type and format of your activities
Inadequate time for reflection	If you move through each of the three parts without pausing and reflecting on the learning that has just taken place, pupils will not have the opportunity for retrieval practice nor to deepen their understanding by connecting new to prior knowledge
Failure to address individual differences	If you focus on delivering each of the three parts to the allocated time (15, 40, 5), you may not address the learning readiness and learning pace of different children. Pay attention to pupils who may need more time or additional scaffolds to fully internalise the lesson content
Incorrectly estimating prior knowledge	If you assume what pupils already may or may not know without finding some way to check or confirm your assumption, some pupils may struggle to grasp the new concepts because there may be too many gaps in their knowledge
Lack of consideration of cognitive load	A three-part lesson may inadvertently overload working memory because the lesson steps are too large with too much content at each stage
Overemphasis on procedural knowledge	If the parts of the lesson focus on procedural knowledge without also addressing deeper conceptual understanding, pupils may memorise steps but not understand the underlying principles
Lack of connection to pupils' interests	It is important to include at each stage of the lesson a reference to pupils' interests and experiences so that pupils can relate to the content and connect it with what they already know

Key Takeaways

- Decide what kinds of things your pupils are expected to learn or remember over time.
  - What knowledge will your pupils learn through the different topics?
  - What concepts will be secured through those topics?
  - What vocabulary will need to be taught in this current year to help your pupils learn better in subsequent years?
- Always ask yourself why might pupils find learning the particular lesson content hard.
  - Where and when will the current content be revisited? Why is that the best approach?
  - What evidence of learning will you be looking for?

Conclusion

Famous basketball coach John Wooden is attributed as saying 'I haven't taught it, if they haven't learned it', but it might also be said that your pupils have not learned something, if they cannot remember it! It is therefore important to decide which key knowledge you expect your pupils to remember in the long term. The best way to approach this is to be clear about what knowledge will be revisited, and how, over time. Spend time analysing a scheme of work to identify which crucial content or essential knowledge you will need to emphasise and repeat. Include in your lesson plans how you will check what knowledge has been secured by your pupils in the long term. Share with your pupils what they need to remember. Balance time in your lessons between factual recall and the opportunity to develop an understanding of disciplinary traditions, processes and concepts to ensure both systematic repetition and the development of deep understanding.

References

Counsell, C. (2003) The forgotten games kit: Putting historical thinking first in long-, medium- and short -term planning. In Haydn, T and Counsell, C (Eds.), *History, ICT, and Learning in the Secondary School* (pp. 248–259). London: Routledge

DfE (Department for Education) (2019a) *Early Career Framework*. London: HMSO

DfE (2019b) *ITT Core Content Framework*. London: HMSO

Education Endowment Foundation (EEF) (2021) *Cognitive Science Approaches in the Classroom: A Review of the Evidence (Summary)*. London: EEF

13
HOW TO PLAN SO YOU CAN FIND OUT IF YOUR PUPILS ARE LEARNING

Why is It Important to Know if Your Pupils Are Learning in Your Lessons?

Knowing how your pupils are making sense of the lesson you have planned can prove challenging for all teachers. New teachers, who are developing their teaching skills, tend to focus on what is within their sphere of control – their own teaching – and consequently plan their lessons with an emphasis on what they do and what their pupils will do. Another common experience is that new teachers learn to copy obvious assessment activities that they see their mentors use – thumbs up, asking if there are questions, etc. – but struggle to know how to act on the information that comes back to them. Perhaps this can be explained by the language the profession uses: 'I am learning to teach'. However, the reality is that teaching is not a linear activity, but a cycle of planning, teaching and assessing.

Dylan Wiliam, emeritus Professor of Education at University College London and international expert on assessment, argued that:

> Assessment is a central process in education. If pupils learned what they were taught, we would never need to assess; we could just keep records of what we had taught. But as every teacher knows, many pupils do not learn what they are taught. Indeed, when we look at their work, we sometimes wonder if they were even present in the classroom. That is why assessment is the bridge between teaching and learning – it is only through assessment that we can find out whether what has happened in the classroom has produced the learning we intended. (Wiliam, 2013: 15)

In many ways, assessment can be seen as the driving force behind planning and teaching. It provides information to both teachers and pupils about learning, which can then be responded to by planning and teaching. This is because assessment in all its forms is the diagnostic element of teaching. Assessment opportunities should be built into your lesson plan and designed into your lesson's tasks and activities as ongoing processes that provide you with specific ways of ascertaining your pupils' understanding and confusion around the lesson content.

There are two ways you can find out if your pupils are learning when you teach:

1 You can check for understanding (CfU) – usually by asking questions.
2 You can use assessment for learning (AfL) – also known as formative assessment or responsive teaching (now termed in the *Early Careers Framework* (ECF) (DfE, 2019a) and *Core Content Framework* (CCF) (DfE, 2019b) as 'adaptive teaching') and generally described as 'low stakes' for the pupil.

The two processes of CfU and AfL also provide you with information that you can then use to give feedback to your pupils to close the gap between your teaching and their learning, and which can also develop their resilience and metacognition.

However, when teaching is completed, assessment is defined as summative, and is used to establish the extent of pupil learning at a fixed moment in time (usually at the end of a half-term or unit, or for external reporting). Summative assessment is usually described as 'high stakes' assessment for pupils.

How to Check for Understanding

The first priority is to adopt the mindset hinted at by Wiliam in the quote above (Wiliam, 2013: 15): rather than assume that your pupils will have learned what is contained in your lesson plan, assume the opposite! Assume that there are gaps, misconceptions and errors in your pupils' knowledge and understanding after you have taught them, and reframe and expand your role to include the *modus operandi* of acknowledging this and actively seeking them out. For experienced and expert teachers, this is seen in their obsession with whether their pupils are 'getting it'. If the teacher perceives that pupils haven't 'got it', they act there and then so that errors, misconceptions and gaps do not continue and lead to confusion or lack of attainment in the future.

As detailed in Chapter 12, it is assumed that teachers plan to revisit and repeat ideas and content as part of their medium-term planning. Thus, it can be argued that there is no need to check for understanding as you will 'mop things up' soon enough, at a time and in a way that you have already planned. However, this is a huge missed opportunity for learning. Schema are formed at the moment of first teaching, so it is important to ensure that checking for understanding is a continuous thread throughout your lessons, alongside the teaching of each of those small steps. In this way, you will be working to enable your pupils to learn better and without errors the first time, by checking in at each step, and tackling this issue head-on and in the moment.

Checking for understanding also impacts on the climate for learning in your classroom. By integrating checking for accuracy into the learning process, pupils will not feel stigmatised or worried about being wrong. Such a learning environment helps to develop both their resilience and gives a space to practise their development of metacognition. Consequently, your pupils will not berate themselves if they get things wrong, but instead develop a 'silent voice' in their head as they learn to regulate and check their own processes of learning and understanding.

Key Takeaway

- Rather than get into the habit of asking the class *if* they understand, instead check *what* your pupils understand. Thus, engage one or two pupils in short, probing dialogues rather than ask in a general way: Does everyone understand? Does that make sense? Or, if you are getting lots of nods, saying 'Good' and then moving on.

Checking for Understanding: Rosenshine's *Principles of Instruction*

Rosenshine's sixth principle of teaching is: 'Check for student understanding' (Rosenshine, 2010, 2012). He argues that by checking for understanding at regular intervals and at each point of change in the lesson, you can help your pupils to learn the content more accurately with fewer (but not, no) errors. Several of the strategies that shaped his ten principles for teaching are founded on this idea – that teachers should build understanding, check for understanding and then act on what they discover (Rosenshine, 2010: 7). Some of these are set out in Table 13.1.

As Table 13.1 demonstrates, for Rosenshine (2010, 2012), questions are the key way a teacher can check for understanding. He argued that there is a link between the effectiveness of the teacher and the frequency with which they ask questions. He suggested that questioning impacts learning because it has two functions in relation to understanding:

1 It allows the processing time needed to move learning into long-term memory.
2 It allows the teacher to check for misconceptions.

He noted that effective teachers took specific actions to check for understanding. Effective teachers:

- asked questions
- asked pupils to summarise the content up to that point
- asked pupils to repeat information, instructions and methods
- asked pupils if they agreed or disagreed with other pupils and the teacher (and why)

- asked pupils to think aloud as they began or undertook a task
- asked pupils to explain their approach and ideas to others

Table 13.1 Teaching strategies that support checking for understanding (Rosenshine, 2010: 7)

Build understanding	Check for understanding	What to do afterwards
Begin a lesson with a short review of previous learning	Ask a large number of questions and check for understanding	Provide systematic feedback and corrections
Present new material in small steps with pupil practice after each step	Ask pupils to explain what they have learned	Use time to provide more explanations
Limit the amount of material pupils receive at one time	Check the responses of all pupils	Provide many examples
Give clear and detailed instructions and explanations		Reteach material where necessary
Provide a high level of active practice for all pupils		Prepare pupils for independent practice
Guide pupils as they begin to practise		Monitor pupils when they begin independent practice
Think aloud and model steps		
Provide models of worked-out problems		

He explained that the effectiveness of these strategies comes from four sources:

1 Pupils are required to elaborate and make connections between new and old information.
2 Teachers can identify which parts of the content need reteaching.
3 When pupils explain in their own words, they are supported in internalising and externalising the lesson content.
4 Pupils learn by constructing and reconstructing knowledge to form schema, rather than by repeating what they hear word for word. It is by sharing the 'gist' of what they have learned that pupils are able to form such mental models (Rosenshine, 2010: 7).

Key Takeaway

- Pupils should not be left to their own devices when constructing mental models during the course of your lesson because they are likely to make errors in the processing of new information. By frequently 'stepping in', you can support pupils to acquire enough knowledge to avoid developing misconceptions. Supporting them in this way often leads your pupils to have 'aha!' or 'lightbulb' moments as they make their own connections and 'get it'.

Checking for understanding: Lemov's *Teach Like a Champion*

Doug Lemov (2021) regards the central role of a teacher as filling the gap between what you have taught and what your pupils have understood, and that it is important to approach any gaps in a calm and accepting manner. His view is that gaps in understanding are inevitable, so the onus is on you, the teacher, to respond. To grasp the significance of tackling the gap between what pupils understand of what has been taught, Lemov suggests that new teachers should ask themselves the following questions:

- Will you see misunderstandings?
- Will you ignore them?
- Can you fix them?
- Will you blame your pupils and express your frustration?

In his book *Teach Like a Champion 3.0* (TLAC) (2021), Lemov devotes an entire section to 'Checking for Understanding', where he describes nine specific techniques that are used by highly effective teachers. Table 13.2 lists the TLAC name for the technique, its more common term, examples of ineffective practice and how effective teachers use the technique (Lemov, 2021: Chapter 3, pp. 75–138).

Key Takeaways

- Even though Lemov lists 63 techniques in *Teach Like a Champion 3.0* (2021), of which nine relate to how to check for understanding, his view is that every technique come with provisos in terms of making it work for any one teacher with anyone class. In others, no technique is guaranteed to be effective, but is a skill developed alongside the judgement of the teacher, and over time.
- What matters, alongside knowing a range of techniques and perfecting them over time, is the culture of your classroom. Is it 'safe' place for learning? Are your pupils able to articulate their struggles with the learning process, so that you can address them? Lemov argues that this is *the* role of the teacher.

How to Assess

Between 2000 and 2014 the National Curriculum in England was broken down into attainment levels and three big ideas drove teaching:

1. Attainment – the grades attained by a pupil at the end of a Key Stage.
2. Progress – the achievement of a pupil over time between two Key Stages (typically between KS2 and KS4).
3. Achievement – the grades a pupil achieves in relation to their starting point.

Table 13.2 Summary of Lemov's techniques for 'Checking for Understanding' (Lemov, 2021: 75–138)

	Check for Understanding – Lemov (2021), Chapter 3, pp. 75–138		
The TLAC name for the technique	**Its more common term**	**Ineffective practice**	**How effective teachers use the technique**
6: Replace self-report	Targeted questions: specific, objective questions focused on content and asked in an open-ended format	'Does everyone understand?' 'Is everyone clear about x or y?' Questions that ask pupils to evaluate their own understanding which yield false conformation (especially those that can be answered with yes or no) Questions that ask pupils what they think they know For pupils to use a thumbs up as response to the above	Ask questions where pupils are required to demonstrate what they know Plan these questions in advance (because they are hard to make up on the spur of the moment) Note the pupils whom you are going to target the question to before or during the lesson (don't wait for volunteers or hands-up) Act on errors and misconceptions right there and then – do not wait for a 'better' time Ask targeted questions about content and to check understanding before a task Be aware of natural transition points in the lesson and check in with pupils to find out how they are doing
7: Retrieval practice	Recall questions: cause pupils to recall information after a strategic delay	Only asking recall questions about the lesson at the end of the lesson and never returning to the questions in the coming days, weeks or months Only use recall for rote learning	Be intentional about using recall by using it systematically and regularly so knowledge is easily accessed from long-term memory, which helps pupil to understand Devote a chunk of every lesson to recall (but vary it by changing the format or applying concepts in new ways) Gradually increase the amount of delay between recall to support remembering Use recall for elaboration: connecting ideas, reflecting on ideas and expanding the idea
8: Standardise the format	Observation (which takes less time than asking and answering questions and so frees up more time to check on understanding and then act on what you observe)	Having the best of intentions to check for understanding but always run out of time to do it well because it takes too long to get pupils started on their work	Design lessons, tasks and activities to the same format so that they build in an observation check and what they are looking for as a consistent element of every lesson Ask pupils to set out their work to an agreed layout so that it is easier to scan their work for errors and misunderstanding as you walk around the room observing

(Continued)

Table 13.2 Summary of Lemov's techniques for 'Checking for Understanding' (Lemov, 2021: 75–138) (*Continued*)

	Check for Understanding – Lemov (2021), Chapter 3, pp. 75–138		
The TLAC name for the technique	**Its more common term**	**Ineffective practice**	**How effective teachers use the technique**
9. Active observation	Focused observation	Thinking that you will remember what you observed as you circulated the room and engaged in 1:1s with your pupils	Circulate the room with sticky notes or a clipboard and make notes as you go to act as a prompt for planning the next lesson in the sequence Decide before the lesson what you will look out for as you circulate the room so you know what you should see and then look carefully to see if you see it Give feedback immediately to each pupil
10: Show me	Hand signals and showing working (on mini-whiteboards or on paper)	Asking pupils to show a thumbs up or down or allowing them to see others' mini-whiteboards	Use hand signals where pupils answer a multiple-choice question to show their response (one finger for a, two fingers for b, etc.) Ensure pupils hold their mini-whiteboards to their chests, so they are less visible to their friends Review individual work and give feedback so pupils feel seen in the process
11: Affirmative checking	Moving onto next activity (making sure pupils are ready for more complex work and checking how they are doing)	Pupils wasting time waiting for the teacher to tell them what to do next by putting their hand in air, waiting for the teacher to come around, sitting with arms folded and pencil down and chatting	Plan the lesson content to develop in stages. Design a checkpoint at the end of each stage that you can evaluate quickly. Pupils can first self-assess (am I ready for the next step?) and then you can readily check the work. Those same checkpoints can be readily checked by the teacher for assessment by annotating their views on a sticky note or by highlighting completed work by pupils, as evidence
12: Culture of error	Making mistakes is a sign of learning, not failure (teachers expect and look out for errors as joint work to be developed with the class)	Pupils are led to believe that their role in the classroom is to get the answer right and it is best to hide from the teacher if they have any weaknesses	Create a climate for learning where learning is seen as a shared endeavour between the teacher and the pupils. Do this by shaping pupils' ideas about what it means to make a mistake, that being 'wrong' is a positive step to getting things right, and by encouraging pupils not to be defensive about their mistakes and to be interested in them instead. Build on this by encouraging risk-taking

(*Continued*)

Table 13.2 Summary of Lemov's techniques for 'Checking for Understanding' (Lemov, 2021: 75–138) (*Continued*)

Check for Understanding – Lemov (2021), Chapter 3, pp. 75–138			
The TLAC name for the technique	**Its more common term**	**Ineffective practice**	**How effective teachers use the technique**
			Use phrases like: 'I used to make this mistake', 'I'm glad I saw this mistake', 'What I am asking you to do is difficult'.
13: Show call	Not blindly sticking to the lesson plan when you realise that pupils are confused	Sticking to your plan because it is difficult to think of how to change it in the moment and in front of the pupils because you want to get to 'the end'	If an error is spotted when you are teaching, turn the error itself into the focus of attention. Model finding the mistake, studying it without defensiveness and relishing this as a moment of learning There are two key moments in this process: Take – taking the work from the pupil to share with the class Reveal – when you show the work to the class Make this process a regular part of your lesson so that it is safe and not humiliating: 'Can I borrow this?', 'This will help the rest of the class' Do not name the pupils but give pupils direction as to what to look for: 'Let's see if we can see…'
14: Own and track	Reinforcing the correct answers to build long-term memory	Spending lots of time analysing errors without reinforcing the correct answers at the end	Ask pupils to write down the correct answer Ask pupils to make notes about the wrong answers from their new perspective of being 'right' Ask pupils to make notes about the right answer from their new perspective of being 'right'

The unintended consequence of this emphasis was that teaching was assessment-driven. Teachers focused on 'teaching to the test' or the assessment objectives (AO) of their subject and Key Stage. Pupils were labelled in terms of their attainment level (e.g. referring to themselves or having written on their book: 3a – working towards the level, 3b – working at the level, or 3c – exceeding the level). And what was taught was the next attainment level because the expectation was that pupils work through one level every two years, progressing through 1.5 sub-levels every year. In this way, summative assessment – the measurement of or a summary of the pupil's current level of performance – shaped all aspects of teaching. This version of the curriculum and assessment by levels was scrapped in 2014.

The current emphasis is on teaching curriculum content and formative assessment – using assessment to form what comes next in the teaching and learning cycle. Formative assessment is rooted in the moment and takes place in the lesson. Unlike summative assessment, which is undertaken by the teacher about the pupil, formative assessment is typically undertaken by the teacher with the pupil. Whereas checking for understanding (CfU) is an activity to plan into your lessons so that you teach better in the first place, formative assessment helps you to decide what to do next. Clearly, both processes are closely linked and designed to help you to discover if your pupils are learning.

What is Formative Assessment?

Formative assessment was first developed in England in the late 1990s following research by Paul Black and Dylan Wiliam (1998), who completed a meta-analysis of formative assessment. They demonstrated clear links between aspects of formative assessment and improved learning by pupils. While the terms 'formative assessment' and 'assessment for learning' are often used interchangeably, it is important to note that Wiliam in his inaugural lecture (which was published by the Institute of Education) saw significant distinctions:

- Assessment for learning is any assessment whose design and practice are first and foremost to promote pupils' learning.
- Assessment for learning differs from assessment that is designed primarily for the purposes of accountability, ranking, or for certifying competence.
- An assessment activity can help learning if it provides information to be used as feedback by teachers and by their pupils, as the latter assess themselves and each other, to modify the teaching and learning activities in which they are engaged.
- Such assessment becomes 'formative assessment' when the evidence is actually used to adapt the teaching work to meet learning needs.

'Assessment for learning' (AfL) was the preferred term from 1997 to 2011 when the National Strategies shaped how teachers taught. Subsequently, 'formative assessment' and 'responsive teaching' are the terms that now tend to be used by schools and teachers. The latter is because pupils play a key role in formative assessment: the teacher's role is to engage in 'responsive teaching', whereby their teaching and interactions adapt and respond, depending on how the learning is going. However, the term 'adaptive teaching' is now used in both the *Early Career Framework* (ECF) and *Core Content Framework* (CCF) (DfE, 2019a, 2019b).

The big idea underpinning formative assessment is that teaching is adaptive to the pupils' needs. Formative assessment can take place in three different cycles of time:

1 Long-cycle formative assessment – periodic checks to examine that the curriculum content has been taught and analysis of the results of summative tests over time to identify trends for where the approach to teaching content needs to be reviewed. Such work would normally be undertaken by senior staff in a school or Trust and is therefore

not expected to have an immediate impact on learning for pupils. Instead, its impact will be a system or school level.

2 Medium-cycle formative assessment – takes place between one and four weeks where teachers meet together to review teaching and learning. Although a valuable process, it can often result in deciding that even more topics are to be taught, rather than developments to classroom practice.
3 Short-cycle formative assessment – minute-by-minute, day-by-day assessment which increases pupil engagement and improves the practice of the teacher because it is responsive to the pupils' needs. If pupils leave the classroom before teachers have used the information about their pupils' achievements to adjust their teaching, the teachers are already playing catch-up.

Since his work with Black in 1998, Wiliam has gone on to develop a body of work around formative assessment, but at its core, formative assessment is about gaining clarity in three processes:

1 Where are the pupils in their learning?
2 Where are the pupils going in their learning?
3 Which steps are needed to get them there?

And in a classroom, three sets of people are involved in those processes:

1 Teacher.
2 Pupil.
3 Peer.

The three process questions form five key teaching strategies, which are set out in Table 13.3.

Gipps, McCallum and Hargreaves (2016), in their research into 23 highly effective Year 2 and Year 6 teachers in 20 schools in two London boroughs, identified 15 ways in which these expert teachers used assessment strategies. Table 13.4 sets out these strategies and shows how they fall into three broad groupings:

- Teacher–pupil interactions
- The teacher watching and listening
- The teacher 'mentally' considering the evidence

Gipps et al. (2016) found that assessment is a core, but complex, teaching strategy. It forms the basis of the work of the teacher (at the start of the lesson, when summarising the lesson and in how the teacher works with and alongside pupils during the lesson). Good formative assessment rests on the ability of the teacher to be clear about the task, the goal of learning and the curriculum content. These expert teachers were very focused on each individual pupil's learning because they acted on the understanding that pupils learn at different rates and in different ways. They therefore provided a variety of activities, tasks and pace of work, which they constantly monitored and evaluated.

Table 13.3 Aspects of formative assessment (Black and Wiliams, 1998)

Formative assessment teaching strategy	Definition	How to do it
Clarify, share and understand learning intentions	Being clear about what you want pupils to be able to do	Be explicit with pupils about what they should know and what the success criteria for judging quality might be It is not sufficient to tell them; your pupils need to understand the learning intention
Engineer effective classroom discussions, activities and tasks that elicit evidence of learning	Monitoring where pupils are in their learning in relation to the intention through classroom talk and an approach to whole-class teaching that is interactive	Use diagnostic questions Use whole-class response methods Listen in to pair, group and class discussion
Provide feedback that moves learning forward	The main purpose of feedback is to provide the pupil with guidance about what to do next, rather than telling them the weaknesses of the last piece of work. What matters most about feedback is how pupils use it	Design feedback to make pupils think, not generate an emotional response (e.g. leaving pupils feeling like a failure or that they will never be able to complete the task successfully) Express feedback in terms that directly relate to the previously shared learning intentions and success criteria Feedback results in more work for the pupil to complete, not the teacher (this relates to issue of teacher workload and the link to marking – not everything needs to be written down by the teacher or pupil)
Activate pupils as teaching resources for each other	Collaborative and co-operative learning, in which pupils teach and assess each other	Think–pair–share helps pupils to rehearse their ideas before they share them with the whole class Focus peer assessment on improvement: checking answers, spotting errors and applying checklists Pupils teach each other content and skills (and clarify their own understanding in the process)
Activate pupils as owners of their own learning	Developing pupil metacognition, motivation and interest, and identifying to what pupils attribute their successes and failures	Support pupils to check their own progress towards the shared learning intentions, e.g. through self-quizzing or structured reflections

Table 13.4 Assessment strategies used by expert primary teachers (Gipps et al., 2016)

Teacher–pupil interaction	Teacher watching and listening	Teacher 'mentally' considering the evidence
Testing	Observing	Using other teachers' records
Oral testing	Checking	Marking
Delving questions	Listening	Making a mental assessment note
Getting a child to demonstrate	Eavesdropping	Assessing the general level of understanding
		Judging progress
		Looking at a range of work to make a summative assessment
		Working out why a pupil has not achieved

Key Takeaways

- Formative assessment is a continuous, iterative teaching process.
- When you plan and teach, have in your mind the three key questions: Where is the pupil now? Where is the pupil trying to go? How can the pupil close the gap?
- Ensure that your pupils are also very clear about the same three questions.
- The purpose of formative assessment is to adapt your teaching to better meet your pupils' needs at that particular moment in your lesson.
- Feedback should make clear to pupils the gap between the actual and desired level of performance in terms of the previously shared success criteria. It should be expressed as productive next steps (the next steps towards successfully reaching the declared goal of learning/success criteria).
- Next steps are set at an appropriate level of difficulty for the individual child and to motivate their continued effort when they find aspects of the work challenging.

Conclusion

You will understand if your pupils are learning through your use of assessment. Assessment informs your understanding of what your pupils can do independently and with support. It provides you and your pupils with the opportunity to gather specific, personalised and timely information to guide the responses and adaptions needed for future teaching and learning. It is important to create a classroom culture where you welcome pupils saying that they do not understand. Assessment also encourages pupils to take ownership of their own learning. A consequence of this is that your feedback will have the most impact on your pupils' attitudes towards, and resilience in, learning if it addresses their effort, learning strategy and the benefits of persistence.

References

Black, P and Wiliam, D (1998) Assessment and classroom learning. *Assessment in Education: Principles, Policy, and Practice* 5(1), 7–74

DfE (Department for Education) (2019a) *Early Career Framework*. London: HMSO

DfE (2019b) *ITT Core Content Framework*. London: HMSO

Gipps, C, McCallum, B, and Hargreaves, E (2016) *What Makes a Good Primary School Teacher? Expert Classroom Strategies*. London: Routledge

Lemov, D (2021) *Teach Like a Champion 3.0: 63 Techniques that Put Students on the Path to College*. San Francisco, CA: Jossey-Bass

Rosenshine, B (2010) *Principles of Instruction: Education Practices Series – 21*. Geneva: UNESCO International Bureau of Education

Rosenshine, B (2012) Principles of instruction: Research-based strategies that all teachers should know. *American Educator* Spring, 12–18

Wiliam, D and University of London, Institute of Education (2009) Assessment for learning: Why, what, and how? An inaugural professorial lecture at the Institute of Education, London, June, 2009

Wiliam, D (2013) Assessment: The bridge between teaching and learning. *Voices from the Middle* 21(2).

CONCLUSION GETTING BETTER: FIVE THINGS A NEW TEACHER SHOULD KNOW

1. Theory and Practice: Know Your Why

Theory can sound like an obscure term, far removed from the busy life of your classroom. But theory is simply the set of ideas that you work from to make sense of the world. Teaching is a knowledge profession and ideas shape every action. If you just 'do' things, you are simply copying other people without connecting your actions back to your understanding of the four big questions: What is learning? What is teaching? What is a curriculum? What is backwards planning? Then it can be difficult to know how to respond to what happens in your lesson. However, if, for example, you are clear in your own mind that you interpret learning as change, then that deep conceptual understanding will guide your actions, even if sometimes you are not quite sure what to do.

Teaching is an evidence-informed profession, that is, we work with the findings of empirical research as well as theory. However, as a classroom teacher, it is difficult to access educational research first-hand for several reasons: academic journals are often behind paywalls, they are not written for practitioners, and they research very specific questions. But there are valuable ways in which we can look at the evidence rather than the empirical research. First, the Education Endowment Foundation (EEF) website publishes evidence summaries and implications for practice that are easy to access and interpret in terms of what you might do in your classroom. Second, *IMPACT*, the journal of the Chartered College for Teachers, publishes action research undertaken by teachers and easy-to-access think pieces by leading researchers and academics. Finally, the *Times Educational Supplement* summarises research into evidence for practising teachers.

As you get better as a teacher, you will develop more know-how (skills) and know-that (knowledge), but in particular you will focus on developing your know-why (your pedagogical reasoning or professional judgement) so that you can continue to improve.

Further Reading

Williams, J (2020) *How to Read and Understand Educational Research*. London: Sage

2. Be Evidence-Informed: Have a Criticality Mindset

It is important to be able to think through what you read when you access theory, research and evidence. This is known as critical thinking. The ability to think critically is built on and draws from your professional knowledge. It is the application of what you know about teaching and learning. Rather than be presented with and accept a proposal about what you should do when you teach, adopting a critical mindset will help you to know *why* you wish to teach in a certain way at a particular time and in response to a set of circumstances. A critical mindset arises from you asking yourself some of the following questions about a proposal for action or teaching issue:

- Why is it significant?
- What are the strengths and weakness?
- Why is it relevant?
- Why does it work best?
- What timing is most appropriate?
- Are some parts more important than others?
- Why select some options and not others?
- How does it link to other things I know?

Being evidence-informed will help you to become a more effective teacher and will impact the ways in which your pupils achieve.

Further Reading

Perry, T and Morris, R (2023) *A Critical Guide to Evidence-Informed Education*. Maidenhead: Open University Press

3. Becoming Expert: Talking About Your Know-Why With Your Pupils

Some teachers shy away from the term 'expert', thinking that it is related to being a genius and is therefore not relevant to their everyday work. There are two common approaches to being expert in teaching: one is that you should practise for 10,000 hours (nearly nine years) as a teacher, and the other is that you should be able to give an instinctive performance because you have attained fluency in teaching that no longer requires thought. The problem is that both of these models are more relevant to activities outside the classroom, such as playing golf or basketball, perhaps. There is, however, a form of expertise that was developed from research (Edwards, 2010) into the complex work and social understanding required of teachers: relational expertise.

Getting better as a teacher in terms of your relational expertise offers you a way to think about your work. Teachers with relational expertise are aware of what matters to them about teaching their subject. They are aware of what matters to their pupils as learners in their school. They build on this knowledge by looking at what is held in common, and they then find ways to align both kinds of 'what matters'

In particular, such expert teachers use a meta-commentary when they teach, which makes clear to the pupils their pedagogical reasoning (their know-why) as the lesson continues. That is, expert teachers explain to pupils why the task is important, and in doing so they enable their pupils to develop their agency. Pupils can develop their subject agency – the ability to think and interpret the world in terms of their subject – and their future agency – the transformational power of knowledge that expands pupils' capacity to operate in the world because of what they now know. Because expert teachers are aware of what is important to them about teaching the subject matter of the lesson, they are able to share these aims as a 'bigger picture' with their pupils.

Further Reading

Shires, L (2023) *Relational Expertise of Teacher Educators: Theory and Practice.* St Albans: Critical Publishing

4. Developing Teaching Expertise: SEND, Adaptive Teaching and Subject Knowledge

Learning to be a good primary classroom teacher takes time and there are no shortcuts. However, as you get to grips with teaching, you will want to get better at some of the elements of teaching that are at its core, but hard to do at a high level. You will develop your expertise in teaching by focusing on:

- teaching your pupils within the four areas of SEND need – communication and interaction, cognition and learning, social, emotional and mental emotional health, and sensory and/or physical needs
- being able to adapt your teaching in response to the individuals who make up your class by differentiation (see below)
- learning more about the subject content that makes up the curriculum

These are the three core areas that reveal teaching expertise because they progress beyond, and refine further, good whole-class teaching and address the part of the lesson when pupils are working independently within the whole-class situation.

Having mastered effective routines for the beginnings and endings of the lesson, it is time to consider how to differentiate. Differentiation follows the themes and topics of the mainstream curriculum, but a range of approaches and resources that are used that support and enable all the pupils to access learning. It does not work well if teachers prepare lots of worksheets, use a parallel curriculum, or use exactly the same materials for all pupils and everyone is expected to make the best of it. But it can take place within the curriculum if the teacher makes small tweaks and adaptations to support access to the curriculum so that all pupils are included socially and academically. For example, everyone is set the same basic task and some pupils work on more complex aspects and methods, others work independently and others work with modelled examples.

The curriculum can be partially differentiated when some pupils (both SEND and more able pupils) require a different level of learning for much of the lesson. In this case, pupils may need support or adjustment for one or two areas of the curriculum but be at the same level as their peers for others. A curriculum will be fully differentiated for pupils (perhaps those with an Education Health Care Plan [EHCP]) who can learn the same subject areas but at a different level and with different resources. For example, some pupils may work in a focused group (In a group focused on one aspect of a activity or a group of children who have similar next steps or learning needs) or with the teaching assistant.

Different pupils need different levels of support from the teacher to access learning, but it is important that a pupil does not have an adult with them all the time, so that they can develop independence. Support may be put in place for part of the lesson, by using additional explanations and questions, or additional and more worked examples, by working one-to-one with a teacher or TA, or by undertaking different tasks with different materials and resources.

To be able to plan a lesson from a curriculum, you need to interpret the curriculum as a progression map. This means looking at how topics and skills become more complex year by year and what concepts draw the knowledge and skills together. As a teacher, your subject knowledge is not developed by taking degrees in all the subjects of the curriculum but by becoming very knowledgeable about the content that makes up the school curriculum. Each school subject has a Subject Association that develops resources and training to enable teachers to acquire subject knowledge. As such, they are the key point of contact for teachers.

Further Reading

Alston, S and Sobel, D (2021) The Inclusive Classroom: A New Approach to Differentiation. London: Bloomsbury

Council for Subject Associations (CfSA): www.subjectassociations.org.uk

5. Keeping Going: Be Part of Something Bigger, Work–Life Balance and Having Fun

It is important to keep a sense of perspective about teaching in order to do it well and to continue to enjoy it. It can be easy to find yourself in a routine where you work in your classroom at breaks and at lunch and after school, and begin to feel isolated from the rest of the school. A school is a community, and while allocating some time to take part in its wider life is enjoyable in itself, it also mitigates against being focused on completing all your work perfectly. Try to take proper breaks in the staffroom or with colleagues in their classrooms, join in the extra-curricular life of the school, such as sports or arts or sharing a particular passion of your own, and spend time on the front gate with the senior staff now and then as they meet and greet parents. You will always feel you are too busy to do these things, but endlessly working does not increase your efficiency and effectiveness. If you are not careful, you can soon lose sight of why you are teaching in your community's school.

Similarly, set boundaries around your working day and working week from day one – and stick to them. Everyone's commute and personal responsibilities are different – small children, pets, no public transport, etc. So decide what time you want to arrive at work and what time you want to leave work and whether you will ever take work home to complete it. Make sure, as a bare minimum, that you leave work very promptly at least one day a week (perhaps Friday), and that you do no work at all at least one day every weekend. Children need happy, enthusiastic, interesting people teaching them, and if all you do is teach, then you will soon become a lesser version of yourself. Keep up your hobbies and interests, be that reading, sport, cooking, etc., and do not get sucked into thinking that you must always be working or thinking about teaching. Finally, remember the advice of the All-Black rugby player I mentioned at the start of the book: **Work hard on your skills and make sure you are always having fun!**

References

Edwards, A (2010) *Being an Expert Professional Practitioner: The Relational Turn in Expertise.* Singapore: Springer

APPENDIX
42 WORDS TO HELP YOU THINK AND TALK ABOUT TEACHING

Achievement
The grades a pupil achieves in relation to their starting point.

Agency
The sense of control that you feel in your life.

Attainment
The grades attained by a pupil at the end of a Key Stage.

Autonomy
Independence or freedom of will and action.

Cognitive science
The science of learning – two areas of cognitive science are influential in education: cognitive psychology, which is concerned with mental processes such as thinking and memory, and cognitive neuroscience, which is concerned with the brain and biological processes.

Concept
An abstract idea drawn from and used to explain a specific field of study.

Consciousness
How minds are shaped and how the world is conceptualised.

Constructivist theory
Views learning as something that happens in the mind of each learner that is shaped by their own experiences and the prior knowledge they bring to a topic.

Core Content Framework (CCF)
A curriculum framework developed by the Department for Education. The CCF sets out the minimum declarative knowledge (learn that) and procedural knowledge or skills (learn how to) that new teachers are required to learn.

Disciplinary knowledge

Knowing about the origins and social production of knowledge, not just its processes, structures, rules and conventions, i.e. how historians learn about the past and use this learning to construct meaning.

Double move

A teaching process where the teacher is working to advance the subject-matter of the curriculum towards the child's everyday knowledge and to extend the child's everyday knowledge towards the concepts in the subject-matter so that they are integrated.

Education Inspection Framework (EIF)

This sets out in law how Ofsted will inspect schools by explaining the principles of inspection and the main judgements that inspectors make.

Effect size

A statistical measure of the strength of the relationship between different predictors and pupils' outcomes. It is generally recognised that in educational research effect sizes are typically small to moderate.

Effectiveness research

A specific inquiry approach that investigates which teaching strategies achieve certain outcomes.

Epistemic ascent

An understanding of the structure of systematic knowledge from the point of view of the learner rather than the expert.

Error

A mistake or getting something wrong.

Externalisation

Demonstrating or using what has been learned in a new or different context.

Internalisation

The process of making the knowledge, skills and understanding taught one's own.

Interventions

Designed to tackle weaknesses in how pupils do something.

Learning-focused teaching strategies

What you can do as a teacher to support the learning of your pupils.

Mental tools

Allow humans to function beyond the limits of their mental capacities. All devices used to improve mental functioning fall into the category of mental tools.

Meta-(meta)-analysis

A form of research that combines the findings of previous studies that have examined the same research question into a statistical analysis.

Metacognition
Awareness and understanding of one's own thought processes.

Misconception
A view or opinion that is incorrect because it is based on faulty understanding.

Model
A representation of something or an example to follow.

Objective
The learning outcomes that are the focus of teaching. They help to clarify, organise and prioritise learning and help teachers and pupils to evaluate progress.

Outcome
The desired learning objectives and educational results schools and teachers want pupils to achieve.

Pedagogy
The methods of how teachers teach, in theory and in practice.

Professional standards
The minimum requirements set out in law for teachers' teaching and professional conduct. They are used to chart professional progress – including entering the profession – and pay progression.

Progress
The achievement of a pupil over time between two Key Stages (typically between KS2 and KS4).

Progression
Learning more of the curriculum by getting better at the particular subject.

Relational
The aim to bring the pupil into relation with the curriculum.

Schema
How the brain structures knowledge.

School Inspection Handbook
The statutory guide for inspectors on how to carry out inspections.

Second-order concepts
Tools for teachers to grasp what it means to learn a particular subject. They shape the key questions asked in a subject and how the subject is structured. Second-order concepts are tools for learning that generate first-order (or substantive) knowledge, and organise and structure it so that it can be used by the learner.

Substantive knowledge (or first-order knowledge)
The abstract concepts that are used to think like an historian or artist, etc.

Syntactic knowledge

Thinking like a subject expert who is able to infer, evaluate evidence and consider cause and effect.

Technique

The performance of a teaching procedure by the teacher (the teacher's know-how or skill).

Think aloud (think-alouds)

Thinking aloud shows the teacher's thought processes so that pupils can observe the expert thinking that they can't usually access.

Threshold concept

A core idea in a subject, where understanding that concept is key to transforming the way you understand a whole subject, allowing you to move on in your learning.

Transmission

When the teacher talks to pupils, and pupils memorise what they have been told.

Value-added approach

The extent to which, given a defined starting point (i.e. family background or characteristics), children's progress in schools exceeds that which might be predicted by their starting points.

INDEX

Page numbers in **bold** indicate tables and in *italic* indicate figures.